The Colour of Courage

by

Sharon Muir Watson

The Long Riders' Guild Press
www.thelongridersguild.com
ISBN 1-59048-115-1

© Sharon Muir Watson
All rights reserved

All rights reserved. Without limiting the rights under copyright reserved above, no part of this publication may be reproduced, stored in or introduced into a retrieval system, or transmitted, in any form or by any means (electronic, mechanical, photocopying, recording or otherwise), without the prior written permission of both the copyright owner and The Long Riders' Guild Press.

ISBN 1-59048-115-1

Illustrations: Sharon Muir Watson
Photography: Sharon Muir Watson, Ken Roberts
Proof Readers: Janet Leon, Lyn Muir, Ken Roberts

Cover Photo Courtesy 'The Age' Newspaper, Melbourne. Photographer, Sandy Scheltema

Sharon, Ken and their 12 horses cross the Howitt High Plains in Victoria

To the Reader:

The editors and publishers of The Long Riders' Guild Press faced significant technical and financial difficulties in bringing this and the other titles in the Equestrian Travel Classics collection to the light of day.

Though the authors represented in this international series envisioned their stories being shared for generations to come, all too often that was not the case. Sadly, many of the books now being published by The Long Riders' Guild Press were discovered gracing the bookshelves of rare book dealers, adorned with princely prices that placed them out of financial reach of the common reader. The remainder were found lying neglected on the scrap heap of history, their once-proud stories forgotten, their once-glorious covers stained by the toil of time and a host of indifferent previous owners.

However The Long Riders' Guild Press passionateiy believes that this book, and its literary sisters, remain of global interest and importance. We stand committed, therefore, to bringing our readers the best copy of these classics at the most affordable price. The copy which you now hold may have small blemishes originating from the master text.

We apologize in advance for any defects of this nature.

PREFACE

Australia's Bicentennial National Trail stretches for over 5000km from Cooktown in Far North Queensland to Healesville, Victoria. It is the longest recreational trail in the world, passing through some remote and beautiful country that few people ever see.

The trail is most commonly used by people taking short trips, and journeys from one end to the other are a rarity. There are many different ways of travelling: bushwalkers, cyclists and riders all develop their own system and fine tune it as they travel. Some horse riders have a back-up vehicle into accessible places, while others have driven their intended route and organised food and fodder caches.

Our approach is unique in this day and age as we eventually travel with a string of 12 horses. Horsemen from the past compliment us on our 'professional outfit', but many modern day equestrians fail to understand why we have resorted to 'the old fashioned' way of travelling. We used 6 horses each whereas most people are only using three. Money and modern equipment make the BNT within everyone's reach, but for us it couldn't buy the enjoyment and incredible experience of taking a step back 100 years in time.

Many of the problems we encountered were due to our own inexperience and from riding the trail in its infancy, often using incomplete draft notes that were untested. Feedback from past users of the trail has now provided an improved set of guide books, so that future travellers can look forward to a much easier trip than the one you're about to read.

Thanks to the foresight of the founders, the Bicentennial National Trail is helping to keep a small piece of Australia open to the public. The support of the public is paramount to enable this route to remain a wilderness trail and become part of our heritage.

ACKNOWLEDGEMENTS

Whilst this trip was undertaken without the physical presence of a backup crew, the moral support of our families and friends is not to be underrated. Special thanks are due to Sharon's mother, Lyn Muir, who was plagued with desperate reverse charge phone calls from remote phone booths with a jammed coin box and a vague address, requesting maps and contacts at a moment's notice. From the far side of the continent, she somehow managed to manipulate people and postal systems to effect delivery of items and messages. Sharon's grandmother, Betty Ball, achieved the same miracles with film, camera repairs and advice on photography.

Thanks also, to the founders and volunteers who have worked on the Bicentennial National Trail, the property owners who gave access through freehold country, and the townspeople, landowners and tourists who took the time to stop and say hello, offer information or assistance.

Many thanks to the people who gave employment, without which we could not have financed the trip.

To the station people, bushmen, packhorse teamsters and old-time drovers: without your advice we could not have made this journey under our own steam.

And lastly, our most heartfelt thanks to Beth and Clarry Stonehouse who provided a base from which to start, and to Lynne King, who organised our arrival in Healesville and continued to assist us long after the event was over.

Ken Roberts and Sharon Muir Watson

CONTENTS

PREFACE
ACKNOWLEDGEMENTS

Chapter 1 : COOKTOWN
Chapter 2 : RUNAWAY PACKHORSE
Chapter 3 : BUSHMEN OF THE BLOOMFIELD
Chapter 4 : SHERIFF OF THE DAINTREE
Chapter 5 : JUNGLE ASSAULT
Chapter 6 : A BULLOCKY'S NIGHTMARE
Chapter 7 : BANGTAIL MUSTER
Chapter 8 : SHOTGUNS IN THE SKY
Chapter 9 : DROVERS AND POETS
Chapter 10: STORMS OVER THE SUTTOR
Chapter 11: RACE AGAINST THE RIVERS
Chapter 12: A KESTREL FOR CHRISTMAS
Chapter 13: BRUMBIES AND BUCKJUMPERS
Chapter 14: THE MONTO GREYS
Chapter 15: COCKIES AND BLOCKIES
Chapter 16: THE HALF WAY MARK
Chapter 17: ALONG THE GUY FAWKES
Chapter 18: THE VALLEY OF DEATH
Chapter 19: BEYOND THE BARRINGTONS
Chapter 20: BUSHRANGERS AND LANDSLIDES
Chapter 21: MUTMUTBILLI
Chapter 22: KOSCIUSKO COUNTRY
Chapter 23: STALLION ON THE HIGH PLAINS
Chapter 24: BUTCHER COUNTRY SPUR
Chapter 25: HEALESVILLE

EPILOGUE
BIOGRAPHIES

THE COLOUR OF COURAGE

Size, be buggered.....
For it's the size of one's heart,
That tells a good horse.

One that has the pluck,
To never say die.

To take on a half flooded river –
With the hobbles on, of course.

To head across the ridges with knee hobble and sideline,
To be tied up all night on an overhead nightline,
To be ridden all day as your main saddle horse,
Then on the next, to carry the packs for sport.

Then to be told by the next clown you come across,
To do away with that little horse,
And to buy yourself a decent hack –
of course.

Ken Roberts

THE BICENTENNIAL NATIONAL TRAIL

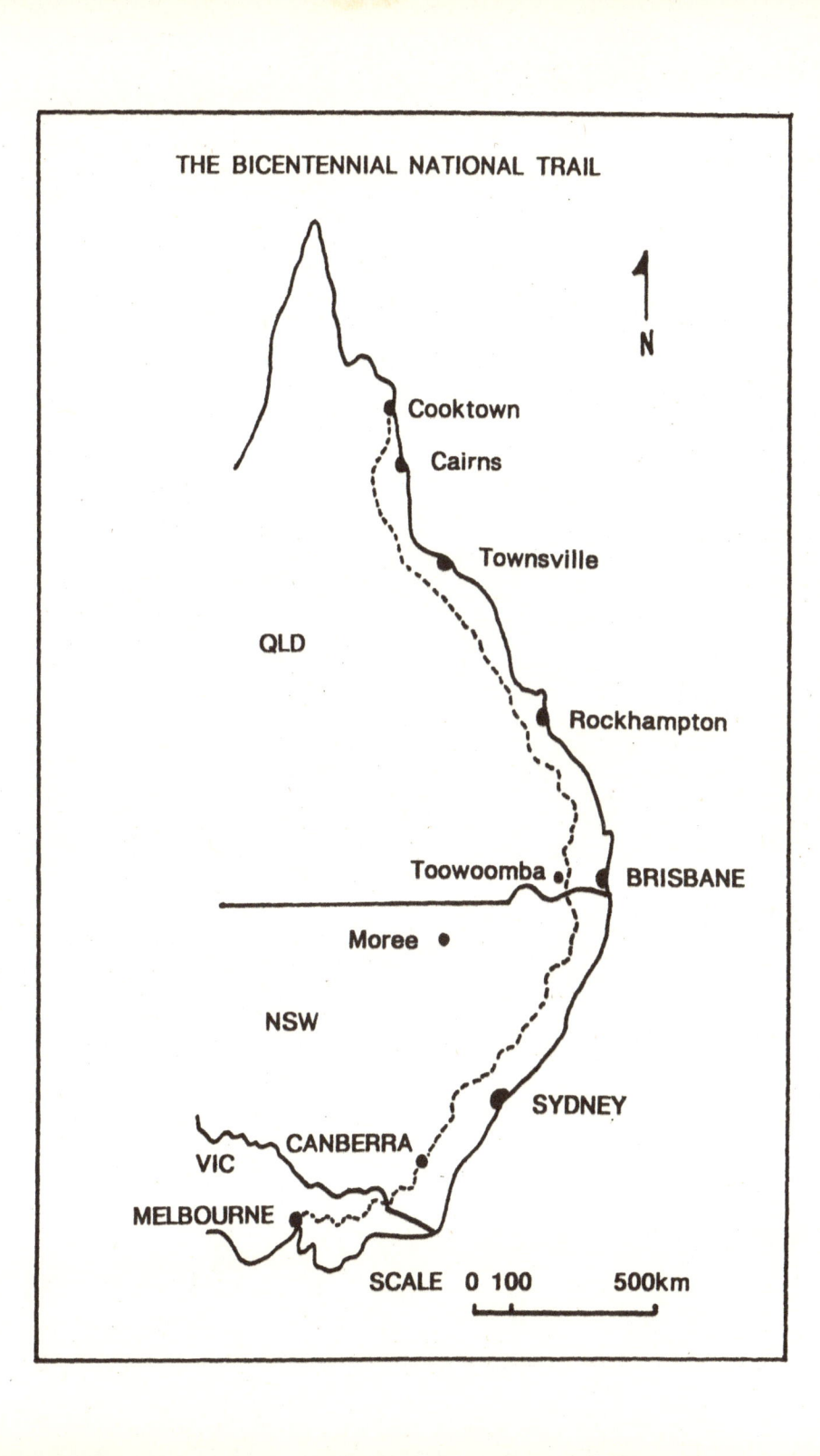

- Cooktown
- Cairns
- Townsville
- Rockhampton
- Toowoomba
- BRISBANE
- Moree
- Sydney
- Canberra
- Melbourne

QLD
NSW
VIC

N

SCALE 0 100 500km

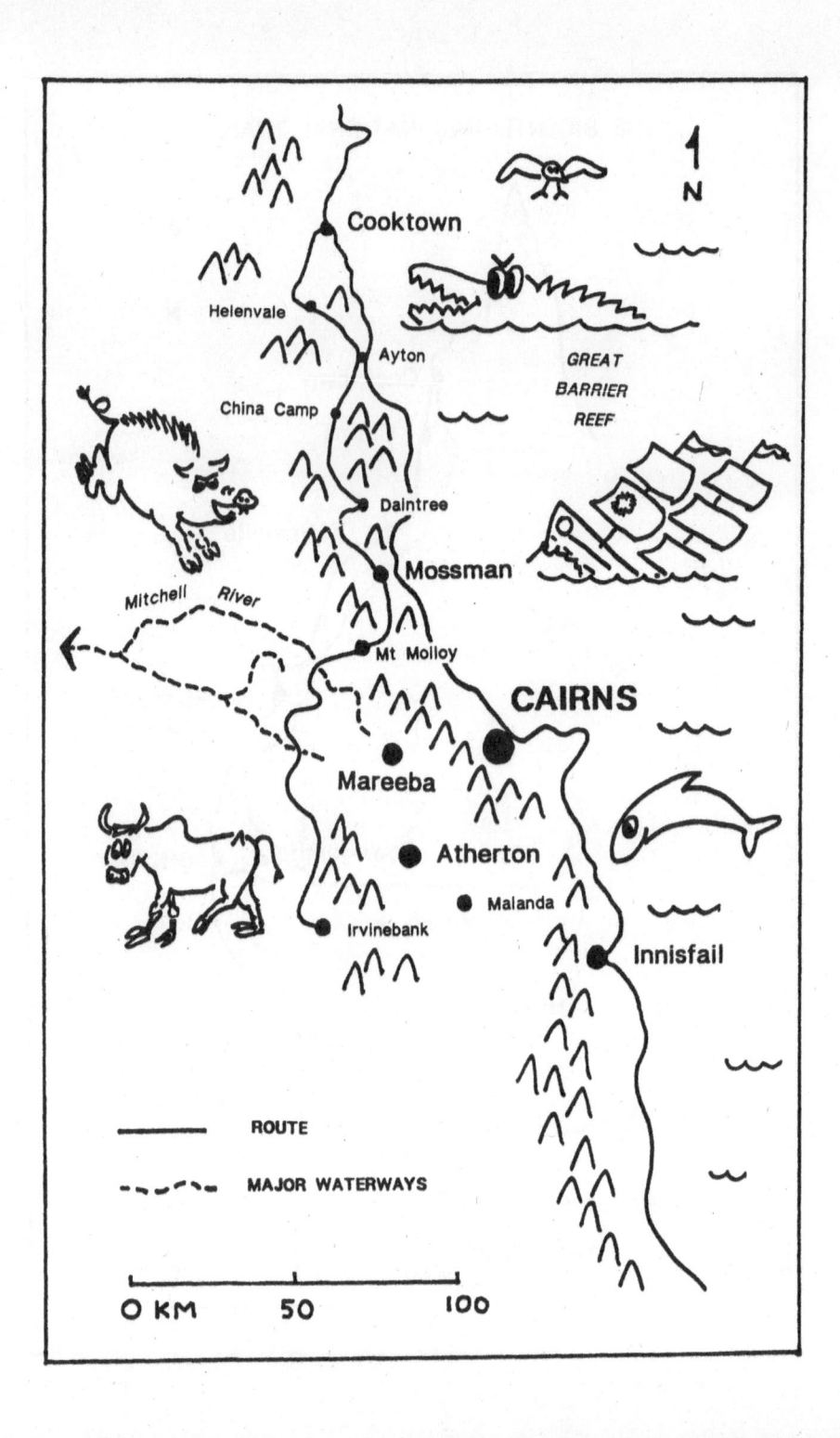

N
Cooktown
Helenvale
Ayton
China Camp
GREAT
BARRIER
REEF
Daintree
Mossman
Mitchell River
Mt Molloy
CAIRNS
Mareeba
Atherton
Malanda
Irvinebank
Innisfail
ROUTE
MAJOR WATERWAYS
0 KM
50
100

Chapter 1: COOKTOWN

THERE WAS SOMETHING irritating on the back of my neck. Preoccupied by the task at hand, I subconsciously ducked my head and delved a hand inside my sweat-soaked collar. Encountering an unfamiliar sliminess, I froze, every nerve ending tingling with electric horror. Panicked into action, I gouged the alien intruder off with my fingernails, unclenched my fist and shuddered in revulsion at the partly engorged leech flip-flopping about on the blood-smeared palm of my hand.

The steady downpour of humid rain eventually prodded me to my senses and I hurled the vile creature back into the wretched jungle.

"Get them off! Get them off!" I screamed hysterically. Tearing frantically at the slug-like vampires clinging to my neck, I lost my tenuous foothold on the muddy hillside. Landing with a heavy 'thump' on my spine I skated wildly downhill, feet first, over coarse-edged bladey grass and churned up mud. Using my arms as rudders and trying to dig the heels of my boots in to slow down, I was regaining control when I floundered off course and finished in an untidy tangle amongst my horse's legs.

The hill had once been rainforest, but the ridge we were climbing must have been cleared for a track at one time. Regrowth plants, grass and Lawyer Vines had since gained purchase, which only happens in a true rainforest where an old tree has crashed to the ground, leaving a hole in the canopy for sunlight to filter through. The undergrowth we were scrambling through was definitely in the 'jungle' category.

"Are you alright?" Ken hollered down to me.

Glancing up at the short, wiry Queenslander I felt a flush of anger at his expression. Doubled up and holding his sides with crossed arms, I could see his face under the water-logged brim of a dripping Akubra felt hat. Red-faced from laughter, Ken struggled to contain tears. The wretch had just about wet himself watching me free-wheel down the mud scree.

Apart from being covered in red mud and my elbows scratched to ribbons from bladey grass, I had sustained no real damage.

"I'm O.K.", I muttered, annoyed at his mirth in the face of my dangerous descent. If nothing else, it had taken my mind off the repulsive leeches. Thirsty for fresh blood and attracted by the heat radiated from living animals, they came springing out of the foliage like a troupe of Olympic gymnasts doing continuous back-flips.

COULD THIS REALLY be happening to me? Maybe I'd fallen asleep at my computer console in the comfortable, de-humidified and temperature controlled operator's room. I must have been dreaming that far-off scene on a hillside in the remote tropical jungle of Far North Queensland. No-one in their right mind would leave such a promising career with one of the largest oil corporations in the world. Especially not to go tripping along the Great Dividing Range down the east coast of Australia on horseback.

No-one except me that is. I'd been having these disturbing dreams since early childhood and instead of growing out of them, they just became more frequent and more compelling. On the other hand, my real-life world became increasingly dreary and routine. Every day, the same thing. Get out of bed, go to the bathroom, get dressed, have a meal, drive to the office in South Melbourne. A machine operating a machine. Knock-off time, go home, have a meal, watch TV, go to bed. No social life, I'm a shift worker.

Plenty of spare brain time for dreaming. Occasionally, I would snap out of it. *Did I just have breakfast?* Check in the sink. *Yes, there's my empty cereal bowl. Strange, I don't even remember what I ate.*

There comes a time when most people evaluate their lifestyle. For some it is a slow, pondering process while for others it may be a sudden assessment. Whatever the cause of an appraisal it usually has the same outcome — do nothing.

Why? Because there is safety in familiarity. There might be a few irksome facets to most people's daily lives, but these are tolerated for the sake of security, that invisible net that we all like to drape around ourselves. Tearing away those invisible filaments exposes the wearer, naked and vulnerable to the onslaught of an unknown future.

Me, I'd had a bad morning at work. One of those days where the 'irksomes' kept nagging, squealing, pinching and pricking me with their sharp little teeth. They won. They toppled the tower. The entire wonky edifice came crashing to the ground, splintering into a myriad of fragments. After being caught and bottled prior to adulthood, my spontaneous instincts burst to freedom once again. Chortling and whooping with delight they struck a match and began to burn the bridge. Unbidden, my hand picked up a pen and drafted a letter of resignation. I signed my name and still in a trance, walked over to my supervisor's office and handed the letter of fate across. The deed was done. I had thrown away my cocoon.

HORSES HAVE ALWAYS been my salvation. As a child in the gold mining town of Kalgoorlie, Western Australia, we always had a couple of horses stabled in the back yard. My younger sister Cathy and I were lucky children living in such close proximity to our beloved horses. Every day after school we mucked out stables and roamed the countryside on *Micky* and *Trigger*. Sometimes saddled, other times bareback with only a string around their noses our four-legged friends were our ticket to adventure. From the edge of town we explored tracks and bushland, rode over the tailings dumps, nearly fell down mine shafts, chased kangaroos and emus through the scrub, swam our horses in the dams and had a truly wonderful childhood.

At the age of 17, the Golden Era came to an end. Our family packed up and moved to the coastal city of Perth. New homes were found for the horses, who wouldn't be welcome in the backyards of suburbia. For me, it was like cutting off an arm.

The city was such a lonely place. When I left home and moved to the eastern states to work in Melbourne, it was even lonelier. In times of sadness, there was no horse to go and cuddle for reassurance. Old *Trigger* had always stood so patiently when I flung my arms around his neck and cried in his mane.

Now that I had burnt all my bridges and shed my cocoon of security, it was not surprising that I should look toward horses for salvation again.

I'd heard rumours about a track stretching from remote, tropical Cooktown in Far North Queensland to the outskirts of suburban Melbourne near the wild, southern waters of Bass Strait. Over 5000 kilometres of trail winding its way along the backbone of the Great Dividing Range. And the best mode of transport? Saddle and packhorse. How enticing! The one thing I longed for, more than anything, was to own a horse again.

I wish I'd been born in the era of horse teams and bullock drays, but alas, I came along about the time Neil Armstrong landed on the moon. How I yearned to go back to those early days, where the pace of life slowed to the rhythm of a horse's step.

Could this rumoured trail be harbouring a hidden time warp? The gateway to the past I had been searching for? Here was my chance, at last, to escape the modern world.

THE NATIONAL HORSE Trail had gained very little publicity until 1988 when it received a grant from the Australian Government as part of the nation's bicentennial celebrations. Re-named *The Bicentennial National Trail* (BNT) it was promoted as a recreational trail for horse riders, bushwalkers and cyclists.

The concept of a National Trail had slowly developed over a period of 20 years. Various riding clubs and individuals, including the legendary R.M. Williams, spent their own time and money finding a suitable route along the Great Dividing Range. Out of mutual interest, the Australian Trail Horse Riding Association (ATHRA) was formed. Its main aim was to unite all the volunteer workers and co-ordinate the mapping of a wilderness trail on existing stock routes, coach roads and fire trails before road closures and new developments made it impossible. The BNT is now independent of ATHRA and has published a series of 12 guide books on the trail from its office in Toowoomba, Queensland.

"How many people have ridden the entire trail?" I asked the administrator when I phoned for details.

"None," he answered to my surprise.

A few had ridden short sections, but never the entire trail. In 1978, ATHRA organised the National Mail Relay Ride along what was then the proposed route of the National Trail. Nearly 1000 horse riders participated in the relay to carry a mail bag, *Pony Express* style from Cooktown to Melbourne.

"How long do you think it would take to ride the whole trail?" I asked.

"Twelve months," was the answer. I ordered the 12 guide books over the phone. "There's only one problem with the books," explained the administrator, "we haven't written them all yet. I'll send you some draft notes when they're available" was his closing comment. The trail was still in its infancy.

When the guide books and rough notes arrived, I eagerly flicked through the pages. The books contained small sketch maps showing a narrow strip of country through which the trail passed. A heavy red line indicated what I took to be the National Trail. Each map showed one day's travel and a recommended campsite and was accompanied by a set of route notes giving distances to important turnoffs. However, on further reading, the heavy red line was not the physical trail, but the surveyed route of the trail. In some areas, the roads don't necessarily follow the legal survey, so I could end up in trouble trying to follow the red line. The National Trail was supposed to be well marked with red and yellow striped triangles at every major turnoff, but there were a lot of gaps in the notes so I purchased 1:100 000 scale topographic maps of the more remote areas.

IN NORTHERN AUSTRALIA, the climate is influenced by the annual movement of cyclones to form two distinct seasons. The Dry starts in May and runs until November and the Wet commences with storms in late October/early November which can flood major roads and waterways for weeks on end.

Australia's highest rainfall has been recorded on the range south of Cairns, where the annual average is about 4500 millimetres (180 inches). People caught travelling at this time of year risk being isolated by rising floodwaters that sometimes stretch as far as the horizon.

The logical thing for me to do was leave Cooktown at the start of the Dry and be out of the north before the next wet. With this aim in mind, I'd bought two horses in Victoria and accompanied them by road transport up to the Atherton tablelands at the end of April. National Trail supporters Beth and Clarry Stonehouse generously allowed me to stay on their dairy property while I organised transport for the horses over the rugged stretch of road to Cooktown. While staying there, I was introduced to Ken Roberts, a local horseman familiar with some of the country through which I planned to ride. My plans appealed to Ken and within a week we'd arrived on the banks of the Endeavour River where Captain James Cook grounded his ship in 1770.

Drawn by the Palmer River gold rush at the turn of the century, over 20,000 people lived in the Cooktown district. It was once the major seaport to the inland, but these days, the population has dwindled to less than 1000 and its main industry is tourism. From the top of Grassy Hill we gazed down on Cooktown and the snaking body of the Endeavour River, where rainforest meets ocean amidst a profusion of tea-tree swamps and mangroves.

Next to Captain Cook's monument on the foreshore, a brass plaque on an unimposing stone cairn marks the official start of the National Trail. On the 12th May, 1989, we filled out a 'Permit to Travel Stock' at the police station, posed in front of the monument while a few tourists clicked away with cameras, then took the first steps on our 5000km plus journey.

Bob, Sharon & Blaze en route to Cooktown

Chapter 2: RUNAWAY PACKHORSE

"FOLLOW ME THROUGH here," directed Ken, leading his packhorse off the Cooktown road and into a tea-tree swamp. "I know a good short-cut that'll give us a break from the dust and traffic." The melaleucas closed in around us giving me an eerie sensation of impending danger. We'd just ridden across the open-sided timber decking of the Annan River bridge, where crocodiles lurked in the water below. This creepy swamp was a likely sort of place to stumble across an old man saltwater crocodile and it raised the hair on the back of my neck.

"I used to do a lot of swamp jobs in this part of the world when I was offsiding for surveyors," Ken explained as he rode along. "Sometimes we'd be up to our necks in water following a surveyed line through a swamp."

He paused for a moment while the four horses floundered across a muddy creek.

"We were doing this swamp job up in the Daintree at Cow Bay," he continued, "and on the survey plan we were following, someone had written "Chainman missing – suspected taken by croc.""

Ken crossing the Annan River Bridge

I was glad of Ken's company, but his crocodile tales were frightening hell out of me as we rode through the ghostly paperbarks. It was a far cry from tearing around the bush on horses in the West Australian goldfields in my youth.

I'd known nothing of the demands placed on travelling horses; in Kalgoorlie they'd always been stabled and their feed came from a produce store. Having no experience on which to base my judgement, I'd purchased two geldings for this trip in Victoria, where I'd lived for the past 2 years. They appeared sound and were around the 8 or 9 year old mark: mature horses, physically able to take hard work and recover quickly from illness or injury.

Blaze really looked the part. A bay gelding 14.2 hands high with a broad white blaze down his face. He had a dash of Arab for endurance and a touch of Clumper for solid bone structure. Quiet natured, he'd been a kid's pony and, I suspect, fairly spoilt.

Bob, I wasn't so sure about. Standing 15.2 hh, the brown gelding with a white star on his forehead might have too much thoroughbred in him to keep weight on if feed conditions were poor. But he was quiet and intelligent, and I needed controllable, trustworthy horses to begin with. I'd recently learnt how to shoe and *Bob* had been a wonderful guinea-pig. For hours on end he'd patiently held up his hooves while I awkwardly rasped, hammered and tapped away.

THE PHYSICAL DEMANDS on my body were far more taxing than I'd imagined. It was only my first day out from Cooktown, yet I felt as crook as a dog. The tropical conditions, compounded by the infected sores I'd created by scratching the heads off my mosquito bites, probably had a lot to do with it. The occasional tug on *Bob's* lead was a further source of irritation, so I tied the rope around his neck and let him run loose.

"I don't think that's a good idea," hinted Ken.

Ignoring the comment, I kicked *Blaze* into a walk and smiled inwardly when *Bob* followed obediently like he always did. But this wasn't his familiar territory. At the next creek crossing, *Bob* stopped at the top of the bank when I rode down into the sticky mud.

"Come on boy!" I encouraged. The brown gelding wheeled and trotted back through the swamp. I swung *Blaze* around and headed after the packhorse, who broke from a trot into a canter and then into a full gallop as I lost sight of the swaying pack bags through the trees. *Blaze* whinnied in panic, needing no urging as he frantically galloped after his mate. I let him have his head and hoped his judgement was sound, as we were going too fast for my unaccustomed eyes to pick up any tracks.

Blaze proved his worth and brought me straight to the spot where *Bob* had pulled up. The wayward horse stood as if rivetted to the ground, eyes wide with fright, muscles trembling and coat shiny and dripping with sweat. It was several seconds before I realised the danger he was in. He must have hit a tree with the pack bags and the entire load had slid around his sweat-oiled ribs. A pack bag hung by one ring underneath his stomach and the big horse was bent at the knees, struggling to remain on his feet. It suddenly dawned on me that a rasping noise was coming from *Bob's* throat. The breast-plate had been twisted around to one side when the pack saddle slipped and it was choking him!

I hurtled out of the saddle, leaving *Blaze's* reins dangling on the ground and sprinted over to the sticken packhorse. Shaking with nervous panic, I tore my pocket knife out of its pouch, dropped it on the ground, hastily retrieved it and fumbled to open the blades.

As if from nowhere, Ken appeared at my side.

"Steady on there with that thing!" He grabbed my wrist before I slashed the breast-plate and probably a big chunk of my horse's flesh.

"Undo that buckle while I take the strain," he ordered calmly, kneeling down, shoving his shoulder under the dangling pack bag and releasing the pressure on the rigging. Still shaking, I unbuckled the breastplate that had been cutting off *Bob's* windpipe. The big horse shuddered as he gratefully sucked air into his oxygen starved lungs.

We undid all the buckles and straps and dropped the pack gear to the ground. *Bob* stood quietly, all trace of his wayward antics gone as he recovered his breath. Disaster averted, the adrenalin dissolved and my legs turned to jelly. I flopped onto the ground exhausted.

"We'll just have to wait a few minutes till he recovers," said Ken tactfully. The brief look of concern that flashed across his face showed that he knew it wasn't just the horse that needed to recover. I waited for the expected "look what happened" and "I told you so", but they never came. My easy-going companion just rambled on about the wild ride *Merlin* had given him and how well the little bay pony had stayed on his feet and dodged the paperbarks. I mentally forgave him for harassing me with crocodile stories and taking a 'shortcut' through the swamp.

Surprisingly, there was no damage to my pack equipment, except for the loss of my camera tripod. Strapped at the rear of a pack bag, it must have torn loose when *Bob* galloped through the scrub.

I picked up my foam-padded woollen saddle cloth which was saturated with sweat and had trapped a vast amount of heat. It was obviously not a good saddle cloth for the tropics, but I had no other padding. Wringing out as much sweat as possible, I plonked the sodden blanket over *Bob's* withers.

Ken hoisted the packsaddle up onto the horse's back. Straps and rigging dangled from the pads which swivelled off a hinged tree. Although I could manage it myself, I was grateful for Ken's assistance as lifting the awkward saddle was a bit like trying to handle a cockatoo tangled in baling twine. I always seemed to get my fingers pinched or bitten.

Leather pack bags containing food and camping equipment

were hooked by rings onto each side of the saddle. A long blue duffel bag stuffed with clothes and other gear was placed crossways on top of the pack bags. A canvas tarp folded across the top and down the sides to waterproof the bags and a surcingle buckled tightly around the entire load.

Perched on top of all this sat a rectangular, hardened plastic, silver camera case, tied on in a variety of ways with about 5 different straps. No matter how tightly I tied the camera case down, it always managed to work itself loose and move towards one side of the horse, upsetting the balance and tilting the load one way.

Bob carried 13kg of packsaddle and harness plus 79kg of equipment. My riding saddle also weighed 13 kg, while *Blaze* was lumping around 71kg of myself and the paraphernalia I'd managed to tie on around me. I had far too much weight on both horses for the long journey ahead, but until I worked out what equipment was necessary and what was junk I wasn't going to part with any of it.

WITH *BOB'S* LEAD rope firmly in hand, we rejoined the main road to see the mysterious jagged outline of Black Mountain rising in the distance. The Aborigines call it 'Kalcajagga' which means 'Home of evil spirits'. Almost bare of vegetation, the black lichen coating the jumbled, white granite boulders, gives the bald mountain its colour and name.

An Aboriginal legend tells the story of two tribesmen arguing over the ownership of a young woman. Each collected a huge pile of rocks to hurl at one another, but before they got the chance, a third fellow came along and stole the woman. Thus ending the fight, they walked away leaving two piles of rocks. The Cooktown Development Road passes through 'The Black Gap' in between these huge piles of granite.

Aborigines live in fear of Black Mountain. Evil spirits are rumoured to dwell in the rock caves and people have disappeared into them, never to be seen again. The scientific explanation upholds the presence of an invisible peril. Gases given off by the granite are highly toxic.

The locals tell of a European woman who was certain an Egyptian pyramid lay hidden under the boulders. She hired bulldozers and spent a fortune looking for it, but her search revealed nothing. There seems to be no logical explanation as to the formation of this granite mountain when not a trace of white granite is found anywhere else in the district. Scientists have their theories, but the secret of its conception will probably elude and intrigue the human race until the end of time.

As we passed through the Black Gap, the legendary mountains added a touch of mystique to the start of our journey.

Ken & Merlin at Black Mountain

Chapter 3:
BUSHMEN OF THE BLOOMFIELD

"THERE'S SOMETHING IN my garden I'd like to show you," announced Wilma Watkins after breakfast. The horses had spent their first night chewing down the grass in the Helenvale rodeo arena, while we'd dined with the Watkins family then camped under a verandah. I'd rung from Cooktown for permission to camp there, but the warm welcome we'd received came as a pleasant surprise. Filing out into the backyard after Wilma, she proudly waved at the Cooktown orchids growing on the trunks of orange trees. The handsome mauvy-pink sprays of Queensland's floral emblem were a pleasure to behold.

It was late morning when we thanked our hosts and departed the rodeo grounds but we didn't get far. Stopping outside the Lion's Den Hotel, we tied the horses up to a rail fence and went inside. Built by a packhorse teamster in the wild days of tin mining over a century ago, the ramshackle old pub retains a colourful atmosphere.

Bob & Blaze outside The Lion's Den Hotel

Lolling about on the verandah were a group from the Wujul Wujul Aboriginal mission. They came to attention at the sight of strangers riding in on horseback. We were hot property and the more outgoing characters asked us all manner of personal questions and introduced themselves and their shy buddies.
"Hey girlie, have you ever met any Murri like us before?" They called themselves 'Murris' in preference to the more derogatory names white people had for them.
"You take my photo, missy. You take my photo." I'd never met Aboriginal people who wanted their photo taken before. Obligingly, I clicked away with my camera while they smiled and posed like professional models.
"You come see us at the mission - we show you waterfall; him Wujul Wujul Fall." This invitation received a great round of agreement from the other Murris.
"What name you, what name?" On learning our names they had great fun repeating them over and over and making playful little sentences with them.
Inside the hotel, a colourful mural covered one wall and old pieces of harness and memorabilia adorned the others.
"They used to have a big python skin hanging up in here," explained Ken, looking around. "It's not here anymore, but this skin was 14 inches wide across the belly and 14 foot long and that was only half the length of the snake because they only had half the skin, aye!"
The town of Helenvale had only the rodeo grounds and the Lion's Den and once we'd visited both, there were no further distractions. We left the pub at midday and headed off along the gravel road to Ayton. Towering, slender trunks topped by a leafy spreading crown crowded along the edges of the road. The creeping vines and burgeoning green lushness of the humid rainforest seemed intent on reclaiming the frail strip of land that had been cleared for human passage. Beautiful, but spooky. It was as though something sinister lurked in those dark silent depths, where plants still exist from before the time of the dinosaurs.
Square concrete paving blocks had been laid to give vehicles traction on steep pinches and looked like a twin trail of footpaths. On one of these hills the minibus from the mission zoomed past. Its dark interior was loaded with smiling white teeth. Spidery black arms waved out the open windows as the inebriated occupants hooted in

recognition.

Blaze had dropped to such a lazy dawdle the previous day that I'd needed to boot him continuously to keep up with Ken's little ponies. This morning I'd switched to riding *Bob* who was far more willing to step out. Ken had swapped his riding saddle onto *Shatah*, a 13.2hh grey Arab crossbred pony he'd borrowed from Clarry Stonehouse. *Shatah* had jig-jogged with the packs on to keep pace with *Merlin* the previous day, reducing Ken's bread to crumbs, flaking his cake of soap and pulverising a packet of biscuits.

Darkness fell when we were still a long way short of Ayton: a small scattering of houses and a shop at the mouth of the Bloomfield River. We'd emerged from the rainforest and were riding alongside cleared paddocks and coastal scrub. The horses baulked at a bridge, which on closer inspection revealed missing planks and gaps wide enough to swallow a horse's leg. We forced them down into a marshy creek instead and they wearily ploughed through and out the other side.

A vehicle drove past with lights blazing, then pulled up and reversed back to us.

"Youse looking for Harlow's?" a voice slurred from within. The Harlows were people I'd rung from Cooktown for information on this section of the trail. They'd invited us to stay with them when we reached Ayton, instead of camping on the beach at Weary Bay. The bush telegraph had alerted everyone as to who we were and where we were going.

The voice gave us directions on how to find the place, but we couldn't really have missed the Harlows' house, even in the dark. A long way off, we heard sounds of raucous laughter, bottles clinking and people talking in loud, animated tones. Guided by the noise and the lights of the house, we steered off the road and into the Harlows' driveway.

As the horses crunched up the drive, a weatherbeaten bushman as lean as a kangaroo dog staggered out in bare feet to meet us.

"Bring them horses around here," he muttered loudly with a wave of his hand. "It's all bloody stuffed up tonight," he cursed, leading us around to a big shed.

I figured this must be Bob Harlow, but had no idea what he was talking about. Perhaps we'd possibly mucked up their plans for the evening meal because it was well after dark and we were several hours later than expected.

"I'm sorry we're so late," I apologised, feeling chastened.

"That's alright; excuse my bloody language," he atoned, "But it's all them other bastards; they've stuffed everything up on me," he grumbled as he helped unload the horses and stack the saddlery inside his shed. I still had no idea what he meant and whether we were in trouble or not.

Bob opened a wire gate in a paddock across the road and our 4 horses quickly disappeared amongst the tall, sedgy fronds of giant guinea grass. On the way back to the house, he tried to explain what had gone wrong.

"We was gettin' a gang ready to go sprayin' fer weeds this mornin'. Well, then the bloomin' skies opened up and it poured rain so's we couldn't go. So's we had ourselves a beer instead; and that was 9 o'clock this mornin' and I can't get rid of the bastards. And when everyone heard youse were comin', a heap more came around and got on the grog. I was gonna have a feed an' all ready for youse, but these layabouts 'ave been in me way all flamin' day."

I sighed with relief. Bob Harlow was only upset because he'd wanted to give us the best hospitality and had been hindered by his other guests.

"Come inside and meet my wife, Vivian," invited Bob, ushering us into the kitchen of his galvanized-iron clad home.

Seated around a long wooden table, leaning against walls and occupying nearly every inch of space were about 20 people, talking, drinking, laughing, swearing, smoking and sweating amongst the claustrophobic press of other human bodies. Cigarette smoke wafted and whirled into every vacant air space, coming to rest in a thick fog screen that hung from the ceiling. There were no glass windows in the external walls and a thin wisp of smoke from the fog cloud trickled out into the night air through a corrugated iron shutter that had been propped open with a stick of timber.

Bob elbowed his way about finding chairs for us and I found myself sitting next to Bob's wife, a vivacious Aboriginal/Malay woman.

"I normally don't drink," confided Vivian in loud tones, "But tonight it's Mother's Eve, so I'm goin' to celebrate," she laughed rowdily. Several other women lifted their glasses and toasted to the health of having a few drinks on the eve of Mother's Day.

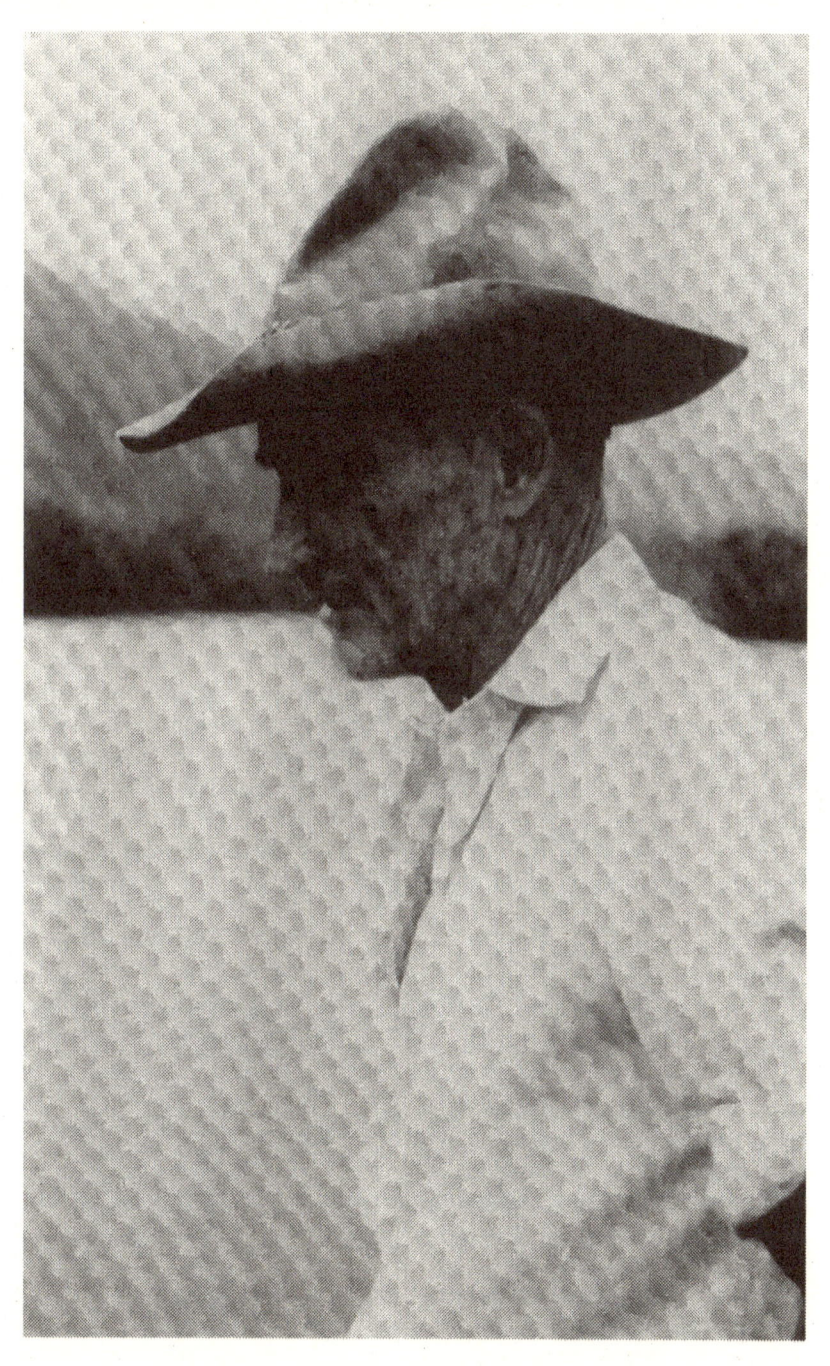

Bob Harlow beside the Bloomfield River

"C'mon Bob," she hollered above the noise, "Recite some poetry for the visitors .... give us "*Reared Upon The Daintree.*"

Bob slouched back in his seat, rolling the base of his half-empty beer glass around in a little jig on the arm of his chair. Waiting till all eyes were upon him in expectation, he glanced down and shook his head.

"Nah," he drawled.

"Ah, come on Bob, don't be a piker," taunted Vivien and her request was echoed from all corners of the room.

"Yeh Bob, yer silly old bugger. Tell us that poem yer Dad wrote."

"Nah," drawled Bob slowly, teasing the crowd.

"O.K. you mongrel old coot, I'll tell 'em!" stated Vivien, giving me a wink as she purposefully attempted a woeful recitation of the poem. Bob slammed his glass down on the table, slopping beer theatrically over the tabletop.

"Bullshit! It doesn't go like that at all!" he squawked. "Ya don't know what ya bloody talkin' about woman. Shut yer face and listen .... this is how it goes."

The noisy crowd silenced instantly as Bob launched into an expressive and colourful rendition of how his father wasted youthful years milking cows on the family dairy in the Daintree Valley. Once Bob got started on his poetry, the ceiling could have fallen in and he wouldn't have missed a beat. His audience fuelled him with lines from a massive tome on the poetic works of Banjo Paterson and Henry Lawson. Bob possessed the uncanny ability to read a poem once and commit it to memory forever. Without looking at the book, he listened to a couple of lines from a verse then reeled off the ballad word-for-word.

In the morning, the Harlows surfaced along with quite a few party guests who were very quiet and subdued. Nursing sore heads and looking rough and unkempt, a number of fellows had grass, twigs and other vegetation in their hair and soil on their shirts, obviously having spent the night in the garden.

Bob was cooking something in a heavy, cast iron griddle pan over the wood stove, determined to have a decent breakfast ready for us.

"Bloody disgusting," he muttered softly, ladling spoonfuls of gravy, onion and meat onto plates and passing them around to those who could stomach food at that hour. "I'm a bloody cattleman and I haven't got a bit of beef in the place."

I chewed hungrily on the stringy lumps in the gravy, not really listening to what Bob was saying or trying to identify the meat content of the meal.

"You know what you're eating, don't you?" questioned Ken, when I'd nearly finished.

"Not really," I answered.

"Well, have a look in the window above the sink".

I gasped at the sight of a huge, hairy black leg with trotter still attached, hanging under the open shutter.

"I bet that's the first time you've eaten wild pig!" chuckled Ken, delighted at my shocked reaction. I was glad I hadn't noticed the hairy leg of pork earlier, because I'd enjoyed the meal.

Seated in the kitchen with only a small group of friends that evening, Bob gave us some advice on how to tackle the next section of the National Trail.

"Don't go down the zig-zag whatever you do," he warned, referring to an old stock route that was no longer used. "I don't know why they mapped the trail through there because it's so overgrown you'll never push your way through. I put a fire through a couple of years ago and took some riders along it, but the spur's so overgrown now you won't even find the turn-off. Take the CREB (Cairns Regional Electricity Board) track instead. It's a much better ride and ya can call in at the old tin minin' show at China Camp."

LEAVING AYTON THE next morning, we followed a track along the mangrove-lined Bloomfield River and came upon a most unusual sight. From around a bend in the road appeared a worried looking group of Aborigines, mounted on a motley assortment of horses. All unshod, with matted coats and prominent hip bones, there were even a couple of old swaybacked pensioner horses shuffling stiffly along. Saddles and bridles were in a derelict state, held together with bits of wire and baling twine, green with a thick coating of mildew and haphazardly arranged. Several bridles were too long, and the horses slobbered and lapped their tongues over and around low-slung, rusty old bits. Some were too short and creased the corners of mouths into a smile. A couple of bridles hadn't quite made it over

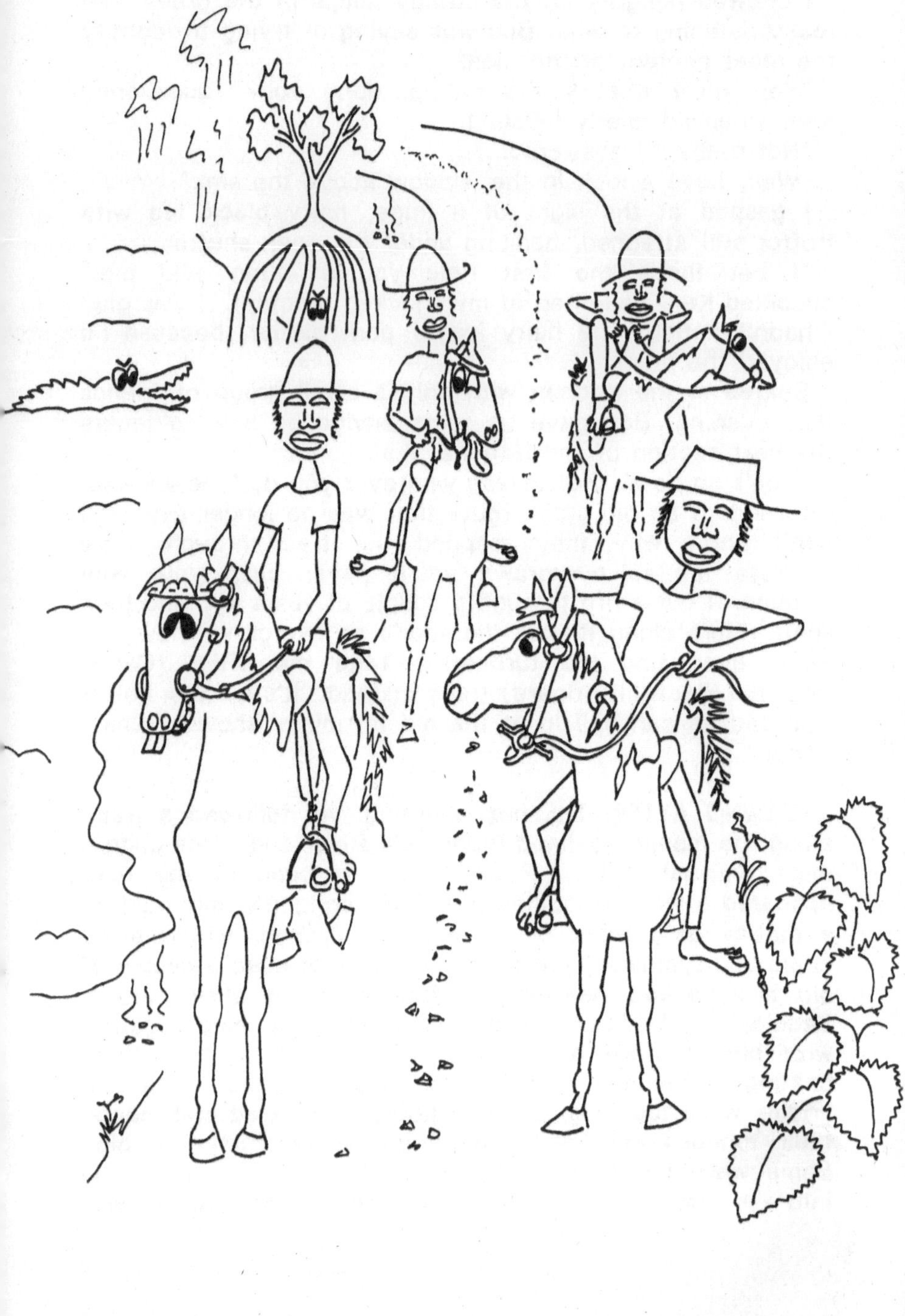

both ears and hung skew-whiff. One man rode with his knees up near his chin. Another couldn't reach his stirrups which flapped loosely against his horse's bony ribs and one fellow must have had about 6 holes difference between the length of his two stirrup leathers as he perched at an angle from the saddle, looking ready to topple over. All were barefoot and those who could reach the stirrups rode with only the big toe hooked in the iron.

Recognising our rowdy friends from the Lion's Den, we pulled up to say hello and ask where they were going. Instead of their usual loud banter, one fellow muttered "goin' musterin'", and without pausing or raising their eyes, the entire subdued cavalcade shuffled past.

"What's got into them?" I asked Ken as we rode on. Their behaviour was rather strange considering they'd been so keen for us to call in and see the waterfall at the mission.

"Remember we heard on the wireless about a stabbing at the mission? These fellas aren't goin' mustering. They're doing a bunk 'cos they think the coppers are on their way down from Cooktown. They'll come back home in about a week when they think things have cooled down. Then the coppers will quietly drive into the mission, pick up the blokes they're after and take 'em back to the Cooktown lockup."

Glancing down at the track, I watched muddy red ribbons of water twisting in and around our horses' hooves. I'd hardly noticed the soft, steady rain, but it had stealthily increased its tempo. By the time I unbuckled my oilskin from the front of the saddle I was soaked to the skin. The rain was surprisingly cold, sending a shiver through my body and bringing my arms out in goose bumps.

Not wanting to vacate the saddle and let the rain soak the seat, I draped the oilskin over my head, removed my saturated shirt and shrugged into the raincoat. Wringing as much water out of the shirt as I could, I stuffed it into the saddle bag with my maps. The plastic wallet in which I kept the maps would keep them dry. At least one of my preparations had been practical.

THE CREB TRACK climbed steeply into the McDowall Ranges beyond China Camp and the horses found it hard going on the slippery red clay. *Blaze* was proving an extremely lazy packhorse, constantly lagging back on the lead rope, stretching my arm out at an awkward angle and playing merry hell with my shoulder muscles and rib cage. Ken rode behind him a couple of times, growling ominous threats and booting him in the hindquarters. After this, Ken had only to raise his voice from nearby and *Blaze* obediently caught up.

Our ascent of the McDowalls was so steep in places that Ken's voice failed to affect my lagging packhorse. My shoulder socket could take it no more, and in desperation I tucked *Blaze's* lead rope under the surcingle. He dropped back and I lost sight of him around a bend, but not for long. When *Blaze* looked up and couldn't see *Bob*, he whinnied in panic and scrambled along the greasy track until he caught up.

I only wished I'd let him loose sooner. My lazy packhorse behaved as if he would follow *Bob* to the end of the earth. As I'd already discovered, this relationship didn't work in reverse and *Bob* didn't give a damn whether his faithful mate was there or not!

The next hill proved too much for the bonds of friendship. Ken had given me his packhorse to lead and dropped to the tail to make sure *Blaze* didn't turn around and head back for China Camp. We leant forward in our riding saddles, shifting our weight over the shoulders of our mounts to assist their climb. But the shod hooves of the packhorses struggled to gain purchase on the hard wet clay as the dead-weight of their loads pressed down on their loins.

It required more effort than *Blaze* was prepared to give. Throwing in the towel, he stood with all 4 legs spread-eagled, trembling like a young colt. Gravity took over and the horse skated backwards down the hill, leaving four long skid marks in the clay before him!

Ken was waiting for the sliding packhorse and shunted him off onto a narrow strip of spongy grass on the edge of the track. Pulling the lead rope from under the surcingle he growled at *Blaze* to move off. The stubborn animal refused to budge. Ken booted, kicked and threatened to feed him to the dogs, but all to no avail.

While I watched from above, Ken hitched the lead rope up again and hunted *Blaze* from behind. Without warning, the brainless horse leapt off the side of the track and crashed down into the undergrowth. The downhill side of the road appeared to be a sheer drop-off but when *Blaze's* ears and terrified, white-rimmed eyeballs plunged out of the bushes I knew his hooves had miraculously landed on solid ground.

I watched helplessly as Ken urged *Merlin* in after him. The vegetation was so dense that it was impossible to fathom where the solid ground fell sharply away. Like a hound after a fox, Ken bounded through the treacherous undergrowth, cursing wildly and driving the petrified packhorse upwards. *Blaze* emerged from the scrub beside us, scaling the embankment to stand trembling from fright and exertion beside his mate.

"Mongrel, bloody horse!" Ken swore as he appeared out of the shrubbery, unconcerned at the risk he'd just taken. "He's a spoilt, bloody kid's horse who's never been made work in his life!" Ken went on. "Get goin' ya lazy mongrel!" *Blaze's* eye's widened at the sound of Ken's voice. He scrambled to the hill top, giving no more trouble that day.

The tortuous mountain range slowed us to a snail's pace and the sun dipped over the horizon when we were still a long way short of our campsite. Ahead, loomed the disheartening sight of a long, steep pinch. We'd just passed an accessible grassy clearing under the powerlines. Having recently drunk from a puddle, the horses weren't thirsty so we decided to camp in the clearing and tackle the climb tomorrow.

There were very few regrowth saplings strong enough to support the nightlines for the horses, but Ken came up with an ingenious anchoring method. The nylon ropes radiated out from a couple of sturdy trees to be half hitched around bunches of thin, whippy saplings. Each line was pulled taut and anchored to the base of another sapling a few yards away. The whole affair looked like a booby trap waiting to be sprung.

Each horse was hobbled then tied to a running ring on the nightline so that its muzzle could just reach the ground. The bladey grass had little nutritional value but at least would fill the horses' bellies.

"What type of horse feed are you carrying?" Bob Harlow had asked us at Ayton.

"None," Ken had replied. Horse feed was too heavy a burden for our packhorses in the hills.

"Good," Bob had answered. "A group of trail riders came through about 10 years ago. They reckoned they weren't carrying any feed, but I still have to go and spray the weeds that have grown out of every pile of manure they left behind."

Horses have an inefficient digestive system that allows seeds to pass through and germinate. Only crushed or processed feed is guaranteed not to spread weeds.

Aided by a firelighting cube, we managed to coax some damp wood into a timid fire with enough heat to cook some noodles and a billy of tea. Finding a reasonably level patch of ground, I settled into my swag and flicked the canvas cover over my face to keep out the dew. I lay awake for a while, relishing the cool touch of the evening air, the beauty of the bush around us and the expectation of adventure that lay ahead.

Here we were at last, camped out on the National Trail with our beloved horses atop the magnificent crown of the McDowalls, listening to the comforting clink of hobble chains as they moved about on their nightlines. It was to be the most reassuring sound to my ears for the many nights that lay ahead.

Chapter 4:
SHERIFF OF THE DAINTREE

"LOOK OUT!" CRIED Ken.

I reefed *Blaze's* lead rope towards me, swinging his head away from a broad, heart-shaped leaf the size of a dinner plate. It harmlessly brushed the side of a pack bag, narrowly missing his rump.

"That was a close shave!" remarked Ken. *Blaze* had come within a few inches of a fatal swipe from a stinging tree leaf. The emerald-green leaves looked similar to those of other plants flanking the edges of the overgrown CREB track. Now that I'd seen one close-up, I would recognize it again by the serrated edge and microscopic dusting of fine white hairs.

Sometimes towering several feet above us, other times only inches high and concealed in the grass on the ridge between wheel ruts, the spiny hairs of this regrowth menace inject a virulent poison into anything unfortunate enough to brush against a leaf. A reddish-purply fruit resembling a cluster of raspberries can also conceal stinging hairs, yet strangely, birds can eat the fruit without being affected.

Stinging Tree

People affected by a major sting have gone raving mad, exhibiting all manner of erratic behaviour to relieve the pain such as trying to burn the spines out of their skin. There is little that can be done to achieve relief. The pain eventually eases, but can be felt for weeks afterwards and is rekindled by contact with water.

A horse receiving a bad sting will go berserk, galloping blindly through the scrub and crashing into trees, fences or anything in its path. The sweat from its exertions intensifies the pain and the frenzied animal usually mutilates itself to death.

On the alert for venomous, heart-shaped leaves, I didn't even see the wispy, barbed tentacle that latched onto my throat.

"Hang on!" I called to Ken. "Steady boy, take it easy now," I soothed, as *Bob*, sensing my panic, edged nervously back and forth. Delicately unhooking the barbs, I sacrificed my fingertips to cast the wretched tendril aside.

"Nasty stuff that lawyer vine," said Ken, as I sucked my bleeding fingers. "Now you see why they call it *wait-a-while.*"

Another regrowth plant, the base resembled a young palm tree until it sent out spidery, hooked fingers. Climbing creeper-fashion from tree to tree, these fronds thickened into porous canes popular for making whip handles, cane furniture and woven baskets.

The wait-a-while took its toll on our equipment, leaving deep gouge marks in my leather pack bags and across the toe of my boot. The horses panicked when entangled, lunging back and losing bits of skin when the vines tore free.

What a relief when a ray of sunlight lit the track ahead and we rounded a bend to find an open green, scrubby hillside sweeping down into the beautiful lush-pastured Daintree valley. I'd had enough of the rainforest with its smelly, rotting vegetation, closed in humidity and traps for the unwary.

"Watch out for logs floating against the current!" warned Ken as we descended to the crossing. I'd been primed to the eyeballs with Ken's crocodile tales over the last week, and here we were, 50 metres further north than I wished to be. In between us and the south bank, the dangerous, concealing waters of the notorious Daintree River sluggishly churled their way to the Pacific Ocean.

"Isn't there a ferry across this river?" I asked nervously.

"Yes," replied Ken, "but it's nearly 20 km downstream, there's no road on this side of the river and you'd have to scrub bash through the jungle to get there."

I knew this alternative was impossible with horses. It would probably take a man with a machete a month to cut a foot-track through and he'd be ripped to ribbons by wait-a-while vines. If it had been virgin rainforest instead of jungle, there would have been no tangle of undergrowth and we could have ridden through at a canter. Numerous cyclones had decimated the true rainforest by tearing open the canopy and letting in the sunlight that encouraged regrowth.

Leading *Merlin,* Ken rode *Shatah* into the river. The water lapped at the chest of the small grey pony as he strained against the current in midstream. Bending at the knees, Ken drew his feet up behind the saddle to keep his boots dry. The threesome made it to the opposite side unscathed.

"Come on *Bob!"* I urged, wanting to spend as little time in the water as possible. My trusty mount waded out strongly, spurred on by the urgency in my voice and his desire to join the mob of horses on the far side. *Blaze's* timing was impeccable. Always picking the worst possible moment to do the wrong thing, he chose this one and lagged back on the lead rope. I had my feet up near the knee-pads and the sudden tug on the rope threw me off balance. My heart pounded as I grabbed for a handhold, but *Bob* had felt my weight shift and swung upstream, preventing me tumbling over the back of the saddle. I risked a glance up and down the river, then kept my eyes dead ahead, not really wanting to see the ugly snout of an approaching crocodile because there was little I could do about it.

"I forgot to tell you," yelled Ken from the safety of dry land, "the crocs never go for the first one to cross, they always wait for the last!"

Hearing Ken's voice, *Blaze* quickened his pace as though he understood the meaning of the words. He came alongside *Bob* and the two horses laboured through the main current, waded into shallower water to climb dripping and puffing up the bank. Mumbling about the disadvantages of riding small ponies, Ken emptied the water out of his saddle bags and we set off along a well used road to the Daintree township.

TRUDGING ALONG THE bitumen, we'd been for a trip across the river on the barge and it was still a fair hike back to our horses. When a Toyota ute pulled over, we gratefully accepted a lift into Daintree, a small village comprising a few scattered houses, a museum and a general store with a liquor licence. Ken jumped into the back while I climbed in beside the driver, Maurice Mealing. Although small in stature, this dark-headed man handled his vehicle with the precision and power of one accustomed to much larger machinery. Not game to break his concentration and perhaps a little fearful of the brief penetrating glance he cast over me, I held my tongue until he pulled up outside the store.

"Coming in for a beer with us?" invited Ken, as he jumped down.

"Sounds like a good idea," replied Maurice with a sly grin and a glint of secrecy in his dark eyes. There was something mysterious about him that I couldn't quite fathom.

"Are there many crocs in the river?" I asked, feeling a bit braver with Ken seated beside me at a table.

"Only a couple of years ago," he replied, "a crowd of us were down at the river after a terribly hot day and a few went in for a swim. I walked out on a jetty and stopped before the bottom tier because the tide was in and it was covered in water," he remembered. "Only a few inches though, because one of the girls was standing there in ankle deep water and splashing herself to keep cool. Well, an ol' man croc' reared up out of the water beside me, lunged over the bottom tier, grabbed the girl and dived down into the river on the other side. It happened so quickly she never had a chance to scream or anything. They wiped out quite a few crocs after that incident, but it was a while ago now, and there's still a lot of them big fellers pokin' around in that river. I won't swim in it, that's for sure. And I always carry a gun down there, just in case."

At first I thought he'd made up the tale to scare me, but something I'd once read in the newspaper jolted my memory. The dreadful story was true. I was relieved that we were already safely across the Daintree with our horses.

"Come with me and I'll show you something," instructed Maurice. We filed out into the dusk and he opened the driver's door of his vehicle. I headed for the passenger door.

"We're not taking the vehicle this trip," he explained, pulling out an enormous pistol in an ornately studded holster. "This way!" he ordered, closing the door and heading off across the car park. I wasn't sure whether we had any choice.

Following Maurice through a dark thicket of timber, we came onto a sandy beach which sparkled like diamond dust in the fading glow of an orange sunset. But the lazy, swirling Daintree was a shimmering, malevolent ebony and looked as inviting as a bathtub full of death adders.

"Give us a hand will you Ken?" asked Maurice as he fiddled about in the shadows. I heard the sound of something light and hollow being dragged over the sand. The two men appeared, pulling a fragile, tin-pot dinghy down the beach and into the water.

"Come on!" Maurice called to me. "Hop in."

The horrifying thought of bobbing about in that frail little tub over those sinister, inky-black depths was too much for me.

"There's not enough room for us all," I called out, "I'll stay here."

"Garbage, there's plenty of room," Ken assured with a grin. I had the most awful feeling that I was being manipulated by two lunatics. Unwillingly, I climbed aboard.

"Here, hold this!" commanded Maurice, thrusting the monstrous cannon into my lap. He took up the oars while Ken cast off from the shore and jumped in over the stern.

"Best time to go croc-spotting now," offered Maurice, effortlessly dipping the oar blades as the little boat glided smoothly over the sullen stretch of water. "If you were to shine a torch around, you'd see hundreds of pairs of red eyes watching us."

I shuddered at the thought. The Daintree River was dangerous enough in broad daylight. What on earth was I doing floating around on its menacing waters at night like a tantalizing morsel on a tin plate?

An eternity passed before the boat scraped bottom and

nosed into the wet, sandy shore. Abandoning the little vessel, the two men dragged it up out of the water, and we climbed through a fence and followed Maurice up a grassy hill.

"Here he is, over by the tractor." Maurice walked over to a bulky, grey body and slapped it with his hand. "Meet my prized Brahma bull, 'Fritz'! Come and give him a pat. He's quiet as a lamb."

Watching Maurice scratch and tickle the mean looking monster, I tentatively put out a hand and touched him on the nose. He snorted and I jumped back with a squeal.

"It's O.K.," said Maurice, "he's just being friendly. Tickle him behind the ears like this – he loves it."

Bravely, I reached out and touched the smooth grey coat. The skin moved under my fingertips, and I rolled the soft, fleshy hide as though it were not attached to the animal, but merely a rug thrown over him. It was so different to the tight skin of a horse.

Fritz stood relaxed and calm, one tonne of solid bull capable of goring each of us into the ground with a twist of that brutal head. I tousled the long, floppy rabbit ears and wobbled the massive hump behind his short neck.

Like the whirling skirt of a flamenco dancer, a loose flap of convoluted skin ran from under the bull's chin and down in between his stumpy front legs. His light hindquarters looked out of proportion with the rest of the body as though he'd been crossbred with a greyhound.

"Go on, hop on his back!" Maurice invited. I wasn't *that* stupid.

"No thanks," I replied.

"He won't do anything; look how docile he is," Maurice insisted.

"Well if he's that quiet," I argued, "why don't *you* get on him!" I challenged, pleased to have come up with a good excuse. But I didn't count on Maurice taking up the challenge.

"Easy boy, nice boy," soothed his owner, leaning over the bull's back and lifting his feet off the ground. Scratching, tickling and talking softly to the enormous beast, Maurice gingerly swung his leg over, breaking into a nervous sweat as he slowly sat upright.

"See – no trouble at all." Having proved his point, the man wasted no time in getting back onto the ground. "Now it's your turn," he demanded, giving me a wicked grin.

I'd run out of escape routes. "Here goes nothing," I thought as Maurice bunked me up.

"You'd better start scratching him and talking nicely," he warned.

"Nice bull, nice bull," I muttered from my vulnerable position, scrabbling my fingers over the ugly hump in front of me. For the second time that evening, I wondered why I'd allowed myself to be cajoled into such a dangerous situation.

Fritz completely ignored the fact that there was a petrified girl on his back. I relaxed a little and began to enjoy the thrill of being mounted on such a powerful beast. No wonder the bullriders came back time after time to ride the big Brahman bulls out of the rodeo chutes. I scrambled down after that thought in case *Fritz* changed his mind and pelted me into oblivion.

When I relayed the stories of our night's adventure to the locals, they thought we'd gone mad.

"You're crazy for knocking around with that Maurice character for starters," said one fellow. "He climbed up on the pub roof one night, fired that flamin' cannon off and started yelling '*I'm the Sheriff of the Daintree*' at the top of his voice."

Sheriff or not, he certainly gave us a night to remember!

Chapter 5: JUNGLE ASSAULT

THE HORSES STAMPED their feet impatiently, and I shifted my weight in the saddle, unsuccessfully trying to find a dry spot under the dripping canopy of leaves. Ken had been gone for over an hour and I was beginning to worry.

"You won't get through to Mossman on the CREB track after Stewart's Creek," we'd been warned at Daintree the day before. They were right. We'd surveyed the track under the powerlines from the creek crossing the night before. It was steep, slippery, overgrown with giant bracken fern and bamboo vines and nobody had been through in the last 10 years. The long bitumen detour around the range was an unsavoury alternative so we'd pressed on to look for another route through the hills we'd been told about.

The horses lifted their miserable, bedraggled heads in unison, interrupting my thoughts. Hearing the faint strains of a cheerful whistle, I caught sight of Ken, carefully picking his way downhill through the dim, rain-misted forest.

"The good news," spruiked my companion as he came within earshot, "is there's no stinging tree. The bad news is it's pretty steep in parts so we'll have to lead the horses on foot. It'll be difficult; but it's not impossible."

It wasn't the trail we'd been looking for, but Ken had found some old blaze marks on trees where surveyors had cut a line through the scrub many years ago. He went ahead to clear a path through the vines while I led *Shatah* in the lead, hoping the other horses would follow.

They didn't. Horses peeled off at right angles, preferring to follow the contour rather than climb. Even more cunning, *Blaze* dropped to the tail, turned around and headed back where we'd come from.

"Hang on!" I called out to Ken. I went back for *Blaze* while he rounded up the others.

"We might have to hold onto them," I puffed, returning with my packhorse from the bottom of the hill.

It was only possible to travel the horses in single file and leading two horses each in this manner was awkward. Continually shuffling lead ropes around trees, we had to be careful not to pull the horses down on top of us.

Climbing the hill above Stewart's Creek

Merlin broke loose from Ken's grasp, skidded downhill, and crashed through the timber until a thicket of sturdy saplings halted his descent. Ken followed close behind, seizing the lead rope and wrapping it firmly around a tree before his packhorse slid further. Abandoning our system of leading two horses at once, we tried shifting them up in stages. We'd come to a grassy patch where the sun would have shone through had it not been raining. Starting up the slope with *Shatah*, I bogged in the mud and he overtook me and disappeared into the shrubbery above.

Ken scrambled to the top of the pinch and I sent *Merlin* up next. He laboured under the packs, struggling to hold his footing as *Shatah* had chopped up the mud and it offered no traction. Ken slid down to assist him.

"Watch out behind you!" I screamed, as *Shatah* appeared out of the vegetation and came slipping and sliding down the mud scree. Ken ducked under *Merlin's* neck, but his foot stuck in the mud and the grey pony skated over Ken's shin on the way past. *Shatah* careered into *Bob*, so I dived on his lead rope and tied him up before he went any further. Ken had managed to pull *Merlin* to the top where he tied him to a sapling.

I sent *Bob* next, but he scrambled up beyond Ken's reach, knocking *Merlin* off his feet on the way past. The sapling to which he was tied bowed over and the knot slipped towards the tip, leaving poor *Merlin* hanging by his chin. As Ken rushed to his aid, *Bob's* head and shoulders appeared above.

"Look out!" I cried. For the second time that afternoon, Ken flew out to one side as a horse crashed over the top of him. Catching *Bob*, I tied him up to let him catch his breath and sent *Shatah* off again. The valiant little pony struggled up through the deepening quagmire. Ken caught him at the top and tied him beside *Merlin*.

Feeling something irritating on the back of my neck, I scraped the skin with my fingers. Opening my palm to reveal a partly engorged leech flip-flopping around in a pool of blood, I shrieked, hurled the slimy creature back into the jungle, lost my balance and fell face-first into the mud. Ken laughed himself silly while I stomped off to get the next horse.

When I led *Blaze* to the foot of the pinch, my packhorse took one look at the daunting hill and threw himself down in the mud. I dived to one side as his flying hooves sailed past, watching in terror as he hurtled downhill in a sickening cartwheel. A thicket of timber checked his fall, and he wedged upside-down between two sturdy saplings.

Ken and I raced down beside him. We needn't have hurried. He didn't plan on going anywhere! Quite content to stay where he'd landed, *Blaze* lay happily on his back, all four legs in the air, my camera case and crushed duffel bag acting as a cushion underneath.

"Never in my life have I come across a horse as lazy as this one!" announced Ken, standing with his hands on his hips and shaking his head in amazement. "He just took one look at that hill and decided he wouldn't have a bar of it!"

Ken hauled the loafing packhorse to his feet and marched him back up the hill. At exactly the same spot, *Blaze* did his lolly and wound up on his back in the scrub again. He lay there and sulked, refusing to budge.

After pulling off the packs and saddle, Ken picked up a hunk of wood and walloped the lounging horse on the rump. The rotting timber disintegrated on impact, having no effect whatsoever.

It took a solid 5 minutes of yelling, slapping and heaving to coax the sullen animal to his feet. Dragging and shoving him back up the hill, Ken had a brainwave.

"We're not thinking straight," he motioned, smacking the heel of his palm against his forehead. "Alls we have to do is send *Bob* up first and bonehead will follow!"

Ken climbed the slope and I sent *Bob* up to him. *Blaze* nearly mowed me down in his effort to climb up after his mate!

"That mongrel bloody horse climbed up there with no effort whatsoever!" he cursed. "And now we're the poor silly bastards who've gotta hoick all his bloody gear up there!"

Shouldering each item, we carried it up piece by piece. With one hand balancing the load on our shoulders and the other digging fingers deep into the mud to gain purchase, it took three trips to cart *Blaze's* load to the top.

If nothing else, I lost my fear of leeches. Instead of picking them off individually, I waited till there was a whole clump on my neck and swiped them off by the handful.

The next stage was even steeper than the last, taking us a couple of hours to reach a timbered ridge line where the horses had solid ground under their hooves once again. We switched back to leading two horses each and made far easier progress until *Shatah* put his foot down a hole and launched himself towards the edge of the narrow ridge. Ken let go of *Merlin* and heaved on *Shatah's* lead rope, spinning him around to crash into *Merlin*. The impact sent both horses sliding front legs first over the slippery track on their haunches, heading for the edge again.

Pouncing on *Merlin's* lead rope, Ken braced himself to take the strain, but the combined weight of both horses was too great. Ken's feet were pulled out from under him and he landed heavily on his backside. He hung grimly on to the ropes, and it was my turn to laugh as the two horses towed him downhill on the seat of his pants!

Ken's weight acted as a brake-log and the horses slowed down enough to gain their feet. Still unaccustomed to balancing himself under a load, *Merlin* stumbled over the side of the ridge. He disappeared from view and we scuttled down after him in the fading daylight, dreading what we might find.

Merlin had slid about 10 metres and come to rest in a dog-like sitting position. He'd turned side on to the hill, but the near side pack bag pushed him away from it and the off side bag hung downhill like a dead weight. Only 5 metres away the slope disappeared over the edge of a vertical drop.

"We'll have to offload him, and quickly," assessed Ken. "I don't know how much longer he can hold himself there!" The helpless horse glanced at us, wide-eyed with fright.

"Steady boy," soothed Ken, crawling over above him. He reached down under the front of the uphill pack bag, his fingers groping for the surcingle buckle.

"Bugger it!" he cursed. "I buckled the bloody surcingle up on the wrong side this morning."

Scrambling down with his head level with the bottom of the horse's belly, Ken kneeled on his left leg and straightened his right leg below him as a brace. Placing one hand on *Merlin's* stomach, he gently pulled the surcingle strap out from the buckle and gave it a tug.

"Holy hell!" he whispered when the slight pressure pulled *Merlin* down towards him.

"Easy boy, easy." Ken thrust both hands against the horse's belly, using himself as a prop. *Merlin* came to a halt.

Bracing himself again, Ken gave a heftier tug on the surcingle strap, managing to undo the buckle as the pair slipped another 6 inches closer to the edge of the drop-off. The pack bags and bedroll were deftly cast aside while Ken coaxed the exhausted horse shakily up to the ridge-top.

Shock had drained all *Merlin's* energy, so we recovered the bags and bedroll on foot and stacked them on the edge of the pad alongside *Blaze's* load before continuing.

What a relief when we finally made it out under the powerlines. We tied our horses up and I looked around for somewhere to lie down. Every muscle and limb in my body ached, and all I wanted to do was collapse onto a sodden clump of ferns and go to sleep.

"If you stop now," said Ken, seeing my intention, "you'll never get going again. We've still got half a night's work ahead of us. We'll have to bring up all that gear, fish out the tent, bedroll, dry clothes and something to eat, otherwise you'll get pneumonia from lyin' out in the rain all night."

He was right, of course. I urged my exhausted body back into the pitch-black jungle. Reaching our stack of gear, we picked up a bag each and headed back uphill. I lost count of how many trips it took to lug, drag and wrestle the remaining gear to the top. My dulled senses were only vaguely aware of the agony of tortured body parts.

"You'll have to set your tent up, because I don't know how to put it together," Ken apologised as we rummaged through pack bags looking for necessary items.

The tent was a tricky little two-man tunnel affair, guaranteed by the manufacturer to outlast a blizzard on Mt Everest. These features weren't much value in the tropics, but I could set up my familiar, nylon fortress with my eyes closed and it was one hundred percent waterproof. Ken's bedroll was soaked right through.

We unrolled his soggy bedroll on the floor of the tent for a mattress and laid my heavy swag canvas on top.

"Yuck, what's this all over my feet?" I exclaimed, discovering a sticky mess when I pulled off my boots.

Ken shone the torch over, illuminating my blood-soaked socks. I shrieked in horror, wondering what damage had befallen my numb, waterlogged feet.

"It's allright, it's only from the leeches!" laughed Ken.

The insidious blood-suckers had found their way inside my boots, squeezed through the fabric of my socks and had a good feed on me. After which, their engorged bodies had been crushed to death and their stomach contents absorbed by my socks. Everything about leeches was revolting!

Changing into dry clothes, we huddled inside the tent, opened a tin of spaghetti and ate it straight from the can. There was no chance of getting a fire going tonight so our dehydrated food which needed to be reconstituted in boiling water was of no value.

We'd stretched out a tarp and managed to catch some rainwater, but it tasted like muddy canvas. Even the horses turned their noses up at it. The ground was so saturated and muddy that the saddles would have ended up waterlogged if we'd taken them off. We left them on the horses to keep their backs warm and dry, tying them to trees as there was nothing to eat that wasn't poisonous.

"COME AND HAVE a look at this!" called Ken. Winding my way through the towering bracken, I traced his voice to the base of a power pole. The hill dropped sharply away, giving us a clear view of the Stewart's Creek causeway we'd crossed two nights ago. Materializing out of the swirling mist, it was so close that I could have landed in the stony-bottomed creek below if I'd taken a running jump. Returning to camp, I consulted the map and calculated the distance we'd travelled. From the base of the hill where we'd started our climb to our campsite was barely 800 metres. And it had taken over 8 hours!

What a slog it had been! Never, ever in my life before had I felt so exhausted, terrified and uncomfortable as I had been yesterday. And yet it suddenly occurred to me that I'd not once thought of throwing in the towel. There had been nothing to stop me turning around, abandoning Ken and heading for the nearest airport and a ticket back to my comfortable job in a comfortable office. I'd given up on much less demanding tasks in the past. Was I really a masochist, or could it be that I was actually enjoying myself? The memory of *Blaze* upside down in the mud and Ken tearing his hair out in frustration, brought tears of laughter to my eyes. It HAD been fun! I'd set out to achieve something and battled against all odds to come up trumps.

What's more, horses had taken on more purpose in my life. I dearly loved horses, but I'd never felt as close to them before as I did now. And Ken? How could I abandon him? In little over a week we'd formed such a strong bond of friendship that I couldn't bear the thought of leaving him. I certainly wouldn't let him or the horses down. We were all in this together: We were not individuals, but a team.

There was little time for any more thought. We needed to quickly pack up camp, get going and find something edible for the horses.

"I'll ride *Blaze* for you and see if I can get the lazy bastard to work," offered Ken.

Passing me his packhorse, Ken booted *Blaze* forward

through the thick undergrowth beneath the power lines. The horse took one almighty plunge and stopped. Ken booted him again, and they plunged one step further, but no more until he got another dig in the ribs. He reminded me of a fat, lazy toad being prodded with a stick.

It was easier travelling for the horses behind as *Blaze* was clearing a track for them. But after one of his jack-rabbit bounds, Ken caught a glimpse of something and hopped off to investigate. He backed hastily out of the ferns, looking a little pale around the gills.

"Bit steep here," he reported. "We'll have to backtrack and find another way down."

We discoverd an old vehicle track, partially obscured by giant guinea grass and ferns. Pushing our way through lawyer vine, we lost a bit more skin and tore a few extra rents in our leather and canvas. A couple of small trees blocked our passage, but we chopped through with a tomahawk.

The track brought us out into a beautiful little gully underneath the power lines. A soft, tender leaved grass grew along the banks of a gently trickling stream, and we pulled up for the horses to drink and graze.

"Have a look where we would have come out if I'd kept riding," invited Ken.

Swinging around I looked back up the powerlines and shivered at the awesome wall of rock that faced us. Fifteen vertical metres above, the thick army of ferns came to a sudden halt at the edge of a bluff. No wonder Ken had looked pale when he'd crawled out onto the unexpected clifftop!

The horses weren't interested in a drink and only grazed a few minutes.

"You'd think they'd be hungry after being tied up all night," I remarked. "This grass looks much tastier than that coarse-edged stuff they've been chewing on lately."

"It's *green panic*," said Ken. "For some reason, horses aren't real keen on it." Pressing on, we picked up the bracken-free vehicle track again which was much easier travelling.

Late in the afternoon, our path was blocked by a massive black bean tree that had fallen across the road. It had caused a minor landslide down the vertical road embankment on our left, while its dead branches disappeared into the steep undergrowth below.

"We might be able to ride around the top of the landslide where those roots are sticking up," said Ken. He coaxed *Blaze* forward, but both front legs plunged out of sight and he bogged to the shoulder. The horse heaved backwards, lost his balance and flopped sideways in the mud.

"Hop off; quick!" I cried urgently, terrified the floundering horse would crush his rider.

"I can't!" retorted Ken. "Me left foot's jammed in the stirrup and stuck in the mud!"

Blaze flung his head up and with a tremendous effort, rolled his body upright. Ken stuck with him as the horse pivoted on his haunches and gave an almighty leap out of the sucking glue-pot.

"Looks like we might have to find another way through," grinned Ken, unshaken by the experience.

There appeared to be just enough room to lead a horse under the fallen tree if we hugged the side of the cutting. Stomping a path through the bracken fern, I stopped short of a small hole, just wide enough to take a horse's leg. It lay directly under the tree trunk at the point of maximum clearance. Water trickling down the gutter had gouged a huge subterranean cavern at least two metres deep beneath the narrow entrance hole. A horse stepping onto that fragile crust would be swallowed up into the bowels of the earth.

Our baby tomahawk wouldn't cut through the massive trunk so we had no alternative. Gathering branches, I placed them over the hidden cave so the horses would steer to one side. This left very little room for a horse to duck under the log, so we offsaddled them for extra clearance.

We led the ponies through within a foot of the underground cavity without any mishaps. *Bob's* wither touched the underside of the log, but he bent at the knees and scraped through unscathed.

Hastily loading up the horses again, we pressed onwards, striking the Whyanbeel Road as the sun's dying rays faded over the main range on our right. We were safely out of the jungle at last!

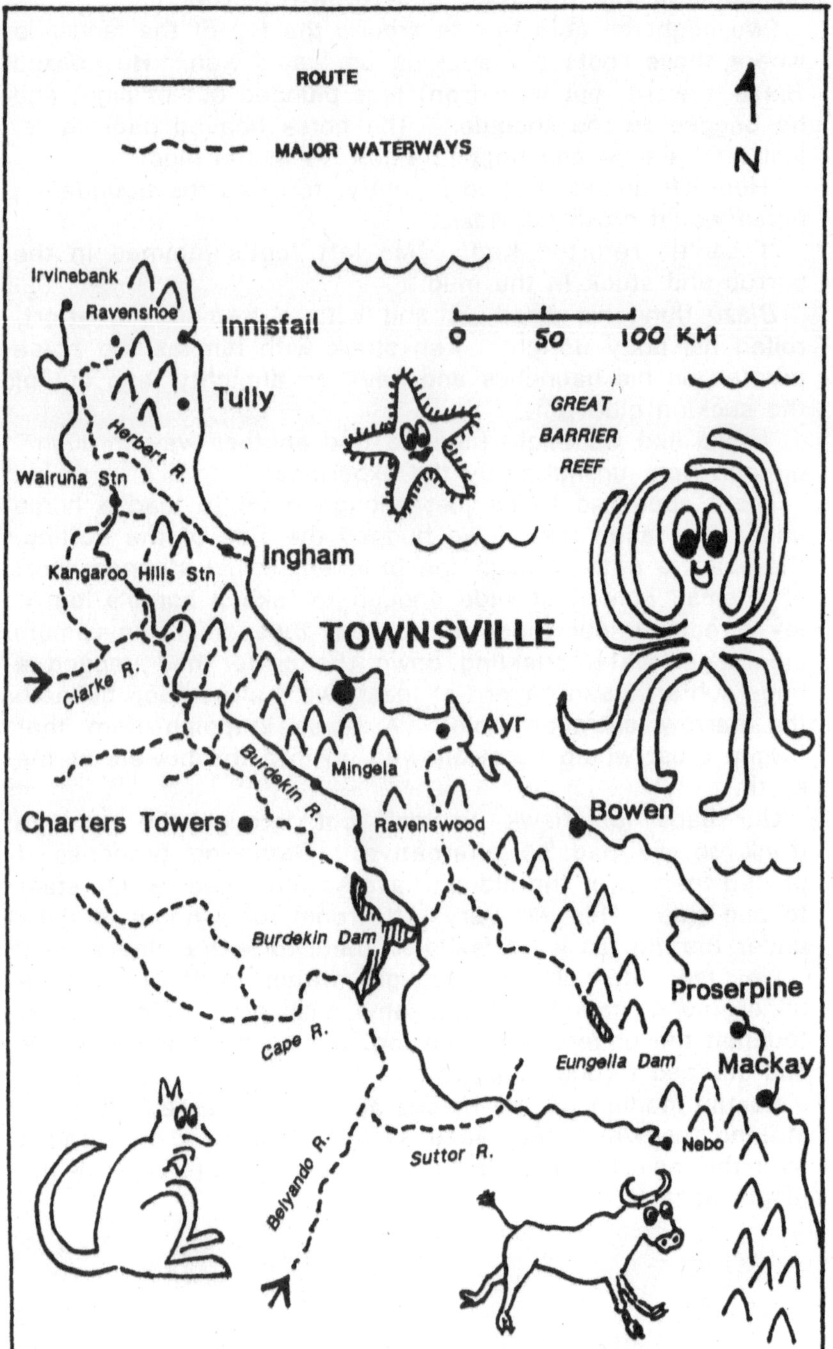
ROUTE
MAJOR WATERWAYS
N
0 50 100 KM
Irvinebank
Ravenshoe
Innisfail
Tully
Herbert R.
Wairuna Stn
GREAT
BARRIER
REEF
Ingham
Kangaroo Hills Stn
TOWNSVILLE
Clarke R.
Ayr
Mingela
Burdekin R.
Bowen
Charters Towers
Ravenswood
Burdekin Dam
Proserpine
Cape R.
Eungella Dam
Mackay
Belyando R.
Suttor R.
Nebo

Chapter 6:
A BULLOCKY'S NIGHTMARE

THE MOUNTAINS GAVE way to rolling coastal hills and an endless sea of sugar cane. Feathery tips shimmered above our heads as we rode alongside cane paddocks, crossing over narrow gauge tramways used by locomotives to pull bins of cane from the paddocks to the sugar mill. The absence of fences gave an air of freedom to the place. Even the stately cane farmers' houses, standing high on stilts, lacked fences. The cane grew right to the edge of the lawns.

Camping overnight in the sugar town of Mossman, we climbed the Rex Range and swung inland to pick up the old 'Bump Road' at the headwaters of Mowbray Creek. Pioneer bushman Christie Palmerston blazed this trail through to the coast off the Thornborough-Cairns pack track in 1877. It opened up a wagon link from the goldfields to the coast, giving birth to the town of Port Douglas.

The National Trail had avoided the beginning of the road near Port Douglas, thankfully sparing our horses from the rigours of Slatey Pinch. This half mile section was so steep that the early model cars had to be towed up with a team of 5 horses. Coach passengers had to both climb and descend this section on foot, while bullock teams travelled in pairs so they could 'double-bank'.

The old wagon road was little more than a track, but quite distinct as it passed through lightly timbered grazing country to the town of Mt Molloy. It was much easier travelling for the horses since the coastal humidity had been replaced by the warm dry air of the inland.

The trail swung south through a waving sea of golden grader grass plains at Font Hills Station. Leaving the Mitchell River valley, we turned west up Dora Creek and climbed the northern reaches of the Hann Tableland. Carved out of the rock on the top side and stone pitched below, the 'Bump Road' was extremely narrow as it scaled the range.

The record load to be carted along this track was a boiler weighing nine tons eighteen hundredweight for a mill at Kingsborough. The 90km journey from Port Douglas took a fortnight and the teamster used two teams of bullocks, yoked four abreast. This Dora Creek section must have been a nightmare for the bullocky. If one of the outside bullocks had missed his footing, he could have pulled the entire outfit over the edge to tumble and smash their way down into the chasm below.

West of the tableland, we sighted our first mob of wild brumbies. They caught one whiff of us in the distance and floated off through the timber like will-o-the-wisps.

Stone Pitching on the Bump Road near Dora Creek

MY LIGHTWEIGHT SURVIVAL rifle was commissioned into active service on the East Hodgkinson River. We'd followed brumby pads along timbered ridges and down onto the sandy-bottomed watercourse. Our horses grazed on nourishing couch grass under their nightlines on the opposite side to where we'd set up camp.

"I think we're in for trouble," muttered Ken as he glanced across the river. "There's a mob of wild pigs heading straight for the horses!"

I looked up from my diary as two jet-black sows and half a dozen suckers trotted in amongst the horses and down onto a pad along the river. Had the horses been fresh and full of feed we might have had a disaster, but they merely passed a fleeting glance over the intruders and returned to grazing.

"Quick, where's that rifle of yours?" Ken demanded when the danger had passed. "I'll go and get us some tucker." I assembled the gleaming black weapon and handed it over.

"Be careful!" I warned as Ken jogged off after the disappearing pigs. "Sometimes the bullets jam!"

I hadn't wanted a semi-automatic rifle, but I'd bought this ultra-light issue because its barrel and firing mechanism could be dismantled, stored in the hollow plastic stock and packed away neatly into a bag. It was intended for emergency use only and the bad habit the bullets had developed of not loading properly from the magazine was not a major setback. They could be loaded manually if need be.

An hour passed and Ken still hadn't returned. I walked down to the river, wishing I could follow the pad and hopefully meet Ken on his way back to camp. Common sense told me to stay put.

My worries disappeared when I caught sight of Ken trudging wearily along the river pad with a black hairy body slung over his shoulder.

"Gave me quite a chase," he panted, draping the dead piglet over a log. "I took a shortcut over a hill to get ahead of them, then stood in the water resting the rifle against a tree with the barrel pointin' out on the pad. While I was catchin' me breath there was a grunt beside me and a big sow nudged the end of the barrel with her snout!" he grinned. "So I pulled the trigger and hit her in the shoulder and bloody piglets took off everywhere! I sprinted up the hill after them and I'd just have a sucker lined up in me sights, when another one'd spring up out of the grass. So I'd line him up, then another one'd take off from somewhere else. I was puffin' and pantin' and tryin' to hold the rifle still when a sucker jumped up right in front of me. I shot him clean through the lung, but when I went to finish him off, I pulled the trigger and it just clicked."

Luckily for Ken it hadn't been a savage, wounded sow that he faced with an empty chamber.

"Isn't a .22 a bit underpowered for shooting pigs?" I queried.

"It's all I ever use," he defended. "Hell, I know of blokes who go in after pigs with only a hunting knife!"

Skinning and gutting the sucker, Ken cut the fillet off the backbone, drizzled liquefied butter over it and roasted it in aluminium foil over the coals. The lovely tender steak tasted no different to domestic pork. The remaining meat was diced up, accompanied by onions and dehydrated beans and cooked into a delicious stew.

Leaving the East Hodgkinson, we found a couple of old markers pointing out a different route from many years ago. Perhaps the National Trail that we were now riding on would also be altered in the future. I'd originally perceived the trail to be a hard and fast line, but already our experience had shown otherwise. The dynamic nature of the trail left it up to travellers to negotiate their way through and around geographical, climatic and man-made barriers.

We could easily have missed someone travelling north. Arriving at a road grid, we might have turned east and travelled say, a kilometre to find a gate in the fence. The other party could have turned west for a distance, dropped the fence, walked their horses over, retied the wires and none would have been the wiser. Yet both parties were still on the National Trail.

Travelling through cattle stations with the goldfields and 'The Bump' fading into the distance behind us, we pressed on past the tobacco fields of Mutchilba and the abandoned tin scratchings of Stannary Hills. In high spirits we rode into the tin mining town of Irvinebank where a picturesque tailings dam rimmed with reeds and waterlilies lay nestled in amongst surrounding hills and gullies. I was expecting letters from my family in Perth, so we followed a sign to the Post Office: a unique tin shed with lift-up garage door propped open with a piece of timber.

We hadn't planned where to camp for the night, but when we rode up to collect the mail, we found that we'd been expected and all our needs had been catered for.

"You're staying at Bill and Anne Byrnes' place across the road," informed Jackie, the postmistress. "They're not home at the moment, but there's beds on the verandah so youse can put your gear up there and stick your horses in the paddock opposite. Come over for a hot shower when you're ready; me husband, Phil, has just gone to get a load of wood so's we can light the donkey."

Ken picks up the mail from Irvinebank Post Office

These 'donkeys' were a common hot water system for people living in the bush. The standard 'donkey' comprised a 44 gallon drum with 4 steel legs welded on to raise the drum and make room for a fire underneath. A pipe from an overhead tank pushed cold water into the bottom of the drum, while the heated water was drawn off from a pipe at the top when the hot water tap was turned on inside.

"I'm sorry I haven't got a meal ready for you," apologised Jackie when we came across for a shower. "But we didn't know you'd be comin' this evening when the Byrneses aren't home. Of course you're quite welcome to stay and have tea with us a bit later."

These people had little in the way of material wealth, yet they couldn't do enough for us or make us feel more welcome. We'd already decided to lash out and have a meal at the local pub, so graciously declined Jackie's offer.

The National Trail guide book told us that Irvinebank had a shop and a horse feed outlet. But the shop had closed years ago and there was nowhere to buy feed for our hungry horses. Jackie took us into Herberton the next day when she went for the mail, but picked up such a huge load of groceries for the other townspeople that there was no room for a bag of horse pellets.

The Byrneses returned home that afternoon and Bill gave us a bale of hay left over from the days when their daughter had kept a horse. *Bob* had lost a great deal of condition in 4 weeks of travelling through country where feed was scarce. He was covered in grass and cattle ticks and I spent hours pulling them off. They hadn't affected the other horses so badly.

It was a two day ride to Beth and Clarry's place on the Atherton tablelands where Ken's borrowed horses could be returned to their owners. *Bob* would have himself a well earned rest and be handfed every day, while we bought some horses for Ken, reorganised our gear and got rid of a great deal of unnecessary junk.

Chapter 7: BANGTAIL MUSTER

"HANG ONTO HIM girl, hang on!"

The nylon lead rope sizzled through my clenched hand as *Riley* bucked and plunged through the timber. Blowing and spitting on my rope-burnt palm, I urged *Bob* around to block him. Flanks heaving and eyes wide-rimmed with fear, *Riley* flung his head up, snorted and spun around, slamming the off side pack bag into a tree. The load tilted and the swag on top rolled forward just enough to loosen the surcingle.

A few more bucks and the surcingle flapped uselessly in front of the swag which flip-flopped about like a demented sausage. Catching sight of the bouncing bedroll out of the corner of his eye, the terrified packhorse arched his body into a horse shoe shape and took off like a bolting fiddler crab, one eye glued to the frightening apparition which relentlessly pursued him.

The pack bag chains jingled and clunked on their hooks, driving *Riley* as fast as a hobbled horse can go sideways until he ran smack-bang into *Blaze*, dozing under a tree. His halter smashed by the marauding packhorse, *Blaze* headed bush, spinning around to see what had hit him when he'd gone a safe distance, but *Riley* was by then out of sight. He gazed dumbfounded at the spot where he'd been standing.

We eventually bailed *Riley* up and resecured his load. By the time we reached Irvinebank, *Riley* had settled into his new role as a packhorse. I'd bought this barrel-chested part Arab at the Mareeba horse sale for $300. He was a lively type, which suited us fine. The last thing we wanted was another gutless *Blaze*. Ken had swapped an old mare for a bay 4 year old gelding named *Tex*. He'd been too slow for a sprint horse but looked like a promising addition to our team.

But for the life of me, I couldn't fathom what had prompted Ken to buy *Lonely*. This lanky bag of skin and bones had spent 5 of his 7 years in Australia's highest rainfall region at the foot of Mt Bartle Frere. The rain had matted the hair on his back so badly that we feared his entire coat would lift off if we touched it. He'd been living in a paddock of bracharia, a grass with coarse, hairy leaves that damage a horse's lips and stomach. Only the seeds are edible, so the starving grey gelding existed on weeds most of the year.

"Why didn't you report him to the RSPCA?" I'd reprimanded Ken. Not only was the horse starving to death, he was unbroken and Ken had paid $150 for him.

"I couldn't do that!" said Ken. "They'd only put him down; at least we can get him out of that paddock and give him a chance."

We really needed a spare horse, but thanks to Ken we ended up with a charity case instead. *Lonely* gangled along happily on the end of his lead rope, grateful to be with other horses again and away from his wretched starvation paddock.

"WE'VE GOT ABOUT a fortnight's mustering and the boss wants to know if you're interested," asked Robbie McDowall, the manager of Wombanu Station. The National Trail directions had been incorrect from Woodleigh Station, leading us down onto the Herbert River instead of cutting across country. We'd covered a lot of unnecessary extra miles, and the five horses could use a rest.

The nights were chilly, but warm daytime temperatures and the heat from the foam saddlecloths had begun to scald the horses' backs. After I'd dispensed with the foam and switched to woollen cloths, the packsaddles rubbed *Riley*, *Tex* and *Blaze* on their withers. *Blaze* had a sack of fluid under his skin, running half way down his ribs from the wither, so we'd been unable to use him. Every night I'd strapped a poultice on his wither to draw out the fluid. *Bob's* face was nearly bald from Queensland itch (an allergic reaction to midge fly bites), while the rest of his body was covered in lumps from fly and tick bites. My two Victorian horses were not standing up to the northern conditions at all well.

Our first day on the 100 square mile cattle station was spent running in horses and shoeing them. Robbie considerately gave me the quietest horse to shoe, but with my limited practical skills it took me all afternoon.

The horse had a bad habit of stomping his foot to the ground when I tried to hammer the nails in. I used a trick that Ken had shown me on *Blaze*. My lazy packhorse had refused to hold his front foot up while I hammered, and had slammed it down on mine, breaking my little toe which went a lovely shade of purple. Ken had strapped *Blaze's* front leg up with a stirrup leather and he'd hopped around for 10 minutes until he learnt to stand on three feet. I'd walked in and effortlessly slapped the shoe on while his leg was still strapped up.

Using this trick on the station horse, I scored a psychological win and progressed to the hind feet without too much argument.

The station building was an 'L' shaped tin shed, the short side being the kitchen area and the long side filled with single beds with a shower and toilet at the far end. There were no dividing walls and the inside of the 'L' was open to the weather. There were 6 of us in the mustering team, plus another 4 men camped under the one roof. I was the only woman in the place, so Ken and I decided to camp down the flat under a cattle crate where it was less crowded.

The first winter frost woke us just before daybreak, giving us enough time to get dressed and walk up to the camp for breakfast. The cook had already been up an hour, the fire was going and steak, sausages and eggs sizzled away. Breakfast was a hurried affair and each person had to make their own sandwiches for lunch, wrap them up and head down to the yards, leaving the cook to do the dishes and tidy up.

Robbie allocated two horses for each person and told us which to ride for the day. Each rider caught and saddled this horse and led it onto a truck. The property was so large that it would have taken half the day to ride to our destination, so the horses were trucked instead.

It took all day to muster a 10 000 acre paddock. Splitting into groups of two or three, we combed sections of the paddock, picking up any cattle we found and meeting the others at prearranged points.

It sounded easy, but it wasn't. Some of the younger cattle had had very little human contact and took off at a gallop when they saw us. The two riders that chased them might end up a mile away from the rendezvous, unable to move the cattle becasue they were so spooky. So they would have to sit and wait.

Meanwhile, another two riders might be holding an edgy mob of cattle at the pre-arranged spot, wondering where the others had got to. If one rider left his mate to go looking for the others, the cattle would bolt off in all directions!

The best option was to head in the direction of the holding paddock (50 acres), and get whatever cattle there you could. The next day, the same paddock might be mustered again to pick up any stragglers. Sometimes an adjoining paddock would be mustered and the cattle yarded into another holding paddock. Every couple of days, the mobs in the holding paddocks were picked up and started on the long walk to the main yards.

They were a mixture of Santa Gertrudis and Brahman stock and weren't content to plod along. The ringers (stockmen) in the lead zig-zagged to block the high-headed wild cows that continually tried to gallop past. The men in the wings dashed off in pursuit as cattle tried to steal away through the scrub. Ken and I croaked our dusty voices hoarse at the calves and lame beasts lagging at the tail. If we let them drop too far back, the mob stretched out to an unmanageable length, making it easy for a beast to break away.

Travelling with the packhorses, we'd been spending about six hours a day in the saddle. But some days mustering we were getting close to ten. My backside was becoming

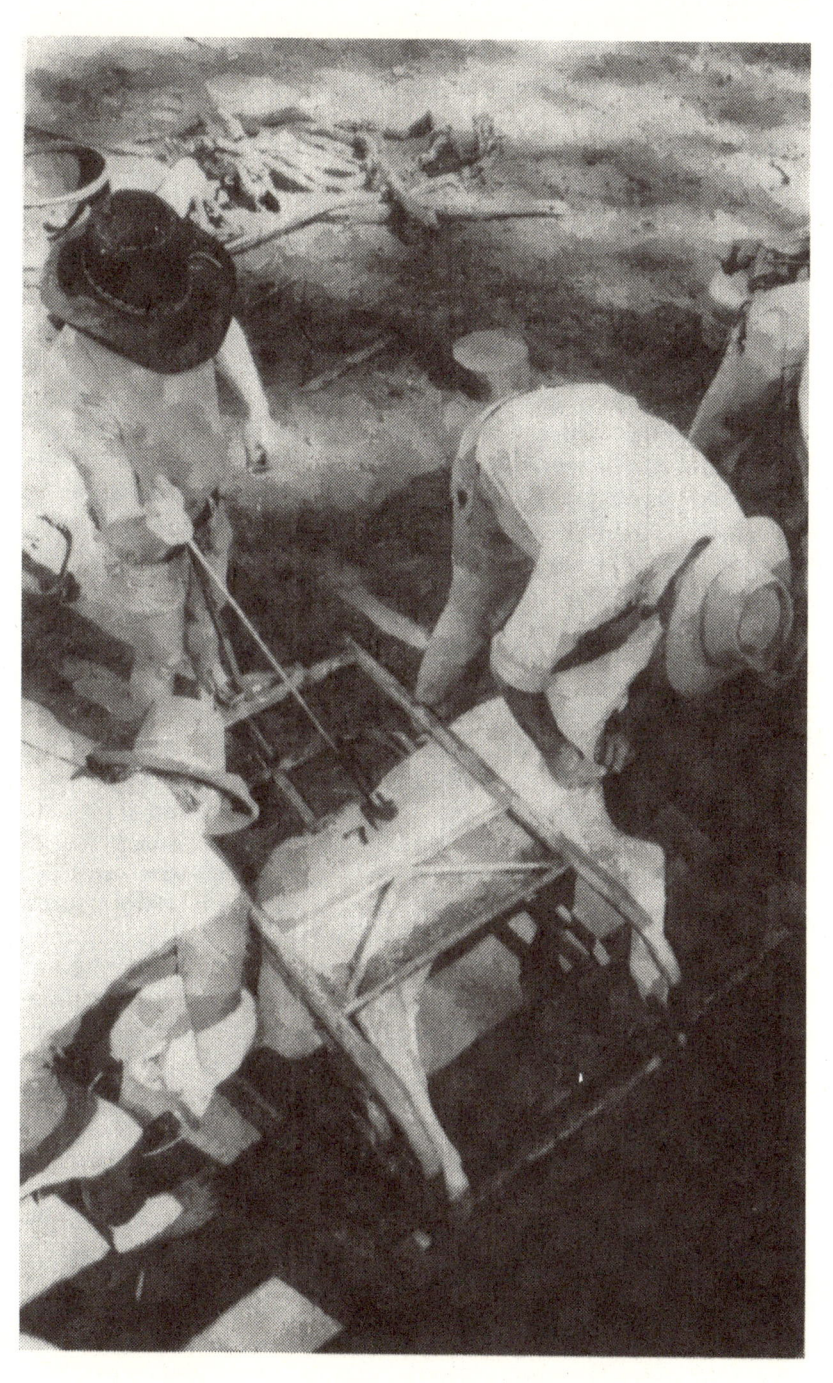

Ringers marking calves on Wombanu

extremely tender. I'd discovered my riding saddle had an uncomfortably narrow tree and it was like sitting on a ridge pole.

Our days of yardwork were a welcome break from the saddle and an opportunity for the ringers to leave their boots behind. I couldn't cope with the thought of what those hard hooves could do to bare feet, so looked the other way each time a man dived out of the way of a beast. Cattle were drafted through a round yard, run into a crush, vaccinated, had horns tipped, were sprayed for flies and ticks, then bangtailed.

I had the job of bangtailing. Wrapping the tail hair around a razor-sharp knife, I jerked the blade upwards, leaving a neat, square finish to distinguish the animal from the scraggly-tailed ones that had missed being mustered.

It was inevitable that cattle from neighbouring properties jumped the boundary fence and ended up in the Wombanu muster. When a stray brand came through the round yard, Robbie called out 'stranger' and the beast was drafted into a separate pen. The calves weren't branded until after lunch, giving the ringers time to observe their behaviour. If a calf showed familiarity with a 'stranger's' cow in the adjoining yard, it was drafted in to see if she'd let it drink off her. If successful, both belonged to a neighbour.

The Wombanu calves were individually run into a 'cradle' which was dropped on its side while the calf was branded, ear-marked and, if a bull calf, its testicles were removed.

At the end of the fortnight, trucks from neighbouring stations rolled in to pick up their strays.

"I hear you two chap are after another packhorse!" boomed Col Campbell from the window of his truck. "Call into my place on the way past; I've got an appaloosa that might do the job."

It was obvious we needed more horses. Even though our team had been spelling a fortnight they'd continued to lose condition. We couldn't carry enough feed to sustain our horses while they travelled, and didn't want to annoy station people with requests for horse feed. Increasing our numbers and sharing the workload would enable us to be self-sufficient.

Blaze's back needed more time to heal, so I left Wombanu on foot, my riding saddle perched on top of *Riley's* load like a maharajah's throne. There was a long, dry stretch of country ahead, so I'd pruned our luggage back to basics. The station people had offered to post my 22 kg parcel of clothes, tarpaulins and 'luxury' camping equipment next time they went to town. We were down to carrying 3 sets of jeans, shirts and underwear, one pair of boots each, a communal towel and toiletries, food and eating utensils, horse shoes and shoeing equipment, bedroll, Ken's .22 rifle, nightlines, 3 billy-cans, rivets, saddler's string and needles. Each horse carried its own set of chain hobbles around its neck and Ken and I strapped a set of dinner hobbles each around our waists where they were always handy. These leather hobbles were used above a horse's knees and only for short periods because of their restrictive nature.

In Malanda I'd done away with the waterbags, sleeping bag and mat which had been tied to my riding saddle. My raincoat and first aid kit were now in a pack bag making *Bob's* burden much lighter with only a few maps in his saddle bag.

"HE MIGHT HAVE a bit of a go" warned Col, trying to corner the prancing, wild-eyed horse with a halter. "He hasn't been ridden for 12 months."

"We won't bother hoppin' on him" explained Ken. "We'll just stick the packs on in the yards and see how he goes."

Bob was two inches taller, but looked feeble alongside the chunky gelding. *Joe's* shaggy grey coat did little to hide the powerhouse of muscle and bone that quivered beneath. He tolerated the harness, but flared his nostrils at the pack bags and swag. We'd only managed to buckle the surcingle when *Joe* tore the lead rope from Ken's hand, dropped his head between his front legs and bucked furiously. As the load toppled sideways, metal groaned, leather tore and timber snapped while pieces of pack saddle rained all over the yard.

Joe heaved to a halt and stood gasping, the breastplate twisted across his chest cutting off his windpipe and the remains of a packsaddle hanging under his belly. Slipping the hobbles on, we cautiously unsaddled the trembling horse and inspected the damage. Metal rivets holding the steel frame onto the timber tree had popped out; one side of the tree was splintered into three pieces and the buckle tongues in every girth, breeching and crupper strap had torn through the leather like a knife through soft butter.

"Oh, well" sighed Col as he opened the gate, "'spose I'd better bush him."

"Quick! Shut that gate before he gets away!" cried Ken.

"What for?" queried Col as he swung the gate closed. "You don't want this horse; he's just wrecked all your gear!"

"He's just the horse we're lookin' for: strong, powerful and spirited," grinned Ken. "We'll take him!"

Greenhide, furniture glue, tank bolts, a bit of bush ingenuity and we were under way again. Our new packhorse found it difficult to buck with his front legs hobbled and one back leg collar-roped off the ground. We loaded him in this fashion for three consecutive mornings and led him with two ropes; one of which passed under *Bob's* neck to be twisted with the other so Ken could hold them both in one hand.

Riding *Tex*, I led *Riley* with the packs on and let *Blaze* and *Lonely* run loose. They dropped so far behind that I rode back and hunted them along. *Blaze* trotted straight up the road, but *Lonely* was becoming cheekier as his health returned. He headed bush and I chased him back and forth until he tripped over a rock. Somersaulting onto his back he lay with legs kicking in the air and head bent awkwardly under his body. I was certain he'd broken his neck. But after a few more kicks, he curled his gawky neck around and lurched to his feet. He stood subdued, like a naughty schoolboy waiting for punishment. Apart from grazed knees, cuts to the face and a blood nose, there was nothing wrong with *Lonely*, but I led him for the rest of the day to put an end to his shenanigans.

Chapter 8: SHOTGUNS IN THE SKY

CHOPPERS DRONED, BULLS roared, shotguns blasted, men swore, dogs barked, and cattle bellowed.

"Sounds like a helicopter muster," said Ken. "We'd better cut through the bush else we'll end up in the middle of it."

Ken had little patience for the sketchy, incomplete trail directions, so navigation fell to me. Taking a rough bearing off the sun, I glanced at the map and headed off into the dry bloodwood and ironbark scrub, rejoining the road further on. Wairuna homestead loomed up ahead, perched high on an anthill partially hemmed in by sun-scorched ridges. Waterlilies mushroomed across lush, sparkling lagoons stretched in between, where sleek station horses grazed belly-deep amongst swamp couch and water weed. A pair of black swans and a flock of waterfowl took flight as we approached, then abruptly veered off as a helicopter hummed overhead to land in front of the buildings.

Stopping at the cattle yards to say hello, we were invited to put our horses in the lagoon paddock and stay overnight. After tea, the manager, John Logan, asked if we'd stay on for a while and help with the muster.

Horse paddock lagoon on Wairuna Station

"We can't pay you anything, but your horses'll have a good feed in that paddock and Dad can fix a bit of saddlery for you."

The horses were in for a good holiday amongst the waterlilies as it would be two weeks before we left. During our stay we were given invaluable advice from John's father. A retired station manager and bush saddler, Alec Logan was a tall, energetic gentleman, still lean from years of hard work. He'd acquired a knowledge of long distance packing from a lifetime of practical experience.

"Your packhorses are overloaded to buggery," he informed us. "Those military packsaddles were only designed for carrying 90lb (40kg) Vickers machine guns. They're no good long distance because the horses are bound to lose condition and the swivel tree will pinch their wither. They were O.K. in the war, as the pack animals carted equipment over short distances from one front to the next. Once the soldiers dug in and set up, they were in the one spot for a while. I'll counterline these saddles of yours, but you'd be best to pick up a couple of station packsaddles if you don't want any more back trouble. They're heavier, but you can pack up to a hundredweight (50 kg) on them."

Alec Logan fixing our packsaddles

At first I'd been offended at the brusque way station people criticised our outfit. But when I learnt that their blunt manner was part of everyday speech I was grateful for their willingness to offer straightforward advice.

We helped Alec pull the cow hair out of the pads, retease it and stuff it back in. After weighting them down overnight, Alec threaded a long needle with butcher's twine and quilted the hair into place.

"Don't be afraid to do this yourselves" he instructed. "So long as you don't leave any lumps in the stuffing, you can't do any harm. Now, how do you use these double girths?" he queried, measuring the straps *Joe* had split.

I explained how we crossed the girths under the horse's belly.

"That won't stabilise the load," he explained. "You must use the shape of the stomach to hold the packsaddle on. Do the front girth up in the normal position, then slip the back girth behind the flank. Don't muck about when you do this for the first time – the horse will be a bit ticklish, but make sure you buckle it up tight, otherwise he'll wreck everything."

Alec laughed on hearing how *Riley* had bucked, slipped the surcingle forward and loosened the load when we first packed him.

"The surcingle only goes around your pack bags," he explained. "The swag is tied on independently so that the pack bags don't jump off the hooks if the swag rolls forward."

I asked him if we should use a saddle blanket on the packhorses as several people had told us we shouldn't but couldn't offer a reason why. "We never used saddle cloths on a packhorse because they'd slip out and we wouldn't notice them because our packhorses ran loose," Alec explained.

I decided to keep using the cloths because we weren't having this problem and it was easier to wash the sweat out of the cloth than out of the saddle lining.

WE'D SENT FOR a spare saddle of Ken's to replace my uncomfortable one, but he nearly needed it himself. Pulling up for dinner one day, the cattle were held in a corner while we boiled a billy and ate our sandwiches. Tied to the fence, Ken's horse lunged back, broke the bridle and galloped off. An aboriginal stockman leapt onto his mount and took off in pursuit, returning empty handed after 10 minutes.

"That one too fast for me, boss!" he muttered to John.

Ken foot-slogged behind the cattle all afternoon and the chopper went out in the evening to look for the horse.

"We found your saddle, but it's still hanging under the horse's belly," the pilot apologised on his return. "He's way up on a timbered ridge and we couldn't find a cleared spot to land."

John went out on a motorbike and came back 2 hours later with Ken's saddle.

"Where's the horse?" I asked.

"I let him go" replied John, casually. "He'll come home when he's ready."

The only damage was a missing stirrup and a torn out saddle 'D'. I sent my own saddle home and used Ken's 1964 Northern Barcoo Poley which felt like I was sitting in an armchair instead of riding a rail.

MUSTERING WITH HELICOPTERS was a lot quicker than scouring a paddock on horseback all day. Our job was to quietly shepherd along a mob of coachers (quiet cattle) on horseback. Helicopters chased the cattle towards us and gave directions over a walkie-talkie so that we could shift the coachers and merge the two mobs.

Selecting a 'killer' for the table

Sometimes a sulky old bull would bail up in the timber or hide in a patch of lantana and the chopper couldn't shift him. The pilot would fire a shotgun at the beast and if that didn't have any effect, he'd radio for the horses to come in and hunt him out. Occasionally a bull still refused to budge except for charging at the horses. The ringers would throw a rope over his horns and either tie him to a tree or toss him on the ground and tie his legs together. The animal stayed that way until the ringers returned with a truck and winched him up the ramp.

We drove out one morning to load some wild cattle that had been yarded by helicopter. It hadn't been prudent to round this mob up with coachers as they would have taken one look at the mounted riders and tame cattle and bolted in the opposite direction. As these animals had no understanding of conventional fences, two wings of flimsy, hessian cloth had been used as a visual barrier to funnel the galloping cattle into a set of portable steel yards. Constructed from two inch square box section pipe, the panels had been assembled then hinged together with steel pins.

"Don't remember the yards being over there," said John, drily. "They weren't such a funny shape when we left 'em either."

Having never been yarded, the cattle had charged the steel rails and the entire structure was pushed out of shape and wrapped around a clump of saplings. To load them into an old Bedford, a ringer stood in the ramp entrance, taunted a beast until it charged, then dived out of the way as the animal thundered past. Each truckload was driven out to the main (gravel) road and transferred onto a double deck semi-trailer destined for the meat works.

The weaner calves had been drafted aside and were now loaded onto the Bedford. Kirin climbed into the driver's seat and headed for the main yards where the calves would be branded. Ken and I hopped into John's ute and followed the truck up the road. Reaching a steep pinch, John slowed down while the Bedford chugged back through the gears for the climb. She'd almost laboured to the top when the engine cut out.

"He's missed low range first gear and stalled her," cringed John, slamming the ute into reverse and whining back down the hill. "Her brakes don't work real good!"

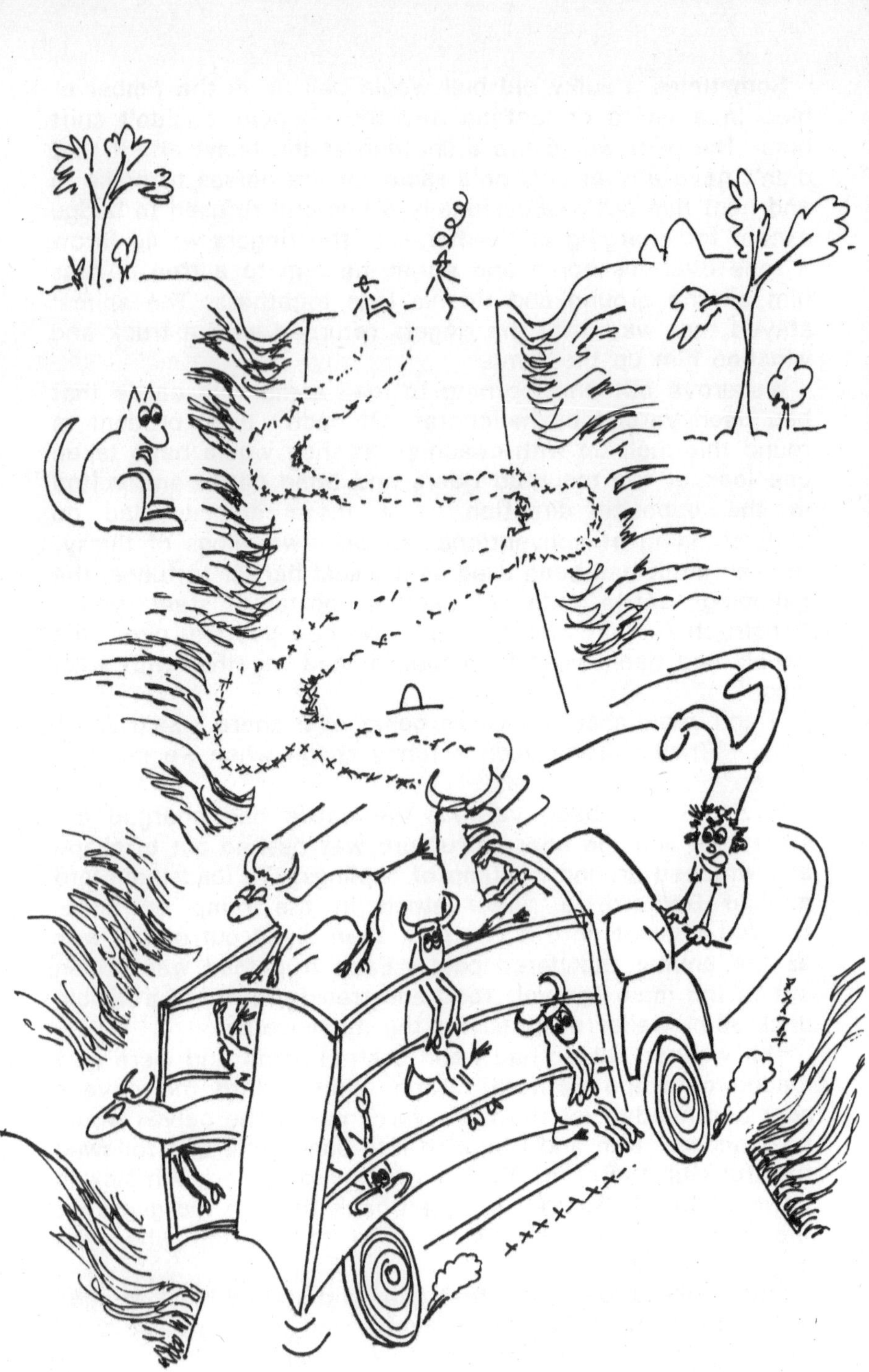

Up ahead, two puffs of dust appeared on the road as the ringers jumped out through the non-existent windscreen. Like a drunken snake, the truckload of weaners weaved wildly back down the hill while Kirin fought the steering wheel. The tyres caught in the spoon drain, whipping the old Bedford around and spitting the driver out through the vacant doorway.

John swung the ute to head bush, but it leapt backwards up the ditch and bottomed out helplessly on the chassis.

"Run for it!" he yelled as we flung the doors wide and bolted.

I risked a glance upwards to see Kirin sprinting down the hill, yelling and swearing as he hurled his hat after the runaway machine and hammered the grille with his fists.

Fast approaching our abandoned vehicle, the rear corner of the tray bit into the road as the truck reared up in the table drain, finally see-sawing to a standstill. Miraculously, none of the calves had been injured, but one of the front wheels had an unhealthy lean. John took the wheel and with a great deal of luck, managed to turn the truck up the hill without tipping it over. The weaners made it safely to the yards, but a couple of days later the stub axle on the Bedford snapped and the 'wonky' wheel rolled for 100 metres before winding up in the horse paddock lagoon!

BLAZE'S WITHER HAD nearly healed by the time we left Wairuna, so we recommissioned him to lighten the load on the packhorses. On the advice of a livestock nutritionist we'd organised 20kg of high protein feed to be sent out for *Lonely* which we divided into a split bag made from a potato sack. It straddled the swag which was folded lengthways and held off *Blaze's* injured wither by a crupper. A breast plate prevented everything from slipping back and a surcingle secured the load a foot back from where the girth would normally go.

Encased by the swag which nearly met under his stomach, *Blaze* resembled a snail carrying its shell. This saddle-less system worked remarkably well although its bearer was not impressed, lying down and rolling in the first waterhole we came to.

We took Alec's advice and flank girthed the packhorses. *Joe* snorted and jumped about as we buckled the girth but *Tex* didn't seem to mind.

Blaze looked like a snail carrying its shell

"That flank girth will help keep the pressure off the wither when you get into the hills," Alec told us. "And if you want to be self-sufficient, you'd better ditch that horse feed and get a few more horses instead."

No doubt he was right, but we didn't have the extra horses and we felt we were doing the animals a good turn by carting feed for them.

Leaving Wairuna in the sweltering afternoon heat, we crossed the headwaters of the Burdekin and camped on Lucy Creek after dark. The horses drank from a mud puddle in the creek bed where the wild pigs had been wallowing. We nightlined them amongst tufts of wiry grass in a belt of timber, leaving *Blaze* off in hobbles as he never strayed far from *Bob*.

Straining the muddy water through a handkerchief, I boiled it up and made a cup of tea, but it tasted like salty pig's pee. Ken added a few more tea leaves and a heap of sugar, but the brackish water was undrinkable. The juice from an emergency tin of plums was enough to sooth our parched throats. We packed up and left early in the morning in search of water.

Water was too heavy a commodity to carry; a horse can drink 16 gallons on a hot day, so it was imperative that we found water every night for them. But from then on we decided to keep one litre in a pack bag for emergency use only as the horses could drink water that we couldn't. We disciplined ourselves to go all day without a drink by consuming huge quantities of black tea at breakfast. If I had coffee or water instead, my tongue would be swollen, lips dry and throat parched by midday.

Our travelling routine changed as the September daytime temperature crept towards 40°C. At 3 a.m. we'd let all the horses except one off the nightlines. There was little grass as the country had been drought-stricken for years, but the horses were so hungry they'd put their heads down and eat whatever vegetation, leaves and bark they could find. After a couple of hours, they'd hobble off in search of better feed so we'd catch them, get packed and start travelling.

From 10 a.m. onwards, we'd be on the lookout for water. If a bird flew out of a dry gully, we'd investigate in case there was a rockpool holding water. Sometimes we'd be lucky and find a dam, but whatever water we came to, we offloaded the horses, hobbled them out to graze and had a long dinner camp during the heat of the day. A 'nighthorse' was tied up and swapped every hour, so we had a horse handy to round up the others if they took off.

Our main meal was eaten at dinner camp, usually a stew of potato, onion, dehydrated peas, rice, packet soup and a duck or pigeon if we'd been lucky. Ken baked a damper in hot ashes to be eaten with jam (butter only lasted a week from town) for tea and breakfast. Cheese was another mainstay food. We cut a hole in the plastic covering and the heat inside a pack bag melted the oil from the cheese and was absorbed by a newspaper wrapping. The cheese improved with age, losing its oiliness and acquiring a 'vintage' flavour.

Although we would have liked to rest in the heat of the day, we were kept busy repairing equipment, shoeing and shifting horses. In one pack bag I carried a black plastic bucket made from an iodine container which I used for washing clothes, saddle cloths and dishes so we didn't pollute any water source. Washing was hung on a nightline or strung out on a barbed wire fence to dry.

At 4 p.m. we loaded up as the shimmering heat haze

faded, sometimes travelling late into the night because many permanent water holes no longer existed due to the severity of the drought. Our torch had packed it in long ago, so we shuffled along in the dark, watching for the simultaneous tell-tale swing of our horses' heads or the glint of starlight on water.

DESPITE OUR BEST efforts, feed and water were scarce, the heat drained our energy and the horses lost condition. We'd decided that *Lonely's* special handfeed be shared with the other horses since they were doing all the work. It only lasted a week. Alec Logan was right. We couldn't carry enough feed to sustain our horses and its weight had been an added burden. Instead of travelling three days and resting on the fourth, we were down to two days' travel, then one day's rest. Covering anywhere between 20 and 35 km a day, it would take forever to reach our destination unless we increased our number of horses. It was too much of a strain using the same animals every day. We passed through Kangaroo Hills Station, which had been drought stricken for the last 6 years and lost thousands of head of cattle. Pathetic piles of sun-bleached bones beckoned and taunted us with the threat of a familiar fate. Only in the dry, sandy-bottomed creeks where the water still ran underground, did we find the occasional blade of grass.

Since following Alec's instructions, our pack loads had stabilised and we felt confident enough to let the horses run loose. I rode in the lead, Ken rode at the tail and after a few breakaway attempts, the horses trundled along happily in between. Until I lost my camera lens cap.

"Wait here!" I called to Ken as the horses stopped under a shady tree, "I'll go back and see if I can find it."

I trotted off on *Bob*, found the lens cap only 100 metres back and dismounted. Hearing a horse whinny, I looked up. *Blaze* was cantering after his mate and mayhem lay in his wake. *Riley* snorted and galloped off into the distance, Ken was chasing *Lonely* around a tree and *Joe* bucked around in a circle, the breeching jammed up under his tail and billy-cans rattling and banging against his neck.

By the time I rode back to help, Ken was on his knees beside *Joe* who lay on his back kicking all 4 legs in the air with gear strewn all around.

"What happened?" I cried, fearing the horse was injured.

"He's fine; just bucked himself off his feet," grinned Ken.

"Thank God its only the gear that's wrecked," I sighed.

"He hasn't wrecked anything." replied Ken. "I've just pulled everything off because he's stuck upside down. I dunno if your camera case is alright, 'cos it's still jammed underneath."

Pushing the trembling horse onto his side, we pulled him to his feet and retrieved the camera case. Opening it, I found the contents unharmed.

"Must be a tough case" said Ken, looking over my shoulder. "It had half a ton of horse on it, and there's not even a dent in the cover!"

The billy-cans hadn't fared so well. Not only had *Joe* crushed them flat, he'd landed in the only patch of wet cow manure to be seen. The squashed contents of three neatly plucked pigeon carcasses and a sprig of gum leaves were coated in revolting green slime!

"Don't worry," laughed Ken as I pulled a face. "I can panel-beat those cans back into shape and we'll wash the pigeons when we find water; its only chewed-up grass!"

Our directions told us we'd find a shop at Ewan, but all that remained of the ghost town were a few rusty bits of corrugated iron that banged eerily in the still afternoon heat. Around the old township grew hundreds of spiky bushes with miniature apples on them. Hungry for fresh fruit, I cut one open and found a stone inside instead of pips. The flesh tasted like a tart apple, but we weren't game to swallow any in case it was poisonous. I later found them to be edible Chinee Apples, commonly called 'Chinky Apple'. They would have been delicious stewed with rice and sugar. Instead, Ken found a sour old bush lemon, which we ate, rind and all.

Our food supplies were running low. Most of our potatoes, onions and pumpkin had rotted, unnoticed, in a pack bag whilst on Wairuna. We had to ration what remained. My past impression of hunger was a grumbling stomach when late for a meal, but it was nothing like the hunger I now experienced. Our dwindling sugar supply was reserved for cups of tea. The gluggy, bland mess of rice and sultanas that passed for a meal did little to appease my appetite. I felt giddy, strained and feeble and the bones of my backside sharpened to uncomfortable points that ground painfully against the seat of the saddle.

"Why am I doing this?" I thought to myself. How easy it would be to pack it all in and go home. But where was home? There was no job and no house waiting for me anywhere. I'd burnt all my bridges. I was stuck. The swag bobbing along on the packhorse beside me caught my eye. There was my home! As I cast a glance over my companion and our horses, the cheerful tone of Ken's whistle washed over me and released my anxieties and discomfort. I had everything I'd ever wanted right alongside. There were no bills, no mortgage, no stressful drives through peak hour traffic and nothing much of value for anyone to steal. We had so little, yet we had so much.

That evening we arrived at the Running River where a grid-type bridge blocked our passage along the track. Designed to withstand floods and commonly used on property boundaries, these bridges are built out of railway iron. The six inch gap between the bars puts an end to horse travel in this district when the rivers are up.

The narrow trickle of water in the river bed was hardly threatening, so we took the horses down across the sand and climbed up the steep bank on the opposite side, setting up camp well above the high water mark. Even under these scorching conditions it was a necessary precaution as the waterways inland of the Great Dividing Range have a vast catchment area. The country can be as dry as a bone, yet a storm over 100km away can send a flash flood roaring down a river bed.

While we were travelling, *Lonely* developed a bad habit of ambling up the fenceline each time I stopped to open a gate. The other horses wandered after him and there always ensued a chase with horses ending up on both sides of the fence. After spending 15 frustrating minutes at one particular gateway we switched back to the arm-aching job of leading two horses each again.

Trudging along a parched track late one afternoon with a cloud of dust and flies hanging around us, we saw what appeared to be a mirage. Shimmering on the horizon was a distinctive yellow and black XXXX sign, the trademark of Queensland's Four X brand beer. Drawing closer, the small railway siding of Mingela emerged from the heat haze. Seventeen days after leaving Wairuna Station we wearily plodded into the oasis of civilization.

Chapter 9: DROVERS AND POETS

"DID YA CATCH them coupla bulls that got out?" asked the lanky, weather-beaten driver, jumping down from the cab of his truck and landing in a puff of dust on the thick pads of his bare feet. Clad in habitual dress of blue Jackie Howe singlet and Stubby shorts, Graham Smith sauntered over to his 18 year old daughter, lifting the crown of his battered felt hat to run calloused fingers through a shock of silver-grey hair.

"Got one tied up on the common," drawled Wendy, a rakish slip of a girl who looked like the last person you'd imagine to be tying up one of her father's stirry rodeo bulls.

"Where's the second one?" asked Graham.

"Down the back of the common in the scrub" answered Raelene, the 14 year old. "We had to tie that first mongrel up 'cos he kept jumpin' the fence onto the highway."

"How'd ya get 'im down?" her father questioned.

"Put the dogs onto him."

"Well I hope youse found a decent tree to leave him under," he remonstrated, giving us a wink with a twinkling blue eye.

"Course we did," growled Raelene. "Don't go tellin' us how to do things."

"Youse can see why I don't have to employ any blokes," Graham laughed to us. "I've got four daughters who can ride a horse better than any fella around here and they've got far more brains as well. C'mon girls, take that Toyota and we'll go bring that bull back to the yards," he waved as we hopped on board a second utility.

Wendy and Raelene jumped into their vehicle, slammed the doors, spun the wheels and stormed off in a cloud of dust. We waited for the dust to settle then followed them down to the common where ugly looking rodeo bulls, buckjumping horses and town livestock scratched the powdery earth for the elusive grass seed or thistle stalk that another animal might have missed.

The girls pulled up under a towering gum and were in the process of throwing a rope over a solid branch when we arrived. At the base lay a bedraggled looking Brahman bull with scratch marks on his nose, chunks torn out of his ears and legs trussed up like a Christmas turkey.

"Friggin' hell!" laughed Graham, looking at the fang marks on the bull's hide. "How many dogs did you let orf?"

"Half a dozen," replied Raelene.

"Ya might as well 'ave let the whole lot go!" stirred Graham.

"Ah, shut ya trap!" barked Wendy.

One end of the rope had been tied to the bull's legs then thrown over the branch and tied to the kangaroo bar on the front of a utility. Wendy gently eased the Toyota back and the rope pulled the massive beast, legs skywards, off the ground. She stopped when the animal hung suspended halfway between the earth and the tree limb.

While the bull oscillated in mid-air, Raelene ripped the other ute into reverse and roared the machine backwards. She tromped the brake pedal just in time to prevent the bulky animal smashing through the back of the cab. Right on cue, Wendy eased forward, lowering the beast onto the tray of Raelene's ute. The two girls deftly untied the rope, lashed the beast firmly to the back of the vehicle and drove off with the bull after scowling at their amused father and hurling a few departing insults in his direction.

"Wander over for tea with us tonight," invited Graham, dropping us off at our camp.

He'd given us a lift into Charters Towers earlier and we'd bought horse shoes, groceries and two bags of crushed corn. The high starch content of corn gives an instant energy boost to horses but has to be fed in small quantities so it doesn't cause colic or overheat their blood.

The horses came running for their nosebags when I called and tucked in heartily, except for *Tex*. His jaw had not developed fast enough to accomodate his last two permanent molar teeth. They'd grown down through the jawbone instead, plus he had bridle teeth coming through and was too sore in the mouth to eat properly. Because of this he'd lost an abnormal amount of condition for the work he'd done.

Being pink-skinned, *Joe* had lost a bit of hair from the rubbing action of the back of the packsaddle. I'd been carrying sulphur powder to dry the horse's backs when we were short of water, as it absorbed the sweat and could be brushed off. It had hardened *Joe's* back a little and he was only a touch tender on the rub marks. I'd bought a bottle of

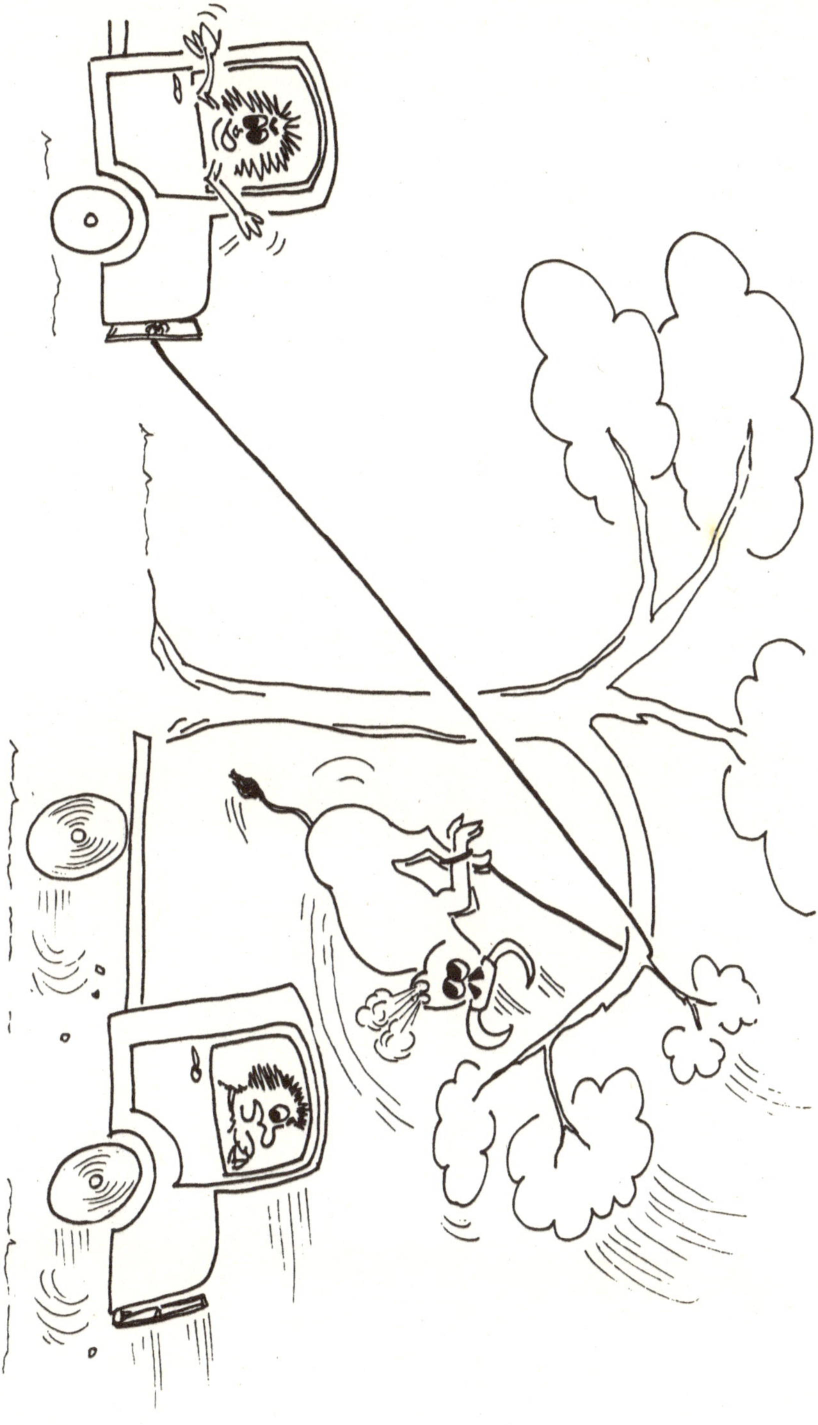

methylated spirits in Charters Towers and poured a capful each side of his spine, a treatment to be continued for the next week to speed up the toughening process.

Buying a carton of beer at the Mingela Hotel we headed back to the rodeo grounds for tea. The Smith family didn't have a house in the normal sense but slept in separate one roomed cottages and congregated in the kitchen: a vast, concrete paved, semi-enclosed carport. Graham's wife, Elaine, ignored the foal that 12 year old Natasha coaxed up to the kitchen table, but the monstrous bull snuffling the clean linen hanging on the washing line was forcefully whacked away with a straw broom. Chooks, peacocks and guinea fowl strutted through like they owned the place, a pink and grey galah fluttered onto people's shoulders, tweaking an ear until he scored a titbit, dogs and puppies gambolled around the furniture, a cat slunk out from behind the deep freezer, followed by another dog and then a couple more cats.

Graham and Elaine barbequed large steaks on a massive hot plate. Along with a few other identities who seemed to live there as well, we helped ourselves to the meat and salad. After the meal, I was standing at the sink helping with the dishes when something latched onto my toe.

All our gear at the Mingela Rodeo grounds

"Yow!" I shrieked. Everyone roared with laughter, but I couldn't see what had bitten me.

"It's only a guinea pig," explained Debbie, the Smith's eldest daughter. "The mongrel thing lives under the sink cupboard and darts out to nibble your toes when you're washing the dishes. You'll have to watch out for ol' E.T. when youse go back to your camp tonight though. I've been standing around mindin' me own business and he'll come up behind and bowl me over every time!"

E.T. was an exceptionally ugly rodeo bull with short, stumpy legs and a face like a hammerhead shark. He'd been retired from Graham's bucking string for many years, but was much in demand for his performance with the rodeo clowns whom he chased and tossed professionally to the delight of the crowds.

Powerful, lumbering bulls that had broken the teeth and bones of those who tried to ride them were chased daily from Elaine's washing line with a broomstick, yet little E.T. was treated with cautious respect. We walked nervously back to our camp that evening, jumping at every sound and ready to take flight if the stumpy-legged marauder came charging out of the darkness.

DESPERATELY NEEDING A replacement for *Tex* we bought a 12 year old grey piebald gelding off Graham Smith. He'd come in with a mob of buckjumpers from south of Cloncurry by mistake but Graham assured us he was as quiet as a lamb.

The nervous animal eyed us with suspicion and slunk away at our approach. Not what you'd call a handsome horse, he had the heavy body of a draught, the short solid legs of a pony, a head like an oversize ironing board and the long, floppy ears of a mule. His entry into a dressage arena would give any self-respecting judge a cardiac arrest, but he looked like a good, tough packhorse so we made a deal. *Malcolm* was his name and with his long face and sad countenance, he resembled a former Prime Minister, so we left it at that.

Cornering *Mal* in the yard we tried to put a halter on. Trembling and quivering, he laid back with front legs outstretched and belly almost touching the ground, appearing terrified of being touched by human hands. Come shoeing time, *Mal* knew all the nasty tricks. Stiffening his front leg he refused to bend at the knee, and when his leg was brought forward to clench the nails over and rasp off excess hoof, he'd bring all his weight down and try to stomp Ken on the knee. Between the two of us, we dragged each front hoof onto a block of wood to clench and rasp. When Ken picked up a hind leg, *Mal* leaned so heavily that when Ken dropped the leg and scooted out from underneath the horse sat down on his haunches. He proved difficult to saddle, jumping sideways and tipping the packsaddle into the dirt before we could buckle up the girths.

We now had 7 horses; *Bob, Blaze, Riley, Joe* and *Mal* to carry the 4 saddles and their respective loads, *Lonely* our charity case and *Tex* who was suffering from teething problems. Leaving Mingela on the Burdekin Falls Dam road, *Lonely* ran loose and we each led two horses (one either side of our riding horse). The sealed road surface rapidly wears the nail heads off horse shoes which then become loose and fall off, so we avoided the bitumen and rode to one side.

The country had been cleared for grazing cattle and there was no roadside shade. The occasional stunted ironbark growing on the other side of the fence wearily struggled to shade its drought ravaged trunk with a pathetic handful of wilted, windburnt leaves.

Barely noticing the monotony of the landscape, we negotiated our way through deeply worn drainage gullies and around spiky bushes and broken bottles. Rarely would both our led horses cross a gully in the same stride. One would usually leap ahead of the riding horse while the other baulked, twisting the rider sideways whose arms were then simultaneously jerked from their sockets.

By the end of the day we both had badly rope burnt palms and were in dire need of a chiropractor. Hyped up on corn after their 6 day break at Mingela the horses had played up a treat. They sweated more than usual and my legs stung and prickled from the constant rubbing of salt-wet necks and shoulders against my saturated jeans.

Halfway across one of Queensland's narrow-gutted road bridges, a red sports car zoomed up and overtook us from behind; the driver didn't even ease his foot off the accelerator. The horses shied up against the knee-high guard rail in fright and we were incredibly lucky not to be killed or lose horses over the side of the bridge. The driver probably didn't realise how near to death he came. If a horse so much as stepped sideways, his speed and close proximity could have wiped out the lot of us. After that experience, we spanned out across the road at every bridge crossing, leaving no gap for ignorant motorists.

Camping in a cleared stock reserve on the banks of the sandy bottomed Kirk River, Ken rode off to check the boundary fence while I headed off to a nearby homestead. Even though in a reserve, we were virtually camped in the front yard of a station, so I paid them a courtesy call to tell them who we were and what we were doing.

Riley had a loose shoe, so I tied him beside a log, found the shoeing gear and tacked a few nails in while Ken got a fire going. I'd just finished when Ken wandered over with two steaming quart pots of black tea. Sitting down on the log, we sipped our tea, relaxed, and discussed the happenings of the day. As we chatted I was vaguely aware of something about my calf muscle, but the tension quietly draining out of my body had dulled my senses. It was not until I felt a sudden wicked movement half way up my inner thigh that my nerve endings came back to life.

Throwing my half empty quart pot into the air, I clutched the inner leg of my strides and leapt screaming off the log. Ken looked on bewildered, the shoulders of his shirt stained with the hot tea I'd just showered on him while I danced and wailed like a banshee. *Riley* spun around to face me, snorting and rolling his eyes in fright.

Looking over his shoulder toward the station buildings, Ken grabbed me and tried to cover my mouth with his hand. "If you don't shut-up, they'll think someone's being murdered over here!"

Kicking off my boots, I unzipped my jeans, pulled them off and shook out an **enormous** centipede! It was at least 6 inches long. Once I'd calmed down, I had a bath in the river, then sat down in the middle of the swag where I could spot any creepy crawlies heading my way. Ken stood at arm's length, handed across a quart-pot of freshly made tea and jumped away.

"Think you can drink this one without me wearin' half of it?" he grinned from a distance.

THE LATE AFTERNOON heat weighed heavily on our burdened animals as they slipped and stumbled down the rutted, shaley shoulders of Mt. Wright. Lean, spindly ironbarks offered intermittent shade, but the glaring sun threatened to suck the very moisture from one's eyeballs. Shutting my eyes for relief, I swatted the biting bush flies with one hand and pressed the heel of the other into the pommel to prevent hitting the front of the saddle as *Joe* lurched his way downhill.

"That's where we'll end up," drawled Ken from behind.

Through a gap in the treetops I squinted at a flat landscape totally devoid of trees and dotted with low, shrubby bushes. The weeping white scars of eroded gullies criss-crossed the open plain while the sun glinted harshly on crushed rock atop hundreds of open mounds pockmarked across the surface. Crumbling fingers of chimneys reached skyward in the distance and on the horizon shimmered massive flat mountains of dirt crawling with ant-size machines.

"Ravenswood," announced Ken. "Biggest inland town in Queensland at the turn of the century."

Blaze helping himself to the water at Ravenswood

The desolate vista before us looked more like the ruins of a nuclear holocaust. It was hard to imagine that this area was once crammed with buildings, teeming with supply wagons and bustling with gold diggers.

The bushes turned out to be Chinky Apples and each one sported a neat 'bobbed' haircut about 6 feet from the ground. All grass had withered and vanished in the drought and the obnoxious shrub whose thorns mercilessly tore through clothes and flesh was at least providing sustenance for grazing animals.

Our horses snorted in fright as a string of goats appeared over a mullock heap. Big ones, little ones, plain black, white, or tan, some multi-coloured, the herd of horny, bearded creatures gazed disdainfully at us as their dusty column filed past on a narrow, well-worn pad.

Shaded by thick rubber vine, a small mob of cattle lay or stood languidly swishing flies in the disappointingly dry bed of a sandy-bottomed river. The township was still some miles away and the horses would have benefited from a drink. Spotting a windmill nearby, we detoured across and found a mob of horses gathered around a water trough. A couple challenged our approach while the rest drifted lazily into the shade. Amongst them was a solid skewbald pony we liked the look of, so I wrote down his brand with the intention of finding the owner to see if he was for sale.

Two hotels, the Post Office and General Store, a few scattered buildings, crumbling ruins and a set of steps that led to nowhere were all that adorned the lonely main street of Ravenswood. Yet the spirit of a roaring frontier town lay quietly pulsing beneath the decaying piles of rubble, not ready to die out while people and buildings still remained. Standing on the pavement outside the Imperial Hotel, I would not have been surprised if the louvred batwing doors had been flung open and old John Wayne himself strode out with loaded sixguns swinging on his hips.

THE MOB OF horses running on the town common belonged to an assortment of people, but we were able to trace the skewbald's owner through the brand. We caught him at home in the evening when he'd finished work at the mine.

"If you can run in that bay mare and foal for me, you can have the skewbald," he offered. "I've been wantin' them two, but I haven't got a horse that'll get 'round 'em."

In the morning we rode *Joe* and *Mal* over to the owner's house, opened up the wire fence and set off to look for the horses. The next door neighbour, Dick Easton, had horses yarded so we introduced ourselves and let him know our intentions. Straight-backed, lean and sun-tanned, he looked like he'd spent a lifetime in the saddle and moved with the agility and balance of a natural rider.

When we found the horses on the common, they took off in the opposite direction to what we'd planned and split into two mobs. The skewbald went with one group and the two mares were in the other. Going after the mares I hung back about 50 metres, not wanting to push them too fast as *Mal* wasn't fit enough for a hard gallop. Ken and the other mob were nowhere to be seen.

After an initial spurt of speed, the horses in front of me dropped back to a fast canter, deftly negotiating familiar gullies and weaving through Chinky Apples. I realised how far we'd travelled in the wrong direction when bitumen flashed past underneath. I had no chance of galloping around to block the horses, but they seemed to be tiring, so I hung back even further, hoping they'd stop on their own accord. They did. The leader trotted down into Elphinstone Creek for a drink and the rest followed.

Flanks heaving and heart pounding from the chase, *Mal* was glad of a reprieve when I halted him in the creekbed, ready to turn the horses back to the yards if they tried to head west. A thundering of hooves announced the arrival of the second mob with Ken hot on their tail. They pounded down into the sandy creek bottom and kept going, taking the other horses with them. I urged *Mal* up the bank and the horses wheeled away down a dirt road and galloped straight through the middle of town.

Ken shot past me, striving to overtake the horses and turn them in through the wire gate. He didn't make it, but the horses swung left and headed straight for Dick Easton's yards. He heard us coming and opened the gate.

"They're used to running into these yards," said Mr Easton as Ken and I came through the gateway behind the horses. "They always run the same way every time."

We bought a couple of old station pack saddles from Mr Easton that had been hanging in his shed since 1963 when he retired from droving. After hosing off the dust and cobwebs we rubbed fat into the brittle old leather and warmed it in the sun. The original padding had rotted and been destroyed by vermin long ago.

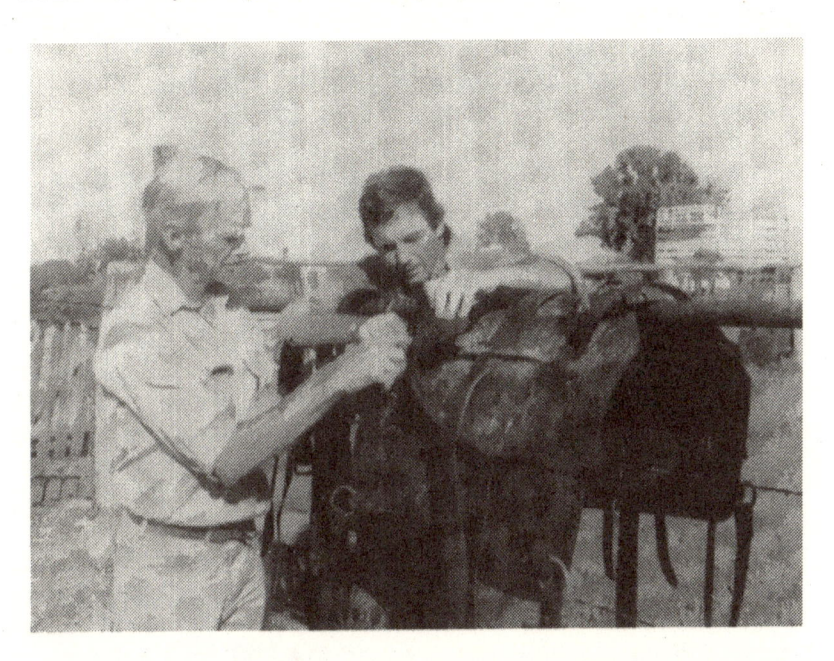

Dick Easton shows Ken one of the old station packsaddles

Back at camp I devised some temporary padding for the ancient packsaddles. Cutting slabs of foam off the end of our swag mattress, I tacked them to the leather pads in conjunction with thick pieces of carpet underfelt. It would take time, effort and the correct materials to restore these old saddles but once they were recommissioned it would hopefully be the end of our horses' back injuries.

Whilst in Ravenswood, *Tex* ate some poisonous leaves from an Oleander bush. His gums and tongue turned blue and he went down with colic. We forced him to his feet and continually led him around to stop him going down again. After two days he was over the worst of it, but we decided to leave him behind in Ravenswood to speed his recovery.

Our new horse we named *Easton* after our retired drover friend. A full brumby, he'd been hand-raised on a bucket of milk, broken-in to ride but never used. We had a struggle putting shoes on the 5 year old gelding, but he was amazingly quiet for his first time with the packsaddle.

The two fragile station packsaddles had to be carried individually but were not ready to take a full load. We didn't have bags for them, so tied the swag across one and a duffel bag and camera case across the other. The military packsaddles were now carrying less than 50 kg and we were using all the horses except *Lonely*.

"COME 'ERE AND have a look at this!" exclaimed Ken.

I couldn't imagine what he'd found of interest in this dry, desolate country, but I turned my horse towards him anyway.

"See this corner peg? I put it in when we were surveying the land resumptions for the Burdekin Dam in 1985."

Ken's personal landmarks and stories about the surveying of Queensland's largest dam helped keep my spirits up while everything withered around us. My father was a surveyor and I'd also studied this subject at college. The knowledge came in handy for navigation and there was always something to learn from Ken's practical recollections.

We reached the dam wall within a week of leaving Ravenswood. The towering concrete citadel spanned over 800 metres to hold back the massive volume of water drained from a catchment area of 114,200 square kms.

Mal carrying a fragile station packsaddle

The dam had been expected to take several years to fill, but not long after completion in 1987, the Belyando and Suttor Rivers came down in flood, filling the storage area in a matter of days. The water is used for irrigating sugar cane, rice and other crops in the coastal Burdekin region.

Pausing at a scenic high spot alongside the road, we marvelled at the contrast between the awesome body of water and the shrivelled, drought-dusted landscape fringing its shores. A utility bearing the Water Resources insignia pulled off the road and a middle-aged man jumped out from behind the wheel before the vehicle came to a halt.

"G'day!" said Tom Oliver with a welcoming smile as he strode enthusiastically over towards us. "I hope you plan on stayin' up at the camp for a day or so."

The dam construction camp once housed over 1000 workers but had dwindled to merely 4 maintenance staff. Tom was the resident gardener-handyman and we followed his directions through streets of empty transportable houses to the caravan park. He was there to meet us, unloading a split 44 gallon drum for the horses to drink from.

"There's no-one else here, so you can camp wherever you like and hobble your horses out on the lawn," he invited. "I'll be back to show you around when I knock off work."

The horses were busily munching soft green couch grass. Apart from their small ration of corn it was the first decent feed they'd had since Wairuna. There was no need to tie up a night horse. They could freely hobble about the streets of this oasis with no intention of leaving. Water was readily available so we thoroughly hosed down each horse then had a hot shower in the immaculately clean ablution block.

Tom was full of surprises. In the evening he ushered us into the cavernous, empty mess room. While I cooked up a meal he told us he'd once travelled the Burdekin district as a horse-breaker, carting all his equipment around in an old Kombi van. It had brought back fond memories when he'd met us coming in with our packhorses earlier in the day.

Retiring outdoors to drink a home brew and watch the sunset, Tom revealed his mastery of words and pen. In a box full of exercise books and scraps of paper was a superb collection of short stories and poetry he'd written about life in the outback. It was a privilege to read the works of this unassuming, quietly spoken man who had also composed the lyrics to 27 songs sung by none other than Slim Dusty.

ROUTE
---- MAJOR WATERWAYS

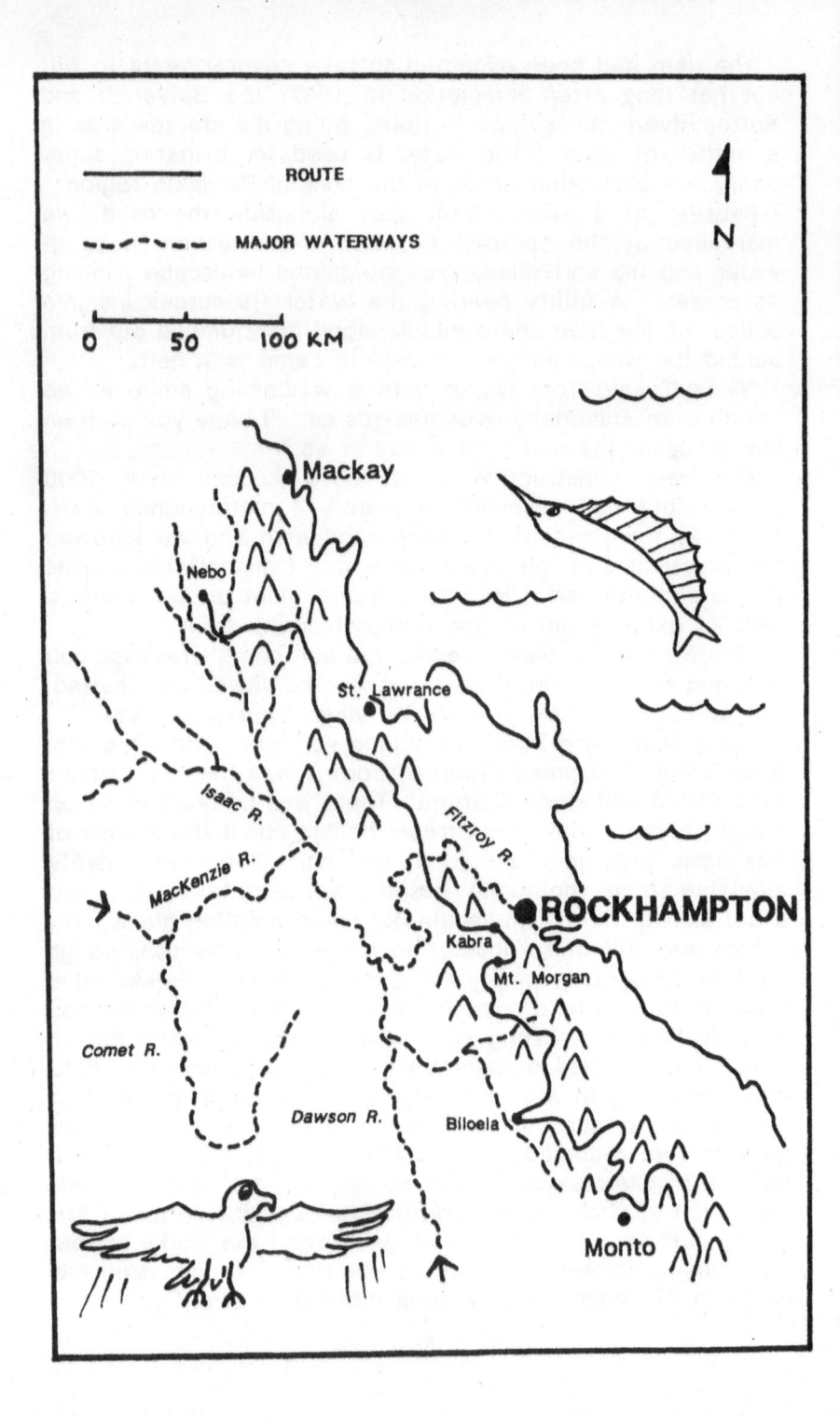

0   50   100 KM

N

Mackay
Nebo
St. Lawrance
Isaac R.
MacKenzie R.
Fitzroy R.
ROCKHAMPTON
Kabra
Mt. Morgan
Comet R.
Dawson R.
Biloela
Monto

Chapter 10:
STORMS OVER THE SUTTOR

HUNDREDS OF THOUSANDS of megalitres of roaring, spuming water came thundering through the air towards us. Yellow raincoats, whippersnippers and flapping plastic bags paled into insignificance compared to the terror instilled by this awesome volume of water discharging from the outlet at the bottom of the Burdekin Dam wall. Our horses had become quivering blobs of jelly.

Unless we detoured hundreds of kilometres, our only alternative was to cross the Burdekin River downstream of the wall. Since the river bed was slippery solid rock and the water full of crocodiles, we urged our seven trembling horses towards the concrete bridge, offering a full-on view of the pounding, gushing maelstrom.

Halfway across we were struck by the full force of wind and spray. Horses danced and slithered over wet concrete, gaping boggle-eyed at the roaring mass of water less than 20m away. Firmly gripping the leads of our packhorses we towed the frightened animals across and emerged soaked but unscathed on the far side of the bridge.

Overlooking the massive Burdekin Dam wall

The success of the northern section of our trip had been based around carefully monitoring our arrival time at this crucial ford. Only two weeks earlier, the dam had been over-full and water flowing over the 500 metre long spillway rendered this route impassable.

With the Burdekin fading in our wake, the landscape became more arid than anything we'd experienced further north. Rock grew on top of rock and the rare tuft of forest grass would not support a wallaby, let alone a horse. The ruthless sun sucked the very sweat from our pores, robbing us of the cooling effect of evaporation and leaving our dry skin to prickle with crusted salt.

We made use of any grass and water we came across as there was no telling what lay ahead. Our first day south of the dam we travelled late into the night to find water. Finally reaching a fenced dam, we tied the horses up and checked the wires. I cursed not having a torch as it was a moonless night and the only way to check the fence was to run a stick along the barbed wire to find the breaks. After much groping around in the dark we discovered most of the back fence was missing. Since there was not a skerrick of grass growing anywhere, we abandoned the fence.

Dishing out the last double handful of corn to each horse, we nightlined them with nothing except bark, leaves and twigs to chew on. Ken boiled up some duck, potatoes and peas, but although we were hungry, neither of us felt like eating. Leaving our meal untouched we turned in for the night, hoping that the morrow's journey would yield grass for our horses.

"IT GETS WORSE!" announced the tall, wiry station manager as he climbed out of the driver's seat. "If you keep heading for Collinsville you'll kill those horses!" he warned. "The water's scarce and there's not a blade of grass anywhere. If you deviate to Mt Coolon you'll find couch grass on the creek. When you go past Terang Station, call in and stay with us; we've got good feed along the Suttor and I wouldn't mind swapping you some horses for those two," he nodded at *Bob* and *Blaze*.

It would have been ruthless to subject our horses to the Collinsville stretch, so we took Sid's advice and reached Terang under our own steam in less than a week.

"I only employ first year jillaroos," Sid explained not long after our arrival. "They're much gentler on the livestock and machinery than blokes and they use their brains rather than brawn to get around most problems. The only catch is that most of them couldn't even ride a broomstick," he grinned. "These station horses are a bit too lively for them, so I'd like to do a swap with you."

I'd been prepared to part with my horses, but when it came to the crunch it was not such a simple matter. Due to his uncanny ability to avoid hard work, *Blaze* was in reasonable condition and capable of continuing the journey. I realised we'd be better off to exchange him for a more willing animal and this decision didn't exactly break my heart. Ken was rejoicing at the thought.

I was more hesitant when it came to *Bob*. He'd been a faithful, hard working horse, but his condition had suffered as a result of his efforts. It would be better for him to be left on Terang and pampered by jillaroos.

Sid gave us a beautiful, six year old, long striding brown mare with a star on her forehead in return for *Blaze*.

"She's tossed off a few jillaroos in her time," he admitted, "but I don't think you'll have any trouble with her." She had a white spot either side of her wither from a badly fitting saddle, but the injury had healed and wasn't tender to touch.

I was given two horses in exchange for *Bob*. A three year old, unbroken chestnut gelding who had identical markings to the *Brown Mare* and his full brother, a six year old liver chestnut with a treacherous eye and the spirit of the devil. He'd been running with a couple of aged unbroken horses on the station across the river and it took a lot of hard galloping to yard him. Black and shiny with sweat, he pranced around the rails when we drafted the other horses out, snorting and casting defiant looks in our direction. His violent aggression and short, spiky mane which stood erect like a dorsal fin, reminded me of a popular football personality. *Jacko*.

"You'll need to stay here for a while and work your new horses," announced Sid. He asked Ken to break in a young filly for him and gave us the use of the horse yards.

We stayed on Terang for a month, working horses and helping Sid with the cattle during the day, then stitching and repairing our station packsaddle for a couple of hours each night. Teased cow hair and serge had been freighted

Rebuilding a station packsaddle

up from Brisbane to restore our packsaddles. We strained our eyes in the artificial light and kept repairing and stitching the fragile old leather until our fingers were rubbed raw.

I organised crushed oats and a mineral block to be sent out from Mackay for the horses as there was very little feed in their paddock. The mineral block was eaten in five days which showed how deficient in nutrients the country had been. Under normal conditions it would have lasted several months.

We named the young chestnut *Morgan*, and once Ken had ridden him a couple of times, he left him alone and concentrated on the filly. The end of October and the start of the storm season were drawing near, so we were keen to get as far south of the flood country as we could. At Terang we were sitting smack-bang in the middle of it.

We only had time to restore one station packsaddle and when it was finished I caught *Riley* and tried it on. The pads stuck out on either side of him like huge surfboards. We'd stuffed in too much hair. Pulling out the surplus hair, we re-stuffed Ken's military packsaddle with it, then tried the saddle on a horse again. This time the pads hugged the horse's sides instead of resembling outspread wings.

There was one other problem we had to deal with. *Lonely* was becoming a terrible nuisance. He coerced other horses into running away, ate grass that the others could be eating and we wasted a lot of effort trying to catch, rescue and shoe him. It was obvious that he wouldn't gain much weight under the harsh travelling conditions and people were beginning to accuse us of mistreating him. Very few believed that we'd saved him from starvation and that his condition had improved.

The owner of a neighbouring station had once experienced similar accusations with a horse he'd pensioned off and understood our concerns.

"I've got plenty of land here," he gestured. "I can't bear to put a horse down, so the place is full of horses that'll never be used. You can turn your fella out with them."

Lonely had a home at last. As we put him out to pasture for the last time I gave Ken a short lecture.

"Next time you want to buy a useless horse, ask me first!" A charity case on our trek was an enormous burden.

The weather had been stiflingly hot, but one morning was hotter and more humid than the rest. About 2.30pm, a few puffs of cotton wool appeared on the horizon. At 3pm the sun was switched off by lumbering masses of ebony-black cloud. Forked lightning lit the heavens and a deafening blast of thunder shook the buildings. Dogs whined in their kennels, cattle bellowed in the yards and horses galloped wildly around the house paddock. Everyone ran for cover as the torrential rain from this violent tropical storm began to pelt down and drench everything in its path.

Half an hour and 100 points of rain later, there was not a cloud in sight. The only indication of the passing storm were tendrils of steam rising off everything wet and the unbearable humidity.

We walked down to the Suttor River for a look. There was no water gushing along the surface, but we knew the river was flowing underneath the sand. Ken had ridden *Joe* across one day and the horse had wallowed into a patch of quicksand. The sandy bottomed rivers can be deadly at any time of the year, but with a few more storms they rise very quickly and present a different threat. It was definitely time to be further south.

Ken mouthing Morgan

Lapping Morgan off Brown Mare in the Suttor River bed

JACKO STUMBLED INTO a pothole, tore the lead from Ken's hand and bucking furiously, swung away and bolted back for Terang. Half a bag of crushed oats worked its way loose from the top of the packs, catapulting into the air to land with a thud in the gutter in the wake of the rapidly disappearing packhorse. Trying to hang onto four jittery horses, I watched Ken gallop off in pursuit.

During our stay on Terang we'd handled *Jacko* every day, sometimes loading him up with pack bags full of salt, then lapping him up and down in the heavy river sand of the Suttor. Yet, that morning, we'd still had to blindfold, dinner hobble and collar-rope the aggressive animal in order to saddle him without being struck, kicked or bitten.

Each time Ken had hooked on a pack bag, *Jacko*, despite all the restraining harness, bucked it off before the second bag could be hooked on. Ken had eventually pulled him to the ground and the horse's head somehow ended up under a yard gate. Feeling much safer on the opposite side of the gate to *Jacko's* thrashing legs, I'd sat on his head while Ken slipped the pack bags on, tying them to the hooks with hobble straps so they wouldn't fall off when the horse stood up. I'd opened the gate and Ken had pulled the rebellious chestnut to his feet. He'd lost most of his 'sting' and stood quietly while Ken buckled the surcingle around the load.

How we would manage to catch and saddle *Jacko* without the use of yards I did not wish to think about.

Shoeing him was a nightmare. Ken had dinner-hobbled the horse and tried to pick up a front leg. *Jacko* had responded by bucking high into the air and rolling his hindquarters sideways. Because his knees were hobbled together, his entire body twisted to a horizontal position in mid-air where I could see 3 clear yard rails between his ribs and the ground. He'd landed on his side with a bone-jarring thud that knocked all the wind out of him.

As soon as he could breathe again, *Jacko* had been up on his feet and looking for a way out. Still dinner-hobbled, he'd reared up, stepped onto the side of a concrete wash trough and tried to climb over the top rail. The empty trough had overbalanced, tipping *Jacko* back into the yard and tearing a quarter out of one back hoof. He'd been as mad as a meat axe and looked like he wanted to eat somebody, so we'd left him to settle down a bit.

It had taken us 6 hours to shoe *Jacko* that day and the

bleeding hoof he'd quartered on the water trough made him extra snaky.

Jacko bucking with the packsaddle on Terang Station

"We're through with carrying bloody horse feed!" fumed Ken when he returned leading *Jacko* after the bucking and bolting spree. "That mongrel bag of crushed oats worked its way too far one side and unbalanced the load before it fell off. We're having more trouble from trying to carry horse feed than what it's worth!"

Jacko was a highly strung stockhorse, the type prone to nervous sweat. Once tilted to one side, the packsaddle had continued to slide around his sweat-oiled stomach. When Ken had finally caught up, *Jacko* was standing outside the fence of his old paddock, rocking backwards and forwards trying to get his balance and jump the wires. With one pack bag nearly under his belly and the other perched awkwardly over his wither, he couldn't quite gain enough balance.

For the first time, *Jacko* allowed himself to be caught in the open. He was so exhausted from the hard gallop he just stood there quivering while Ken slipped dinner hobbles around his knees and pushed the packsaddle back into place. The horse was so well greased with sweat that Ken managed this normally impossible task without having to unbuckle any straps.

"We'll leave those oats where they are," instructed Ken, relieving me of *Morgan's* lead rope. "Sid will be along here a bit later and he'll pick them up."

Sid didn't get the chance. Ten minutes later a vehicle roared past with half a bag of crushed oats, clearly labelled 'Terang Station' visible through the back windscreen!

SILVER STREAKS OF forked lightning pierced the bowels of angry black clouds that menaced overhead. The horses jumped in fright each time a loud clap of thunder rumbled around the hills and shook the muddy ground beneath their hooves. For two days now, violent afternoon thunderstorms had raged all about us, yet we'd managed to miss the showers of rain.

Freshly shattered branches and broken tree limbs littered the road and the shores of Lake Elphinstone as though a mini-cyclone had torn through. We camped here overnight, relieved to have missed the destructive forces of nature. Our tent would have offered little protection from falling timber.

A motor bike chugged up to our camp when we were packing up the next morning. The rider had come down from the nearby mining town of Glendon to go fishing. He'd been caught in the same storm that had hit the lake two days ago.

"Had bloody hailstones the size of marbles," he grinned, removing his helmet. "We were travelling in a bus from the Newlands' mine at the time and the bus copped such a hidin' from the hail that it looked like somebody'd gone all over it with a ball-peen hammer."

How lucky we were not to be caught out on the horses or camped in our flimsy tent at the time.

We'd just finished packing *Jacko* who'd been unusually quiet and hadn't thrown a solitary buck. Ken decided to saddle *Morgan* and give him his first ride since being broken in on Terang.

"Stick around," he invited the bikie, "we might have ourselves a rodeo!"

Blindfolding the near eye of the young horse, Ken slipped the hobbles on, saddled him, then mounted while I sat on *Joe* and held the cheekstrap of *Morgan's* bridle. When Ken's weight hit the saddle, the young chestnut pulled away from my grasp. Ken leant forward and pulled the blindfold off, and the horse bucked high in the air, spun 180 degrees, landed, then repeated the performance while his rider clung firmly to the monkey strap on the front of the saddle. The other horses were all unhobbled and grazing, as we'd planned on leaving as soon as Ken was mounted, but when *Morgan* bucked off across the flat in hobbles, he smashed into his big brother, *Jacko*, and sent the other horses running for cover.

Abandoning Ken, I took off after *Riley*, but when I dismounted to catch him, *Joe* pulled the reins out of my hand and both of them headed for the road. I sprinted through the scrub to head them off and came across *Jacko*, firmly wedged between two trees, so I tied him up where he stood. *Easton* slunk past with his load skew-whiff from nudging a tree and I caught him, righted his load and tied him near *Jacko*. I secured *Mal* after finding him lurking in a clump of bushes, then made it out to the road where *Joe* stood with my saddle hanging underneath his belly and a sheepish look on his face while *Riley* loitered nearby.

Ken appeared while I was rearranging my saddle on *Joe*. When *Morgan* had bucked to a standstill, he'd managed to dismount, catch *Brown Mare* and transfer his saddle across. It hadn't been a wise idea for Ken to ride his young horse. *Morgan* had his big brother's ability to perform corkscrews in mid air. No doubt he would become a useful riding horse in time, but for now he would have to suffice as a packhorse.

Our helmetted friend gave us a wave when he zoomed past us later. His fishing bag was empty, but no doubt he would have a few tales to tell when he arrived back in Glendon.

Chapter 11:
RACE AGAINST THE RIVERS

FINISHING THE LAST few crumbs of our steakburgers, we started on a 2 litre container of ice cream. Resting his elbow on the table with chin in hand, Ronnie watched us attack the contents with the spoons I'd borrowed from the roadhouse, then glanced at his old mate, Blue. Having caught one another's eye, they exchanged a silent thought, politely concealed their mirth with a movement of the hand and resumed their observation. It was 9 o'clock in the morning and never before had they seen two people eat such a huge, unconventional breakfast.

We'd met Ronnie the night before when I'd mistaken the lights of his caravan for the township of Nebo. It is no simple matter to identify a town when you've never been there before, it's a pitch black night, you don't have a torch and you've no idea where you're going to camp. How was I supposed to know that we'd arrived at Lynford Station and still had 3km to go until we reached town?

I'd judged the distance wrong because there were a lot of gates and every catch was different. This slowed our progress as I'd had to grope around in the dark and work out how to open each gate. At one gate I'd disturbed a nest of paper wasps. My compassionate partner had howled with laughter at my shrieks of agony from the repeated stings of the invisible insects.

Homing in on the light from the caretaker's caravan, I sang out to the occupant who beamed a flashlight over us and nearly fell out of the doorway at the sight of our horse team. Ronnie wasn't satisfied with merely giving directions into town. Aided by a walking stick, he shuffled quickly across the yard, shining his torch so that we could see our way back to the stock route. An engine roared to life and a little Daihatsu 4-wheel-drive crept cautiously past and sped off. In his vehicle, Ronnie accompanied us to town, opened and closed all the gates and showed us where to camp near the rodeo grounds.

He returned early the next morning and asked us if we'd care to shift our horses into a small paddock he wanted eaten out.

"I've been meaning to burn it off and haven't got around to it," he explained. "There's legume and couch growin', and your horses'll do me a favour by eatin' it down."

Ronnie's paddock had enough feed to last our horses a week. Camped in a large shed nearby, we had the ideal opportunity to restore our second station packsaddle. If only we could find a successful way of securing my camera case, we'd finally have our loads stable enough to let the horses run loose.

A trip down to Mackay and a visit to a good mate of Ken's provided a solution. Barry and Ken put their heads together and built a rectangular frame from angle iron. When bolted to the steel arches of a military packsaddle, my camera case sat rigidly on top and was secured with a single strap. We'd planned to do away with the two military packsaddles, but kept one to carry the camera gear and posted the other one home.

We only had two sets of pack bags, so fashioned a third out of hessian corn sacks. These would be used to carry light, bulky items such as ropes and tarps on the military packsaddle. As this saddle was designed for a maximum load of 40kg, we'd ensure it never exceeded this weight.

Sharon treating Jacko's injured wither

JACKO'S WITHER HAD swollen from his stint of bolting with the packs under his belly. The swelling had burst open at Nebo, leaving a nasty, weeping wound, so we organised a course of penicillin to be delivered from a vet in Mackay. *Jacko* had to be completely blindfolded, dinner hobbled and collar roped to administer the intramuscular injections. I jammed the first one in his rump, but he bucked and shot the syringe into the air. It was more successful to inject them into the neck muscle.

The wound was bathed twice daily with warm water, then treated with a few drops of hydrogen peroxide which frothed and bubbled as it killed the infection. The injury was serious and it would be many months before *Jacko* could be saddled again.

While camped in Ronnie's paddock, we felt sorry for the horses and took their hobbles off. There was no back fence, but we were certain they wouldn't cross the four feet of water in Nebo Creek. But then, horses will always do what you don't expect.

Just on nightfall, we heard the terrible sound of steel-shod hooves galloping on bitumen. Spurring them on was the incessant tooting of a car horn. We sprinted down the road on foot, fearing that the horses might be chased onto the Peak Downs highway only 2km away. Fortunately, they baulked at the bright lights of a power substation, and we found them grazing on the far side of the road.

Catching *Joe*, I led him back while Ken pushed the others along behind. As soon as we filed through a gate next to Ronnie's paddock, the loose horses peeled off and galloped away into the night. They were running in 30 000 acres of timbered station paddocks. All the gates were open, making it into one big paddock, so we had not a hope of getting around them on foot. It took two of us to hold *Joe* who was doing a good imitation of a pogo stick. Securing the appaloosa to a nightline, he kept us awake by pawing the ground and whinnying out for his mates all night.

Ken saddled him at first light, scouring the rocky roadside for hours before he spotted the faint imprint of half a shoe where the horses had left the road. He tracked them down through the scrub and brought them back to camp at midday.

"That'll be the last time we leave the horses unhobbled!" he declared, closing the gate.

I remembered the advice of an old friend, "Never feel sorry for a horse," he'd told me. "They take advantage of you every time." What a pity I had such a short memory.

WE LEFT NEBO with our plant of 7 horses, carrying 30kg on the military packsaddle and 50kg on each station pack. The loads were balanced and stable so we decided to try driving the horses when we found ourselves in a fenced laneway. I rode in the lead to block the horses and Ken rode at the tail to keep them moving. They took off in all directions, but Ken managed to keep them in front of him with a few cracks of the stockwhip and each horse that tried to get past me got whacked on the end of the nose with the dinner hobbles. They settled in quickly to this routine which was much easier than leading three horses.

Crossing a ditch full of water, *Easton* dived in and had a merry roll with the packs on before we could get to him. With all the yelling that followed we had to do much galloping to catch the little swine. He'd been carrying our clothes which were only slightly damp as they were kept in a plastic bag, but our paperwork was saturated. While the horses grazed, we spent a couple of hours laying photos, letters, diaries and maps out on the ground to dry. After this incident, *Easton's* lead rope was left tucked under the surcingle so he could be caught quickly and led across any water.

An English couple in a campervan pulled up to look at our horses and we invited them to camp with us overnight as they were keen to hear about the National Trail. While Ken and I were having a wash in Denison Creek that evening, we found some freshwater mussels in the muddy bottom. Digging them up with our toes, we took them back to camp with the idea of treating our foreign friends to some good old Aussie 'bush tucker'.

We cooked those mussels every way we could think of; steamed on the coals, fried in butter, boiled, stuffed with black sauce, tomato sauce and even a bit of parsley, but they still tasted like gritty mud and were like chewing on a piece of rubber. The English couple were so polite they tried each new variation in cooking, pretending it wasn't that bad, while Ken and I spat them out in disgust. They'd had the foresight to boil a tin of peas and a few spuds which they shared with us; so much for our 'bush tucker'!

*Ken chasing the horses across Tierawoomba Creek
and into camp in the morning*

Once across the treacherous, quick-rising waters of Funnel Creek, we rode through the beautiful valley of Tierawoomba Station and saw the first good feed since leaving the Atherton Tablelands four months ago. The valley led us to the base of the Connors Range where the National Trail followed a bitumen road that we decided to avoid. Making local enquiries, we found an old telegraph line that offered a lengthy but challenging detour over the range before linking up with the National Trail on top.

Following a ridge that wound its way upwards, we had a clear view of the valley for miles behind. The telegraph poles eventually petered out and while we were searching for the old line on top of the range, a loud thunderclap sent us scurrying to make camp. Nightlining the horses amongst sheoaks, we hoped these trees were less likely to crash from lightning strike or lose branches in a storm. Pitching our tent well away from the timber, we zipped ourselves inside after a hurried meal. After all precautions, the storm passed without a drop of rain!

Zig-zagging our way east in the morning, we picked up the telegraph line which led to the escarpment and a view over the coastal plain towards St. Lawrance. There was much whip cracking and bellowing to force the horses down the steep, rocky face of the range, where the stone had been worn smooth by the passage of steel shod wheels. Carved out of the rock, this old coach road must have been a nightmarish hell for pack teams and teamsters alike. Cruppers and breechings pulled tight on our packhorses as their loads shifted forward, but their flank girths stopped the backs of saddles lifting, preventing pressure being transferred to the wither. Sour and cranky from the discomfort of the crupper, the packhorses kicked and bit one another, turning uphill for relief, only to be shunted sideways by the horse behind.

Hordes of hungry mosquitoes welcomed our troupe at the bottom of the range. There was ample feed for horses at the stock reserve that evening, but the water tasted brackish and stayed that way all along the coastal plain. It looked cleaner than the muddy dams we'd been drinking out of, but was heavy in salt and minerals.

Swinging south, the National Trail took us along the Bruce Highway, where the stock route was wide enough for our horses to run loose a safe distance from the traffic. Dancing up and down when a mob of paddocked horses galloped up to the fence, *Joe* didn't look where he was going, put his foot down a hole and did a complete somersault with the dinner packs. Gaining his feet, he walked off completely unharmed. Most foodstuffs were decanted into calico bags or plastic bottles and only a glass jar of vegemite and a bottle of black sauce were in their original containers. Cautiously opening the dinner packs that evening we found the contents shaken up, but thankfully intact.

Upstream of the salty, boggy Styx River we forded Granite Creek then crossed the Styx over a timber decking bridge. Skimming across the muddy brown water came the googly-eyes of a school of mud skippers, disappearing under the bridge and continuing up the tidal river.

Unloading and hobbling our horses at a recreation reserve, we walked into the village of Ogmore and had tea at the Styx River Hotel.

Patronising local hotels was a small price to pay for the support that publicans give the National Trail and the wealth of information found in the public bar. We met a wiry little black-bearded Irishman named Larry Moi in the hotel. He lived up in the hills and saddled his packhorse once every three weeks to come into Ogmore for groceries. The Irish certainly have a way with horses, because the locals often found Larry on the ground, having fallen asleep and slid off his horse. Instead of deserting him, the horse would stand with its head over its owner, waiting for him to wake up.

"A few months back, I come across these two blokes riding north with a pack mule," remembered Larry. "They were trying to shape a shoe on the railway line and asked me whether I knew anything about shoeing a mule," he chuckled. "Yeh, I said. You don't need to shoe a mule, because they've such a depth of hard hoof. But they reckoned you did, so I helped them anyway and rode with them for a bit. This mule was tagging along loose because they couldn't lead him, and at the road bridge over the Bruce Highway, a semi put the air brakes on and the mule turned and bolted. Well, the two of them were gone for an hour trying to round up this mule and left me holding on to their packhorse. There was something funny about this horse, and I kept lookin' at it until I realised there wasn't a hair left in its tail," he laughed.

"What happened to this horse's tail? I asked when they returned. They told me they'd got sick of fetching this mule every time a truck came along so tied him to the packhorse's tail. They gave the horse a hunt, but the mule sat down with the packs on and tore every hair out of the horse's dock!"

We would have liked to stay longer in Ogmore and listen to Larry's yarns, but it was mid-December and the level of the Fitzroy River was starting to go up and down like a yo-yo as a forerunner to the wet season floods. A fortnight earlier, the river had been too deep to cross and we would have had to backtrack to the main road bridge over the Bruce Highway and ride straight through the middle of busy Rockhampton. I rang and found that the level at the stony crossing had dropped to 2'6". If we could make it to the

Fitzroy before it rose again, we were in business. A fair dinkum flood could inundate the country miles back from the river, cutting off access to the main road bridge and taking months for the level to drop low enough to cross with horses.

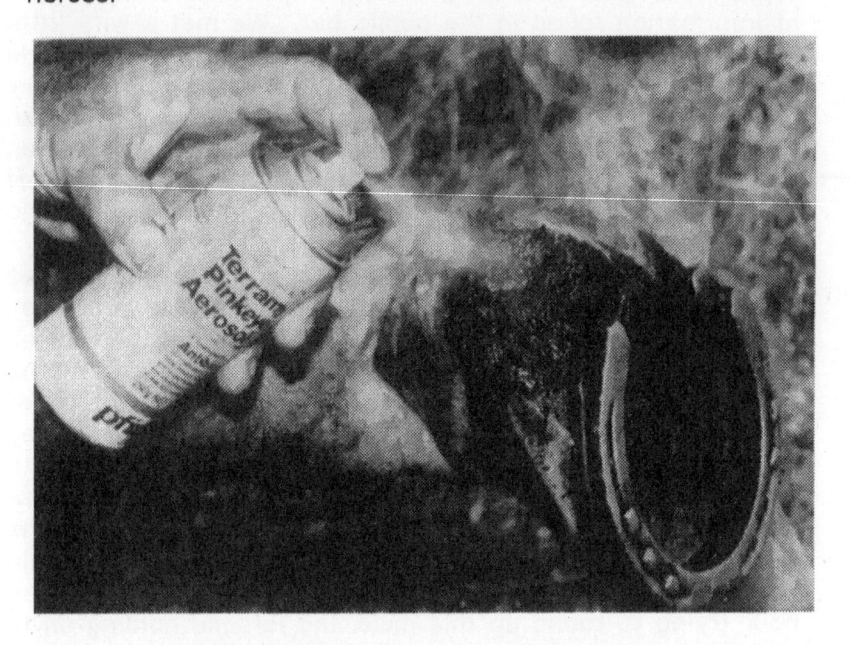

Joe's double shoe for a stone bruise

JOE HAD DEVELOPED a massive stone bruise on a front hoof from the night he'd galloped down the bitumen at Nebo. Several other horses had small stone bruises from that same night, but like *Joe*, they'd shown no sign of lameness, and we didn't know of the bruises until they blew out at the coronet. A stone bruise usually heals itself once this happens, but *Joe's* hoof had infected and hadn't responded to treatment. Larry had a look before we left Ogmore, advising us to cut away the hoof wall so it didn't harbour bacteria, and clean it regularly.

Ken cut away an enormous quarter of hoof with the shoeing nippers. Three times a day we cleaned away all the rubbish with hydrogen peroxide and treated the wound with an antibiotic spray. The hoof looked terrible, but *Joe* never flinched during treatment and only limped when he stood on a rock and it touched the exposed wound. Resorting to ingenuity, Ken used two horse shoes and some extra long nails to 'double shoe' the horse and keep his injury up off the rocks. This idea worked so well that *Joe* never limped in the rocks again and was able to carry a load.

On the 15th December, 1989, our 7 horses waded across the Fitzroy River, where crocodiles lay invisible beneath the shallow, muddy water. A fully grown bull had been taken by a croc only a few kilometres downstream of the crossing. Thankfully, horses and trail riders weren't on the menu today and we rode up through the sand to the top of the low flood bank. The high flood mark was a star picket 3km from the river inscribed with the year '1956'.

The Fitzroy was our last major flooding river system. We'd won our 'race against the rivers', with no more barriers to our progress until snow in the NSW highlands halted us for winter.

Crossing the Fitzroy

Chapter 12:
A KESTREL FOR CHRISTMAS

RIDING INTO KABRA, a tiny hamlet only a stone's throw from Rockhampton, we wondered where on earth we could camp with the horses for a week. They needed a rest and a safe place to graze while we went into town to buy maps and horse feed. An endless procession of coal trains from Blackwater rumbled past the unfenced recreation reserve.

Heading to the pub for information, we rode past a team of blokes building a fence and stopped for a chat.

"Me mate's got a paddock here," offered Barry Brazier, the fencing contractor. "I'll give him a ring and see if you can stick your horses in it."

Not only did Barry find us a paddock, he introduced us to a wonderful lady named Maisie Harris who insisted we stay with her. Everywhere our journey took us, we were overwhelmed by the friendliness and hospitality that was offered. At 64 years of age, amazing Maisie worked 6 days a week in Rockhampton, yet couldn't return home fast enough to make sure that we weren't starving to death.

When Ken went out to feed the horses the next morning, he returned with two dusty, tired travellers. Jenny and Rainald were spending their honeymoon on the National Trail and had ridden from Eungella Dam with packhorses. They were the first people we'd met on the trail and we enjoyed swapping tales with fellow travellers who understood the problems and demands of long distance packing.

Christmas Day was spent with the Brazier family whose generosity extended to giving Jenny and Rainald an ex-trotting mare, and myself and Ken an unbroken Standardbred gelding as Christmas presents. Boof-headed and roach-backed, our *Trotter* looked more like a dinosaur than a horse, but he'd done well in a paddock full of little else but lantana and had the toughness of character we'd begun to look for in a packhorse.

Grateful for the Brazier family's help, we offered to take their 12 year old son, Mike, with us. The fiery little Palouse pony he'd been given for Christmas might learn a few good manners after a couple of weeks on the trail.

When Barry and Mike arrived at Kabra with the Palouse

pony, she had a nasty gash over one eye, having run through three barbed wire fences when they tried to catch her. Hobbling the pony, Barry tried to spray her eye with 'Terramycin', but she reared up, struck him in the chest and knocked him to the ground before tearing off around the paddock. It looked like we had a fair job ahead of us for the next fortnight!

Trotter was remarkably quiet for his first shoeing, but we decided not to saddle him until he'd run loose for a few days. Mike rode a little chestnut pony named *Gidget*, while Ken led the rogue pony mare. Two miles down the track, *Trotter* turned around and made a wild dash for home. Ken chased him on *Brown Mare*, but the little horse went into top gear and took them all the way back to Kabra. Once Ken returned, we kept our guard up all the way to Bouldercombe, trying to keep Mike's pony in tow and thwart more breakaway attempts by the Standardbred before he could hit full speed.

That evening, Mike named his new pony *Blue Heeler* when she tried to bite a big chunk out of Ken as he tied her to a nightline.

Following an old packhorse mailman's track up the Razorback Range, Ken was forced to let *Blue Heeler* run loose on the narrow, winding pad. Travelling in single file, we came to a washaway where the pad had turned back on itself. It was too steep to turn around, so we kept moving and all the horses jumped the three foot gap without losing their footing. To the east lay magnificent views of the coastal plain, with Rockhampton shimmering in the distance.

Giving the horses a spell after the hard climb, we took advantage of our new horses while they were still tired. Ken and Mike struggled to collar-rope and saddle *Blue Heeler*, while she plunged, bit, bucked and kicked. Meanwhile, I dinner hobbled our unbroken *Trotter*, who totally ignored me and continued grazing. Cautiously slipping a packsaddle onto his back, I gently girthed up, buckled the breastplate and breeching on and left the crupper to one side. The horse only seemed interested in eating, so I left him and watched the entertainment: A mere 11hh pony in an oversized stock saddle was dragging man and boy through a huge patch of variegated thistle.

Trotter never batted an eyelid when I hung the pack bags

on and pulled the surcingle tight. Ken led *Blue Heeler* when we set off again, but after leading *Trotter* for half an hour, he proved so placid that I let him run loose. It was hard to believe that he'd never been broken in.

At the mining town of Mt Morgan, we had to ride straight through the middle of town on the bitumen to reach our camp at the showgrounds. Keeping as far to the left as possible, I took off in the lead at a fast trot which had the effect of stringing the horses behind me. Ten horses trotting down the main street in single file turned quite a few heads.

Blue Heeler had settled down after carrying a heavy saddle for half a day, so Ken and Mike decided to shoe her. They tied the aggressive pony up with ropes and straps, but she managed to boot both lads with one well-aimed kick. It took four hours to get the shoes on, but she lost some of her fighting spirit in the struggle.

While this was going on, I'd been busy making hobble straps. Our leather straps had been broken and repaired so many times that I'd bought a roll of plastic coated webbing in Rockhampton in the hope that it was more durable.

"Go and catch me a horse so I can try on these straps," I asked Mike. Instead of going after one of the quiet horses, I heard him trying to catch *Jacko*. He had developed a fascination for our most dangerous horse.

"Here *Jacko*, come on *Jacko*, nice *Jacko*," he soothed, creeping slowly up to the arrogant chestnut, who stood his ground but eyed the boy suspiciously. Even though we weren't using the horse because of his back injury, he occasionally tried to kick, strike or bite. But *Jacko* and Mike seemed to have an understanding right from day one. I watched the boy undo the lead rope from around the halter and cautiously run his fingers down the horse's legs, half crouching and leaning against the shoulder like Ken had shown him while he unbuckled the hobbles. Not trusting the horse enough to turn his back, Mike walked sideways, holding the end of the lead rope and watching the horse's eye. *Jacko* was the last horse I would have chosen for the fitting of stiff new hobble straps, but Mike was so proud of his catch that I couldn't refuse him.

THE LOCALS WARNED us not to water our horses at the Dee River running through Mt Morgan. Unfit for human consumption, it had been contaminated by cyanide from a gold mine on the hill behind the town. The water was crystal clear because nothing lived in it. The fish, aquatic plants and algae had died from poisoning. There were several crossings of the Dee River to be made when we left Mt Morgan, and the horses had to be hunted through with a stock whip so they wouldn't drink the water.

"When can I ride *Blue Heeler*?" Mike had been asking ten times a day.

Pulling up for dinner two days out of Mt Morgan, Ken decided she'd quietened down enough for Mike to ride. Hobbling and saddling the little mare, we left Mike to watch the horses and walked over to a dam for water.

"O.K." said Ken when we returned, "You can put a bridle on her and hop on now."

"I've been on and off her three times while you were gone!" boasted the young rascal. He hadn't had the patience to await our return!

The pony behaved herself until late afternoon of the following day.

"Go on," said Ken to Mike, "Kick that pony into a canter; she's not going to do anything."

At the touch of the heels, *Blue Heeler* bucked and plunged like a miniature version of Australia's famous bucking mare, *Curio*, pelting Mike into a patch of raspberry bushes.

"I would have ridden her but the saddle slipped!" declared her bedraggled owner, picking himself up out of the raspberries. There was no shame in being thrown, as Alan Woods, the first man to ride 'time' on *Curio*, would have been hard pressed to stay aboard the roly poly little horse. Ken tied a monkey grip to the pommel of Mike's saddle, instructing him to hang onto it next time the pony bucked. Two days later, a riderless Palouse pony came bucking past me again.

"Why didn't you hang onto the monkey grip?" scolded Ken, when Mike caught up on foot.

"I did," answered Mike, "but it was hurting my backside too much, so I let go!" Determined not to let the horse get the better of him, we caught the little mare and off he rode, scolding her for misbehaving. That 12 year old boy had more pluck and gumption than most fellows twice his age.

Mike bridling Blue Heeler

"WHAT HAVE THOSE crows got over there?" demanded Ken. "Leave the horses for a bit and we'll go have a look."

Two crows were rolling a squawking mass of feathers over the bare ground.

"It's a poor little baby kestrel!" cried Ken as the crows flapped away on our arrival. The tormented bird raised one wing and made a defensive rush at our horses' legs. The barbaric crows had chewed his other wing down to the first knuckle joint.

"See if you can catch him," I urged Ken, taking hold of his reins when he dismounted.

"Yikes! It's not going to be that easy," he yelped. Brandishing sharp claws and a wicked curved beak, the pathetic, squawking bundle of feathers forced him back. "He's a bit upset at the moment! Pass me that stockwhip, will you Mike?"

Throwing his hat over the injured kestrel, Ken lifted it enough to pin the bird to the ground with his whip handle.

"Jeez!" he exclaimed, jamming his hat on, "Now what am I going to do with it?" The little bird screeched and struggled to attack every time Ken tried to get his hand near. "He's bloody quick with that beak; I'm likely to lose a few fingers."

"We can't leave him here," I pleaded, "the crows will come back and finish him off."

Gently holding the bird's head down with his boot, Ken grabbed him behind the neck.

"Quick!" he cried, "open your saddle bag!"

Unbuckling the straps, I pulled out the maps and thrust them at Mike. *Brown Mare* snorted and sidled away as Ken approached with the screeching bundle of fury.

"You can't stick him in there!" I protested. "This horse is likely to go berserk if he starts squawking inside that saddle bag."

"There's nowhere else we can put him," grinned Ken, stuffing the kestrel inside and slamming the flap, "Besides, this was your idea. Merry Christmas!"

The soothing darkness of the saddle bag silenced the baby bird and I soon forgot he was there. A couple of horses broke away from the mob, and I galloped off through the bush to block them. Once they'd turned and headed back for the road, I remembered what was in the saddle bag that had been flapping and banging against *Brown Mare's* ribs.

"Oh no!" I cried, "You'd better open the bag and see if he's O.K. Ken."

Unbuckling one strap, Ken raised the flap and a furious head popped out and screeched. Ken slammed the flap down as *Brown Mare* jumped away.

"He's alright!" grinned Ken. "We'd better leave him be!"

That evening, the baby kestrel quietened down when we fed him some warm spaghetti sauce and milk. He slept in an old tin stuffed with rag and we caught him a few grasshoppers for breakfast.

"This is the best place to leave him," said Ken. "He'll be able to catch plenty of insects and hide from predators in the long grass."

Mike came walking up from the creek and the little bird squawked and darted out at him from a tuft of grass.

"Did ya see that?" called Mike, dancing out of the way. "He just tried to attack me!"

He'd certainly regained his strength, so we packed up and rode away, at least having given the little kestrel a chance of survival.

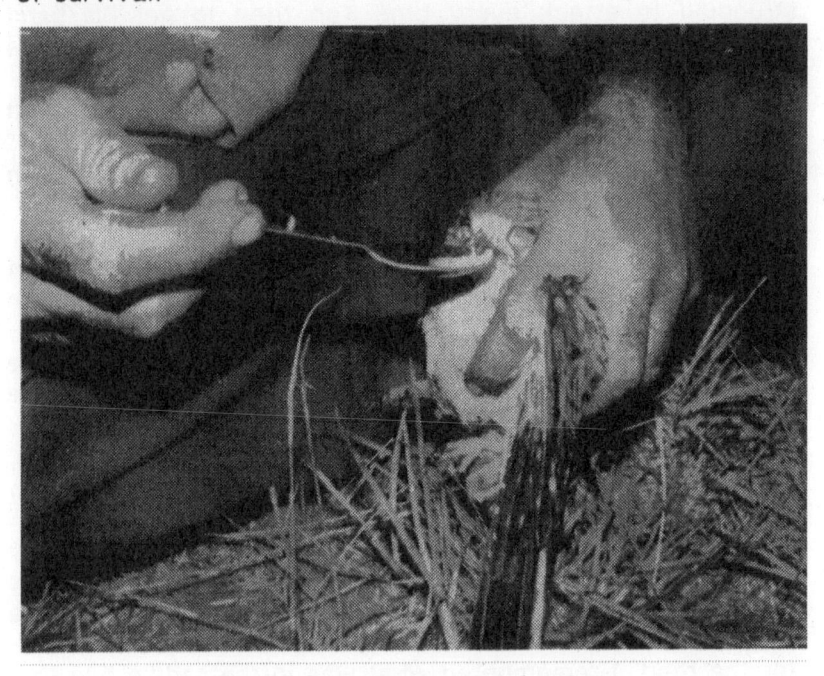

Spoon feeding the baby kestrel

AT THE BASE of the Calliope Range, we caught up with Jennie and Rainald.

"Where's your new horse?" I asked, seeing that she was missing.

"We camped in the Cattle Creek reserve and found her dead on her nightline in the morning!" replied Jennie, puzzled over the death.

"It would have been from Poison Peach," stated Mike, "It was growing all through there and it only takes a few leaves to kill a horse."

During the drought, Mike's family had lost a lot of livestock to Poison Peach. Its botannical name is *Trema aspera*, a regrowth shrub commonly found growing amongst lantana with a similar flower and berry. It was prolific along this section of the National Trail and we were lucky to have Mike with us to identify the plant. Tethered horses are more likely to eat the poisonous leaves because they can't wander far enough to forage for more palatable species.

Mike & Sharon discover an old car

Leaving our fellow trekkers on top of the Calliope Range, we headed south to pick up an old bullockies' track through the abandoned Mt Rainbow gold mines. The horses were hot and tired when we climbed to our night camp on Specimen Hill, finding a Telecom tower and panoramic view, but no feed or water. Retracing our steps it was two hours before our thirsty horses reached a watered stock reserve. The heat and hilly terrain, compounded by the lack of feed and water, saw our horses losing condition every day.

Reaching a sealed road the next morning, our trail guidelines gave us the option of following the bitumen or taking an old wagon road. We opted for the wagon road, but having no directions to find it we ended up beneath high voltage power lines which had probably obliterated the old road. The power lines took a direct path, regardless of hills. Several times we rested the horses in the shade to prevent them overheating. A sheer cliff face brought us to an abrupt halt and we spent an hour picking our way down through the timber before joining the power lines again.

As the Callide Dam came into view, we veered away from the power line and made for the feeder creek. A timbered thicket on the opposite side offered a sheltered campsite, so we went to cross over as the water level was low. Ken rode *Joe* into the creek, but he baulked at the muddy water and soft ground. There were cattle tracks everywhere, so assuming it was safe to cross, Ken urged the heavy appaloosa forward. Against his wishes, *Joe* plunged into the water and bogged straight to his stomach in the mud. Ken slid off the helpless horse, leaving him to catch his breath.

Meanwhile, I cantered off to get a camera, but failed to negotiate a grazing horse's rump. My left knee took the full impact of the collision, smashing into the horse's tailbone with a sickening 'crunch'. Sliding to the ground, I rolled around in agony, certain I'd broken a leg.

When the initial pain subsided, I managed to move the leg and realised it wasn't broken.

"Thank goodness for that," said Mike who'd flown to my assistance and was still holding my horse, "I hate to see women get hurt!"

It sounded so comical coming from a 12 year old that I had to laugh despite the agony. Ken and Mike helped me to get the camera gear and hobble over to photograph our other casualty. After a ten minute spell, Ken stood on a submerged log and let drive with a coiled up whip on *Joe's* saddle flap. The horse gave one almighty heave and lurched his way clear of the stinking, black mud. Exhausted after a long, hot day and with myself a stretcher case, we camped right where we were amongst the reeds, mud and mosquitoes. My knee was so stiff in the morning that I couldn't mount my horse.

"You can ride *Gidget* if you like," offered Mike.

I scrambled aboard the little pony and she carried me all the way to Biloela. This town was a diversion from the National Trail and meant two days' extra travel, but we'd arranged for Mike's parents to pick up their son and his horses there. *Blue Heeler* had become a much milder mannered pony in the two weeks Mike had been with us, but we were sorry to see him go. He'd been a big help with the horses, could make a decent cup of billy tea and had been a character into the bargain.

Ken stands on a submerged log beside Joe

Chapter 13:
BRUMBIES AND BUCKJUMPERS

WE LEFT BILOELA on the Valentine Plains Road, our 8 horses fresh after a five day spell. A couple pranced off onto the golf course fairway and while Ken shepherded them back to the road, the rest took off into a cultivated paddock, looking for a good spot to roll!

Pushing them into a trot to keep them from further mischief, the horses strung out single file, resigned to the fact that it was a work day again. Once they settled down, we dropped back to our normal walking pace of 5km an hour.

That evening, Ken recognised a fellow working in a set of cattle yards. He'd met Ian Crisp five years ago mustering cattle in the Lower Gulf country of Queensland, and Ian invited us to stay the night.

"Would you have any use for a four year old, unbroken filly?" he asked, as we were saddling to leave the next morning. We couldn't believe it when he yarded a perfectly stunning, grey, anglo-arab mare. "She's the last of a line of foals from a stallion we had on Greenvale Station," said Ian, "and I'd much rather see her used than go to a doggers' sale."

She was the most beautiful horse I'd even seen, and when Ken had difficulty trying to lead her off *Brown Mare*, I saw the opportunity to snaffle the filly for myself and offered to lead her off *Joe*. Without hesitation, she led alongside like an obedient puppy, giving the seal of approval to my intentions.

She was not so accommodating when I tried to lead her out of the yards and away from her home paddock. Ian's wife, Desley, rode along with us for half a day, helping Ken control the loose horses while I had a tug-of-war with the filly, whom I named *Jordie*.

We'd had permission to camp at a set of yards overnight, which we utilised to shoe *Jordie*. Since I'd been leading her off *Joe*, she'd quickly formed a bond with him, so he was tied outside the round yard to make her feel secure. Each front leg was strapped up in turn and shoes hastily tacked on before she had time to think about what was happening.

Instead of shoeing her back feet, we turned the filly out into a small paddock with *Joe* for the rest of the day so she didn't 'sour up' from spending too long in the yards.

Thirsty from our efforts, I turned on a tap beside the plunge dip and went to drink out of the hose.

"Don't drink outa there!" yelled Ken, "let's go over and check the water in the tank first."

The creek behind the yards was dry, and the only water available had been pumped by a windmill into a large tank. Climbing onto a fence post beside the tank, we peered in to see a dead parrot floating around in the green scum on top of the water.

"Looks like we get a few extra minerals in this lot," laughed Ken, at the wry face I pulled. "It'll be O.K. – we'll just have to boil it first."

The horses were gone in the morning except for the three we'd left in the small paddock. Ken saddled *Brown Mare* and tracked them 3km back, almost to the spot where we'd had dinner yesterday. Buckling each horse's hobbles onto the one leg, he ran them back to camp, the jingling hobble chains acting as 'shin tappers' to discourage them from galloping off.

The new plastic hobble straps were proving much softer than leather ones. When the horses watered at a muddy dam, the mud dried and fell off the plastic, whereas it used to stick to the old straps, cracking the leather and making them brittle as it dried. Our days of hobble chafe on fetlocks were over!

Using a collar rope, we shod my nervous filly's hind feet quickly and quietly. It was fortunate for us that *Jordie* behaved so well, because if we'd had to be rough with her, she would no longer have trusted us and would give trouble when it was time to break her in. I'd helped Ken break in horses, but never tackled one myself. Perhaps this mare would be quiet enough to be my first?

In the afternoon, we followed an old road that was barely visible in places to the foot of the Kroombit Tops, a rugged mountain range between Biloela and Monto. A wallaby pad took us up a spur before petering out on a rocky hillside. The National Trail directions told us to 'wend our way around a lemon squeezer landmass', and we did just that, our horses slipping and sliding on the loose rocks and scrambling across the many gullies running off the mountain peak.

Our directions were vague and there was no sign of a trail marker on an old ironbark that was mentioned. Wherever we turned, there were steep drop-offs and hidden cliff faces, ready to send an unwary horse into the gorge hundreds of metres below. Our National Trail notes and map were of no further assistance, so I resorted to our insurance policy, the 1:100 000 topographic map series.

Since the northern side of the mountain was a vertical rock face, the only logical route was to descend the southern slope into Dry Creek. If we followed it upstream, we should pick up a small creek that would help us identify a hillside that took us up onto a major fire trail.

Still leading *Jordie*, I picked my way downhill on *Joe*. Ken was busy with the stockwhip trying to drive the horses down after me, as they preferred to follow the contour around the side of the mountain rather than zig-zag downhill. Several thick stands of wattle provided an education for some of the bull-headed packhorses. They learned it was easier to back off and go around trees that were too close, instead of getting jammed trying to barge through.

After half an hour of scrub bashing, we slid down into Dry Creek to find water the colour of black tea in a handful of tiny rockholes. Gently pushing aside the brown frogs, Ken scooped a cupfull from each hat-sized hole, filling our quart pots before the horses skated over the smooth rock and stirred the water up. It was too late in the day to keep going, so we returned a little way up the hillside to camp.

A well used brumby pad followed the creek and there was no grass, so we hobbled all the horses and tied them to trees. *Jordie* had never been tied up before, so we used two halters to secure her. She pulled back and fell on her haunches, but the halters held and she stood quietly after the struggle. If we lost our horses in this wild piece of country we'd never find them again. The mares would end up in a mob of brumbies and the geldings would be killed by a stallion. We lit a big campfire to prevent a stallion sneaking in amongst our horses unseen, but spent a restless night, waking to investigate every sound. The hillside was so steep that we continually slid out the bottom of the swag, ending up on the rocks with a tangled mess of sheets and blankets.

The brumbies left us alone, but our own horses were

hungry and cranky from being tied up all night.

"Mongrel bastard!" yelled Ken while we were unhobbling.

"What's wrong?" I asked, looking up to see Ken and *Jacko* glaring at one another. Hooked on a bush between them were the tattered remains of Ken's shirt.

"This mongrel coot has a streak of dirt in him a mile long," he growled. "He just lunged at me and tore the shirt off me back with his teeth!" *Jacko* was a horse never to be trusted.

As we travelled upstream, the brumby pad along Dry Creek was hemmed in by such dense undergrowth that I had to hop off and waddle along in a crouched position like a Russian Cossack. My riding horse, *Joe*, was the only one I could see behind me. Leading his mount also, Ken could only see the horse in front of him and I hoped that *Jordie* and the others were somewhere in between. When the horse in front of Ken stopped, he had to tie up his mount, scramble through the dense scrub, find the packhorse which had halted the column and untangle him from the thick woody vines.

The undergrowth became impenetrable, forcing us out into the dry, rocky creek bed to risk sprained ankles and fetlocks. Sparks flew off steel shod hooves and the gully echoed with a clattering din as nine horses staggered awkwardly over boulders and loose, jagged rocks.

Travelling in this fashion for two hours, we fought our way through a prickly stand of lantana at the first sight of a clearing, keen to vacate the dreadfully stony river bed. Nearby we found signs of a fresh campfire. Jennie and Rainald were several days ahead of us and we could see where they'd tied their horses up to trees overnight. They'd obviously been having trouble finding their way also. Mounting up, we climbed a ridge to establish our bearings, holding our breath when the pad narrowed to a width of one metre. I prayed for the horses not to slip when they scrambled over a pile of loose rocks with a sheer granite walled drop-off on either side.

The ridge flattened out on top, but we couldn't identify any landmarks through the timber and descended into another dry creek. Scouting about on foot for waterholes, Ken discovered a deep catchment under what would normally be a waterfall if the creek were running. He stayed there to water the horses, while I continued across the creek to look for a way out. Reaching an impassable cliff face, I returned and we headed off upstream in search of our fire trail on a ridgetop.

Carrying the dinner packs in the climb from the creek bed, *Easton* tried to overtake *Mal* when the pad widened across a flat-topped boulder. There wasn't enough room for two horses, and *Mal* bumped the skewbald's pack bag as he squeezed past. *Easton's* back legs slid sideways in a 'two-wheel drift', skating over the edge of the rock face to dangle in mid air as the horse landed on his stomach, front legs outstretched before him. The tough little pony strained as hard as he could, his front hooves finding enough purchase in the pitted rock to heave himself back over the lip and away from the twenty foot drop to the creek bed below.

Upstream, we found the National Trail landmark: a fig tree growing by a waterhole. I'd already ridden past it before I recognised it as such. We'd been looking for a fig tree fifty feet high by forty feet across and this puny specimen was three feet high with about two leaves. The waterhole was full of green slime and barely enough water to put out a match!

Trotter stops for a rest on a narrow ridgetop

Crossing the creek bed we zig-zagged uphill to join our long-awaited fire trail, grateful that our horses had come through this rugged section of the Kroombits without injury. It was easy travelling on roads from here, so I caught *Jordie* in case she tried to slip away. Beginning to relax after the ordeal, I rode around a bend and there, not 10 metres away, challenged a wild-eyed black stallion.

"Get out of here, you mongrel black coot!" I screamed, taking a firm hold on *Jordie's* lead rope.

He pranced off into the bush, but circled in from the side and came straight for me.

"KER-RACK!"

Ken had come galloping from the tail and let drive with the whip. The stallion wheeled and plunged off over the side of the ridge with two bay mares. A minute later, we could still hear them crashing down through the undergrowth and over rocks, way below.

"That frightened the living daylights out of me!" I told Ken. Shock had set in, my legs had turned to jelly and I was shaking like a leaf.

"I figured it must've been a stallion when I heard you yelling," he grinned. "More better we get you a stockwhip to protect yourself – I mightn't get there quick enough next time!"

FRINGED WITH SHADY trees, the grassy, level clearing beside Griffith Creek looked like a beautiful spot to camp. Hungry after the scant grass of the last few days, the horses were tucking into the flowering clover when we went down for a bath.

"Did you hear a vehicle?" hushed Ken, motioning me to stop wallowing around in the creek. We both froze, stunned into silence by the sound of an engine drawing closer by the second. We made a dash for the towel, but Ken beat me to it so I jumped back into the creek. By the time I'd dried and dressed, Ken was talking to a bunch of people in a 4-wheel-drive.

"We thought your horses were brumbies," I overheard one bloke say, "I was about to start shooting when I noticed all the greys."

Luckily for us these people were locals and knew there were no grey brumbies in the Kroombits.

"Brumbies come here most evenings to graze," said

another fellow. "I've got a hut and a paddock up the track here – you can camp there as long as you like and it'll be much safer for your horses," he offered.

There wasn't much feed in the paddock, but we gratefully accepted as our horses were exhausted and needed a rest. The Kroombits were so steep that breast plates and breechings had blistered the hide on the packhorses from continually pulling tight. A break from work would give the skin and hair a chance to grow back.

A set of scrubber (wild) cattle yards were at our disposal and with a few temporary modifications we turned them into breaking-in yards and I got to work on *Jordie*. She was a naturally quiet filly and as I'd hobbled and led her already, my task was made easier. Using the Jim Wilton method (a horse breaker on Queensland stations in the 1920's) of blindfolding the horse's eye on the side you're working on, *Jordie* turned out a lovely, placid saddle horse with a beautiful soft mouth. The Wilton method uses no scare tactics, so *Jordie* had no fear of me and I could catch her anywhere.

Sharon nervously puts a crupper on Jordie

Sharon removes Jordie's blindfold and dashes for the rails

Brown Mare with hives

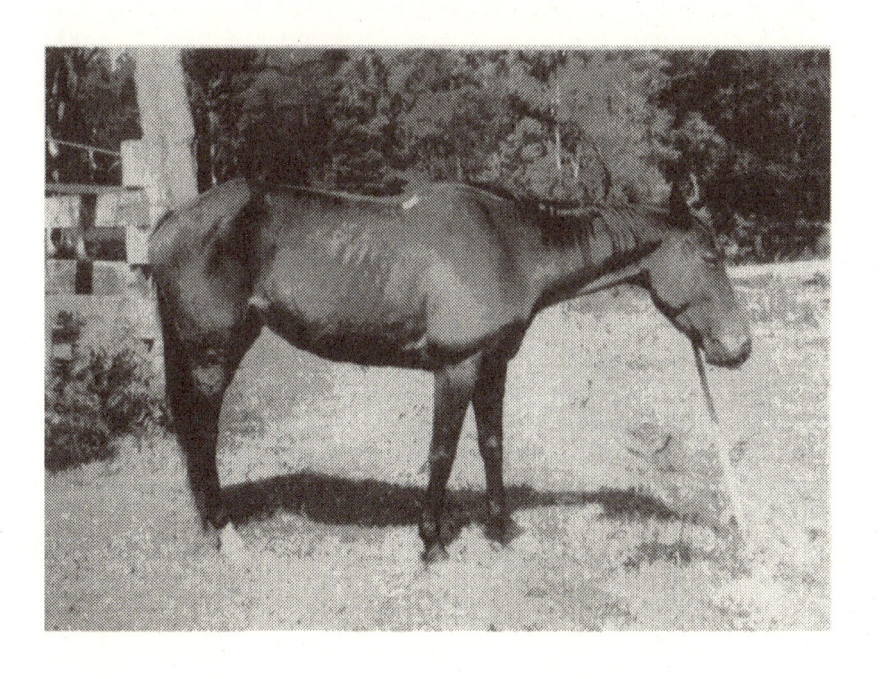

One morning we found *Brown Mare* covered in lumps as though she'd been stung by a swarm of wasps. Her face was so swollen she couldn't open her eyes and could barely breathe through her nostrils. We were miles from any vet or means of communication and we feared she was about to stop breathing.

Resisting the urge to panic, we took a closer look and realised she wasn't acting like a horse in the throes of death; if anything she was just terribly itchy. I remembered she'd been eating the young leaves of a citrus tree, whereas none of the other horses had touched it. Perhaps it was an allergic reaction to the leaves and the lumps were only hives? We roped off the citrus tree and twenty four hours later, *Brown Mare's* hives had disappeared and she was soon back to normal.

When we left the paddock after a week's rest, *Jacko's* back had finally healed enough to use him. He hadn't felt a girth around his belly for three months. Collar roping him in the yards, he stiffened every muscle, but never flinched while we saddled and loaded him. Removing the collar rope, *Jacko* stood as still as a statue, his body as taut as a drum. He wasn't going to budge an inch.

When we were ready to leave, I hunted all the horses into *Jacko's* yard, Ken cracked the whip, and there was a mass exodus through the gate. *Jacko* blasted out like a rocket, scattering the horses and bucking all over the flat as though he'd just come out of the chute at the Mt Isa rodeo. He shot the surcingle over the front of the packsaddle, but thankfully the flank girth held.

Riding along a clifftop, we had fantastic views over the coastal country, but kept well clear of the edge where the wind roared up the rock face from the plains below. The late January weather was warm and muggy and the breeze most welcome. As our track swung into the hillside, something set *Jacko* off. The horse's eye glazed over, he bucked forward with his front feet down the drain, his neck slammed up against the almost vertical road cutting and his head bent right back. As *Jacko's* back legs kicked up, his ears almost touched his rump and we sat there watching, waiting to hear the bones crunch as his neck broke. Unbelievably, the big chestnut shook his head, his eye cleared, he looked around him as though nothing had happened and walked off down the road.

Jacko in the chute

There and then, we decided that *Jacko* was too dangerous a horse to keep. We would advertise him for sale as a buckjumper or send him away for dog tucker.

Although the Kroombit Tops were a tremendous wilderness experience, we were glad it lay behind us and the lush irrigation country of the Cania Dam lay ahead. Camping on a 64acre reserve that hadn't seen stock for years, the horses hoed into a mixture of swamp couch, kikuyu and dry land grasses. While they were happily filling their bellies, we set off to find a buyer for *Jacko*.

We didn't have to look far. A young bloke on a horse rode past and said g'day.

"Have you got any good bucking horses in your plant?" he asked. "I'm looking for a practice horse for rodeo."

Jacko had found his place at last.

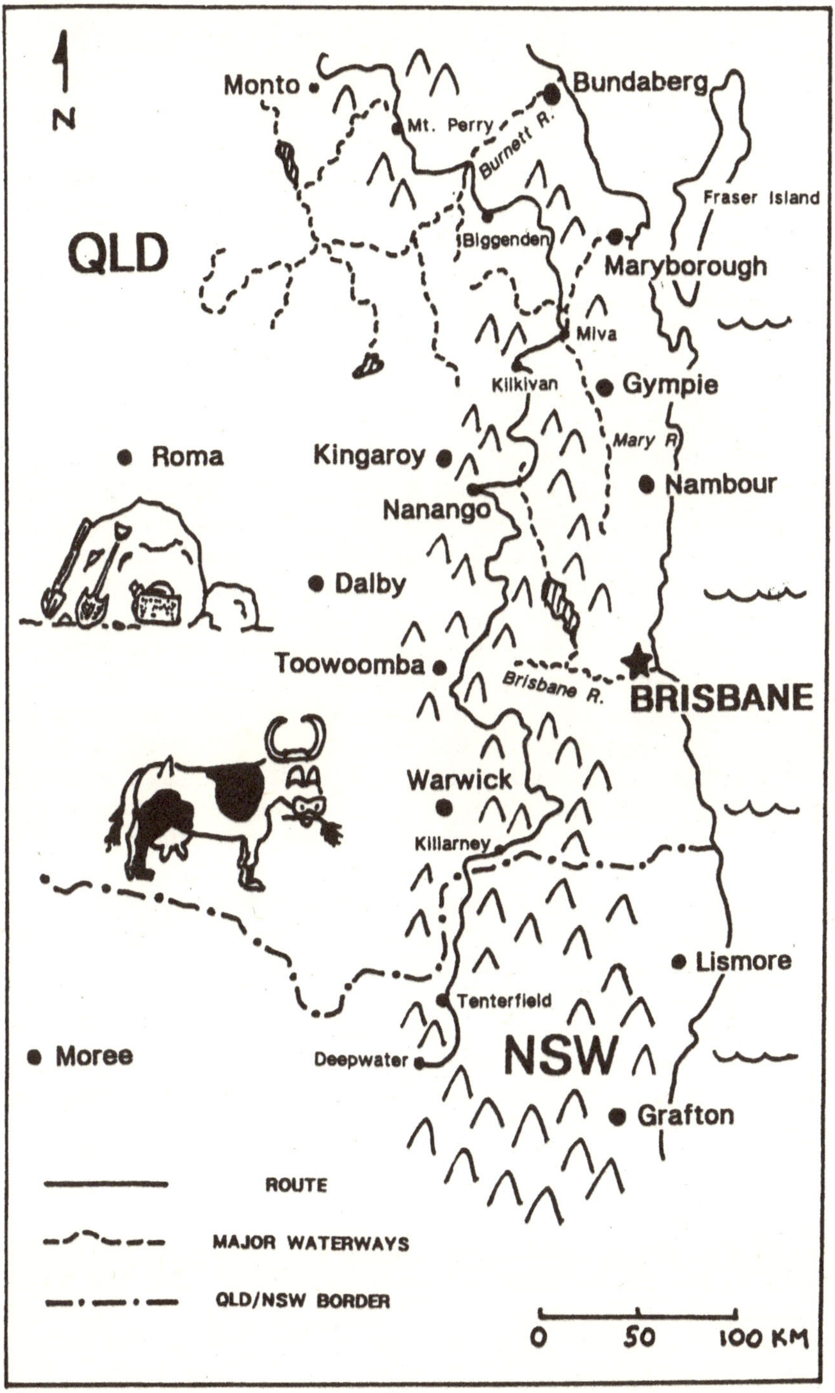

N
QLD
Monto
Mt. Perry
Bundaberg
Burnett R.
Fraser Island
Biggenden
Maryborough
Miva
Kilkivan
Gympie
Mary R.
Roma
Kingaroy
Nambour
Nanango
Dalby
Toowoomba
Brisbane R.
BRISBANE
Warwick
Killarney
Lismore
Tenterfield
Moree
Deepwater
NSW
Grafton
ROUTE
MAJOR WATERWAYS
QLD/NSW BORDER
0
50
100 KM

Chapter 14: THE MONTO GREYS

"I GUARANTEE NOTHING except that they're tough!" grinned Jack Anger. Forty grey horses milled about in the yard behind him: rugged looking crossbred Arab ponies with beautiful hard feet from running in the rocky hills of Cania Gorge. All the mares looked identical and you couldn't pick one gelding from the next, yet Jack had drafted four aside. Our plan had been to buy two horses, increasing our plant to ten. This way we'd be using five fresh horses every day.

"I didn't spend half the morning runnin' this lot in to sell youse one or two," lectured Jack, matter of factly. "Take the lot or none."

Jack loaned us his truck and we drove the four greys over to Parker's yards only 5km from our camp in the Washpool reserve. Offloading them, we ran each horse into the round yard for a closer look. One of the mares was unbroken, but we couldn't remember which as they looked so alike.

First into the yard was a solid looking mare 14hh whom we named *Anvil*. She faced up immediately to the crack of the stockwhip, casting a murderous glare at Ken. Obviously broken in, we hobbled and saddled the mare between us, letting her out into another yard.

The big, raw-boned gelding was drafted in next, prancing unwillingly through the gate, neck arched and snorting like a stallion. Totally blind in the off eye, from running into a stick while mustering, we named him *Angry Jack* after his former owner. The 12 year old horse trembled like a young colt when we caught and saddled him, yet walked out of the yard like a proud, high stepping coach horse.

The next mare was so obese she had rolls of fat in between her back legs and a channel down her spine and rump that would hold half a gallon of water. We thought she might be the unbroken horse, but when she waddled straight up, butted me with her head and nibbled my arm, we didn't know what to make of her. Unlike the other two, she stood relaxed while we saddled her, casually walking over to join her mates.

The last mare came careering into the yard, ears laid back and teeth bared. A shade over 13hh, we had not a hope of walking up to this ferocious little pony. The brand on the near rump read 'B2 Lazy A', and she hurtled around the yard like a *B2* Bomber, earning her this name.

Certain she was unbroken, Ken roped *B2* and pulled her to the ground. Strapping on the breaking in tackle was like wrestling with an octopus. The mare thrashed at the ropes, trying to savage, strike and kick her captors with unabated fury. When released, *B2* flew out of the yard and down to her mates, but without a single buck or sign of discomfort towards the harness.

"Well, which is the unbroken one?" I asked Ken.

"I dunno!" he replied, shaking his head as we watched the four horses standing quietly at the far end of the yards.

One of Jack Anger's sons pulled up to see how we were going.

"That horse with the tackle on is broken in," he revealed, "but that porky one with the saddle under its guts was raised as a poddy by Jack's niece. She's got a dingo bite on the hindquarter, so they didn't bother to break her in."

Poddy ignored the clank and jangle of stirrup irons behind her front legs when we ran her in and removed the saddle that had slipped under her belly. Just to double check, we bridled the mare, who rolled her tongue over the bit and tried to spit it out. With much difficulty, we drafted in and roped *B2*, forcing a bit into into her mouth.

"UNGHKK!" clunked the bit, as she savagely clamped her teeth down onto familiar cold steel.

Our new horses had to lose some weight before we could use them. It is impossible to keep a pack saddle on a fat horse, plus carrying a load in the hills whilst overweight puts too much strain on the heart.

In Monto, I'd bought three bags of feed and a mineral block to help put condition on our old horses. The new ones were on a diet and exercise program. Mounted on *Riley*, I prepared to lead *Anvil* out of the yard for her first trip to the reserve. Running her lead rope across *Riley's* chest, I urged him forward and slapped the mare down the side of her ribs with my reins. *Riley* strained against the rope, but *Anvil* dug in her toes and refused to budge until I slapped her down the flank with a set of dinner hobbles.

Ken was having much the same trouble leading *B2*, but we got them mobile and out onto the road, where *Anvil* bared her teeth and tried to tear a chunk out of my leg.

"Hang on!" I called to Ken, punching the mare in the nose and nearly losing the lead rope as she spun away.

"See if you can get her back to the yards!" he replied.

Anvil led willingly in through the gate because her two mates were still there. Finding a piece of rope, I tied *Anvil's* jaw shut and kept her 'muzzled' all the way to the reserve.

We camped on the Washpool reserve for three weeks, busy looking after our 12 horses, helping Brad Parker with a few jobs and fighting a bush fire that came within 200m of his house. Leaving the Monto district, we had many weeks of trauma with the four greys, who behaved more like brumbies than station horses. At the end of each day, we had to saddle a fresh mount, chase each grey pony and catch it with a rope. Our old workhorses were getting knocked up, so in the mornings, we'd let the rebels run the first kilometre in hobbles until they tired enough to be caught.

Whilst staying with Mungungo cattleman Tom Goody, all but our nighthorses disappeared from an unfenced stock reserve overnight.

"They could be miles away down a laneway by now," said Tom. "Hop in this vehicle and we'll go look for them."

Sure enough, we found the horses about 3km away. Because they were so far from camp, we unhobbled them, put hobbles around necks and chased them back in the vehicle.

"When I was droving," explained Tommy, "we used to hunt the horses back to camp in hobbles. That way they never strayed too far because they knew they'd have to hobble back and we could always catch them in camp because they wanted the hobbles taken off."

It was a valuable piece of information. When the horses reached camp we spent an hour trying to catch them because they'd already been unhobbled. We made it a rule to follow Tommy's advice as the variation to our routine had made the horses almost impossible to catch.

Shoeing the Monto Greys was like trying to nail down a snake. They'd never had their feet picked up before, requiring some unconventional tactics on our part to prevent being injured by flying hooves and teeth. It would have brought a smile to Jack Anger's face to see how much of our gear they wrecked, but the Monto greys eventually settled down to become our best horses and live up to his guarantee of toughness.

Tom Goody with a one day old Brahman calf

Ken 'stretches' Poddy between trees to shoe her hind feet

The Monto greys (with Mal in the middle)

"KER-RACK! GIT UP there" bellowed Ken, cracking the whip on foot as the horses milled about in front of the pitch black entrance. Only a pinprick of light indicated the far end of the Boolboonda tunnel, 192m away. Blasted through solid rock near Moolboolaman Gap, it is the longest unsupported tunnel in the southern hemisphere. We were thankful that locos no longer hauled gold bearing ore from Mt Perry to coastal Bundaberg through this old railway tunnel, but the possibility of encountering a motor vehicle halfway through posed a potential hazard.

Finally, one horse took a few tentative steps into the darkness and the rest followed. The ceiling was too low to crack a whip off horseback, so Ken remained on foot, driving the horses forward while the tunnel rang with the clatter of hooves and the volley of the whip. The horses stopped halfway, disoriented by the circle of light at each end and further agitated by the hundreds of bats that flitted and hummed over their ears.

Jack turned and bolted back for the entrance, unnoticed by the other horses because of the noisy racket and mantle of darkness. Reaching daylight, he realised his three sisters were still inside, so wheeled and headed back to the mob. Ken could see the silhouette of the big gelding coming towards him. *Jack* chopped from side to side, continually slamming the packs into the wall on his blind side. There was nowhere for Ken to go so he stepped lively, dodging aside as the one-eyed horse careered past. *Jack* crashed into the back of the mob, shunting them into action down the tunnel and out into the blinding sunlight.

DAYTIME TEMPERATURES HAD fallen to the low 30's and the nights had become chilly when our horses waded across the swiftly flowing Burnett River in four feet of water. Setting up camp, we returned to the river and threw in a fishing line, catching two swallowtail catfish on a piece of kabana. I hopped in for a swim, while Ken fished.

"TWANG!" hummed the line, as it pulled taut and broke. I made a wild dash for the shore as Ken gazed dumbfounded at the weightless frizz of fishing line that sprang towards him.

"I thought you said there were no crocs this far south!" I scolded.

"There aren't," he replied. "I'd say that must have been a

huge lungfish."

These fish are an ancient form of marine life found only in the Burnett River and adjacent waterways. A protected species, they grow to an enormous size for a freshwater fish and must be returned to the water if caught.

The horses quickly tired of eating the watery green panic growing around the campsite, and we heard them hobble down on the river stones on dark. In the morning, we rode the nighthorses across the river, found our team grazing on a patch of couch and hunted them back to camp. We had planned a day off but the depth of water in the river and the threat of rain changed our minds. If the river had risen last night our horses would have been stuck on the far side.

A week later, we crossed the Mary River on an old timber bridge and camped with a couple of fishermen. The horses were hobbled out on the fenced roadway and we'd been given permission to put *B2* and *Brown Mare* into a paddock alongside. During the night the horses created a terrible din, clattering across the cobblestones and rattling the bridge timbers as they hobbled across. Through the racket, we both heard a loud 'splash'.

"Hey Ken," sang out one of the fishermen. "I think one of your horses has fallen in off the bridge!"

Instantly awake, we tumbled out of the tent to investigate. *Brown Mare* was frantically calling out to her mates who had disappeared from view on the far side of the bridge. In the moonlight, a horse's head broke the surface of the water, then disappeared below.

"It's that bloody *B2*," groaned Ken, as the head appeared again a little further upstream. "She's hobbled into the water when her mates went across the bridge."

Unable to swim in hobbles, *B2* was kicking off from the river bottom and porpoising her way along. Upstream of the bridge she made for the bank and tried to launch herself out. She managed to get her shoulders clear of the water, but the bank was too steep and she fell back in at each attempt. Porpoising back downriver, she waded out and stood beside *Brown Mare*.

"Thank goodness," said Ken. "She'll stay there now."

But we weren't used to horses that could 'think' like these little Arab ponies. Whinnying out to the other horses, *B2* hobbled downstream, waded into the river and porpoised across the current. Reaching a gentle slope on the far side, she jumped out of the water, hobbled over a sandhill and disappeared after her mates.

"Bloody horses," grumbled Ken, setting off after them, "When you're riding them, they'll jib and baulk at a piddly little ditch. Then, right when you don't want them to, they'll go places in hobbles you wouldn't think possible!"

Chapter 15: COCKIES AND BLOCKIES

HER TERRIFIED GAZE rivetted on the flapping branches and leaves that followed, *Poddy* galloped around the reserve at Miva, dragging a heavy bough she'd pruned off an ancient fig tree. We'd only just started to put hobbles on when the camera frame on *Poddy's* packsaddle hooked under a low branch, breaking it off and sending the other horses bolting in all directions at the sight of this frightful apparition. Running like billy-ho, Ken blocked *Poddy* while I sprinted in to grab hold of her before she headed after the mob and chased the whole lot through a fence.

Since leaving Monto, *Trotter* had incessantly challenged and fought *Jack* for the honour of shepherding the three sisters before him. The little Standardbred quickly discovered the old gelding was blind in one eye and had beaten him by sneaking up on the blind side and double-barrelling *Jack* in the ribs with both back feet. Sullen and cranky with defeat, *Jack* had resorted to sinking his teeth into the withers of any other gelding that came near him. We no longer had injuries from packsaddles, but *Jack* had chopped out so many backs, we'd had to use *Poddy* while she was still too fat. As we travelled, we'd made frequent stops to push *Poddy's* saddle back into place, but this was the first time she'd really taken fright. Removing the fig tree branch, we unloaded her, rounded up and hobbled the horses and walked into Miva.

Living in this four-house town were an interesting couple named Darrel and Missy. Hanging over their back fence was a beautiful half draught horse and an evil-eyed chestnut mare named *Dragon's Breath*.

"Come and have a look at our harness gear," invited Missy. A spring cart and a sulky were parked side by side in the shed.

"We used to have a bullock for the cart," chuckled Darrel, "but he kept breaking into my vege garden, so we ate him and I had a whip plaited out of his hide! I must get a handle so I can crack the bloody thing."

We camped at Miva for a few days, spending much time in Darrel and Missy's company. Most of our horses needed re-shoeing, so we rode a couple over every day and used Darrel's anvil. It was much easier than trying to shape a shoe on the head of a star picket. The handle of my shoeing hammer had snapped last time I belted a shoe on top of a rock. Selecting a branch from a guava bush, I sat down to whittle it into a new hammer handle, while Ken cut a wattle branch and fashioned a whip handle for the remains of Darrel's pet steer.

Rain had set in and the Mary River flats were dreary with mist when we packed up and left Miva. Feeling fresh because of the cool weather, a spell and a dose of worm mixture, the horses played up and old *Jack* threw in a few bucks. The drizzle kept up for days and we were glad to reach shelter in the showgrounds at Kilkivan. Our horses had to be left in a stock reserve as grazing in the showgrounds was leased out to townspeople. The stock reserve had no permanent water and had been eaten out by cattle, so when we received a job offer from a tordonning contractor (method of ringbarking), we walked the town in search of agistment. We couldn't feed hay to the horses as there were still cattle in the reserve and we wouldn't have enough time to supervise them if we were out tordonning. Finding no agistment, we declined the offer of work and moved on.

The further south we travelled, the more difficult it became to find camping spots close to towns. Horse shoes and groceries were too heavy to carry far, so we needed to camp within walking distance of town centres. As the population increased, patches of grass were scarce and jealously guarded by locals. They wanted us to spend money in their shops, but made it difficult to do so.

We'd always tried to give something in return for assistance, helping maintain goodwill towards future trail riders. Unfortunately, much hostility had already been generated by previous trail users who'd exploited people's hospitality or left without paying their bills.

IN BETWEEN TOWNS, we often found grass much better than any we'd come across in North Queensland, and the horses would have been in prime condition if it weren't for the hills. Winding our way down a spur on the Widgee-Manumbar packhorse mailman's track, we could understand why the posties needed so many horses in the early days. It was hard, tiring work for our horses on the steep, rocky hillside and they only had to come this way the once!

Rounding a corner, the horses stopped dead at the sight of a fully grown stag and three does, only 20m away. Held for a few seconds by the curious sight of our packhorse team, the stag wheeled away, leading his does to the safety of a distant ridge. I could still see the heavy crown of antlers following our progress until we rode around a bend and out of view.

We'd had the foresight to send Ken's rifle home from Mt Perry. The country was too densely settled to be using firearms from here on, besides which, no-one could now accuse us of poaching deer.

Autumn drizzle obscured any view we might have seen from an old stock route along the ridge tops of the Brisbane Ranges. Ironbarks coated in wispy, pale green 'Old Man's Beard' made it an eerie but beautiful place to ride. As soon as we unpacked the horses, tarps were thrown over the gear to keep it dry. While Ken tried to get a fire going, I'd set up the tent, throw in the swag and our bag of clothes, then rig up a few tarps so we had access to our pack bags and could sit in amongst them out of the weather. On our days off, we spent most of our time smoking the washing dry over the campfire, throwing it under the tarp in heavy showers and hanging it out again when the rain eased.

I'd planned on reaching Nanango early in the afternoon as I'd called from Kilkivan and knew that the agricultural show was in progress and we couldn't camp in the showgrounds. Further phone calls had failed to find agistment, so we

Smoking the washing dry

needed plenty of daylight to scout around. However, a muddy, slippery climb through the mountains slowed us down, and it was nearly dark when we arrived on the outskirts of town.

"Where the hell should we start looking?" I asked Ken.

"Let's go down this laneway on the left," he suggested. "It might be fenced down the end and we can hold the horses there overnight."

The laneway only went 100m before disappearing into someone's driveway. While we were sitting there scratching our heads in the fading daylight, a wild looking bloke with long, curly hair and matching beard strolled down the drive towards us.

"You guys are lookin' a bit worried!" remarked Alan Taylor, cheerfully.

"We're in a spot of trouble," I replied, explaining our dilemma.

"No you're not!" he answered, "I've got 20 acres with only two cows in it. You can stick your horses in there."

Alan and his wife Wilma were living in a caravan near the front of the block with their two children, Kaylene and

Lawrance. While we were setting up our tent in the paddock, Kaylene walked across to invite us over for tea.

"I hope you don't mind eating out of margarine containers," laughed Wilma, "But we've not long moved here from Kalgoorlie and I haven't got around to buying plates yet!"

What a small world; they were from my old home town! We sat up half the night talking about the place and all the people we both knew.

"You'd better stay here a few days," instructed Alan. "There's plenty of grass in the paddock for your horses."

A horse eats and tramples into the ground about four times the amount of grass that a cow does, so we hunted around and got permission to put the horses on a vacant building block before we took up their offer.

Wilma came across in the morning, called up the cows, threw them some hay, sat down and starting milking into a bucket.

"Don't you need to tie her up?" I asked, amazed that the cow didn't walk off.

"You can teach them to stand, provided you get the cow young enough," she explained.

After breakfast, we walked into town with the kids, said goodbye at the school gate and continued on to the shops. The Taylors were almost self sufficient with a huge vege garden and plenty of eggs and milk. They were saving to build a house, so we bought a heap of bread and meat and a few luxuries they wouldn't have bought themselves.

"You're either a Cocky, a Townie or a Blockie in this district," laughed Wilma, when we returned. "The Cockies go into a shop in town, book up their groceries and can't pay the bill if they have a bad year. People like us who are starting from scratch are classed as 'Blockies'. We don't get credit. We pay for everything in cash, the shopkeepers willingly take our money, then make snide comments about Blockies when we walk out the door."

It certainly is a strange attitude to take against people who work hard to build a better lifestyle for their families, but the Taylors saw the funny side of things.

"I went to buy a sheep off a Cocky the other day," chuckled Alan when he came home from work. "I grabbed this woolly thing runnin' around the paddock, picked it up in me arms, took a big sniff of air and said 'Now I smell like a farmer'. I don't think he was real impressed!"

"How about when you bought Milo after her calf had died?" reminded Wilma.

"Oh yeh," said Alan. "Some hippies had her on a five acre block and they told me she'd lost her calf in the paddock. I looked around and before I could stop meself, I said 'How could she lose it – there's no grass and there's no trees!'" he roared with laughter.

"I wish you could control your warped sense of humour sometimes" sighed Wilma.

The Taylors were wonderful people and we enjoyed our stay with them immensely. When it came time to leave, I lifted the tarp on our gear to find everything coated with a thick layer of green mildew. We'd only been there four days, yet the gear looked like it had been sitting for months. Wilma came out with a camera when we were packed up and ready to go.

"I want to get a picture of your horses before you leave," Alan had told us. "Then I can send the photo to me mates in Kalgoorlie. I'll say, *Look at all the packhorses I need to ride me boundary fence!"*

Kaylene leading Milo the house cow

Chapter 16: THE HALF WAY MARK

FIGHTING OUR WAY down an eroded gully overgrown with lantana, we pushed the horses across Blackbutt Creek and into a muddy tangle of overhead vines and decaying plant matter. This old coach road had obviously not been used since the days of Cobb & Co.

Riding in the lead, I kicked my feet out of the stirrups as *Joe* gave a sickening lurch underneath me. Bailing out of the saddle as he bogged to his stomach, I frantically tried to block the other horses before they ended up likewise.

"Hold up! Hold up!" I screamed to Ken, trying to be heard above the crack of the stockwhip. It was too late; the horses were already across, but they sensed danger and stayed on a high patch of firm ground. Soupy ground and quicksand lay all around, camouflaged by a superficial crust of rotting leaves and plant matter.

Joe had floundered out of the mud, so I tied the trembling horse where he stood in case he tried to rejoin the mob and plunged into a patch of quicksand. While Ken blocked the horses from returning across the creek, I went ahead on foot to find a route out of the gloomy jungle. An old fenceline heavy with vines and creepers materialised, but no gate. Clambering through the wires and out into the sunshine, an almost vertical rockwall led up to a disused railway line. Even if we did find a way through the fence, the horses couldn't climb the rockface.

We had no choice but to retreat and tackle the Brisbane traffic on the busy D'Aguilar Highway. The most dangerous stretch was 80m of road bridge over the creek and railway line. Waiting for a break in the traffic, we took the bridge at a fast canter, with the horses running single file in the left hand lane. We made it across safely without encountering any vehicles and the line of horses followed me back into the scrub at the first opportunity.

Boggy ground forced us back alongside the highway where we managed to stay on top of the road cutting by pushing through thick lantana. I tried not to watch as the loose horses strayed dangerously close to the 8m drop to the bitumen.

Only a few weeks ago, we had been riding through dry, open country, well away from major roads and camping on reasonable grass. The weather was now cold and wet, oilskins were kept close handy and each pack load was tarped in the morning before we set off. Keeping to the National Trail had become extremely difficult, fighting through dense undergrowth with poor visibility, avoiding quicksand and bog, and the additional stress of encountering fast traffic on narrow, winding bitumen roads. Feed was scarce and of poor nutrient value, while scrambling up and sliding down hills put extra strain on the horses' leg muscles and endurance, making them prone to injuries.

"What's wrong with *Brown Mare's* eye?" I asked Ken one morning. The weeping eyeball was clouded over and had a blue ring around it.

"She must have scraped her eyeball pushing through the lantana," he replied. "Put some pinkeye powder in her eye, but I don't know if that'll save it; she looks pretty bad."

Morgan was limping and Ken found where a broken bottle had pierced the sole of his hoof. He scraped out what broken glass he could and treated the wound with hydrogen peroxide. *Brown Mare's* eye came good after a day or so, but *Morgan* continued to limp along. It was time to start looking for a paddock to spell our horses over winter.

REACHING THE SMALL settlement of Murphy's Creek, we were welcomed by members of the Cumburries Trail Riding Club. They helped find enough laneways and paddocks to give our horses a fortnight's spell, inviting us along to a club night where we showed slides from our trip. During our stay, Murphy's Creek hosted "The Great Divide Challenge" endurance ride. The horses competing were so lean and fit that the winner completed the 120km course through the mountains in just over 8 hours. It would have taken us a week to cover this distance with our packhorses!

Heading south, we came to a stock reserve at Echo Valley near Toowoomba, where a granite marker sponsored by R.M. Williams stood beside the gate.

"Congratulations!" I smiled at Ken. "We've just reached the official half way mark!"

I didn't realise the full significance of our arrival until I penned the date into my diary that evening: The 12th of May, 1990. By sheer coincidence, this was the date we'd started our journey in 1989. We'd arrived at the half way mark 12 months to the day since leaving Cooktown on the coast of Far North Queensland!

The Half Way Mark

The few people who gathered to watch us leave Cooktown would barely recognise us now. Our original four horses had grown to a string of twelve, our style of packing had changed completely and we ourselves looked more trail hardened and competent than the two inexperienced people who'd left Cooktown a year ago.

Between the two of us, we'd been able to meet our initial shortfalls with improvisations and alternatives. By listening to the advice of ex-drovers and stockmen and learning from our mistakes, we were gradually learning the skills of long distance packing.

The risk of spreading TB and the onset of modern road transport put an end to the packhorse droving days. We'd met many self-proclaimed 'experts' on packing, but the extent of their experience had been no more than a recreational two or three week trip, quite often with a backup vehicle, a food cache, or several towns en route. On this type of trip, most people can get away with incorrect packing procedure, as horses will be back home in a few weeks recovering from the trip.

The packhorse drover, however, was out on the road with

the same horses month after month. This was true long distance packing, where there were no vets or farriers, you had to be self-sufficient and it was weeks or months between towns. You couldn't get away with overloading a horse and using a cheap, lightweight packsaddle that would give no problems on a two week trip. And you certainly couldn't use the same horses every day as horse feed is logistically impossible to carry and the horses will only be grass fed.

It had taken many months for us to learn all this and come up with a successful outfit, and we turned a deaf ear to the inexperienced 'experts' who kept telling us we were doing it 'all wrong.' The golden rule with packhorses is, *When you find a system that works, stick to it,* and we did just that.

The National Trail stays in 'dirty' (tick infested) country all the way through Queensland until it crosses the Great Divide into Killarney. We'd arranged for a DPI (Dept of Primary Industries) inspector to spray our horses at Lake Moogerah. Unfortunately for us, the tick spraying procedure in the guide book was incorrect and we had to camp by the roadside for four days and await a second spraying before moving on. We hadn't allowed enough food for this delay and tightened our belts another notch after a couple of days on cheese and damper. Nor did we have enough money for both sprayings, but the accommodating DPI inspector gave us credit and arranged for the balance to be paid in Killarney.

"It's the scrub or paralysis tick that causes the most problems," explained the inspector. "One scrub tick is enough to kill a cat, dog, foal or calf. They're only a tiny little mite, but you'll often find them on livestock where they've burrowed in underneath a cattle tick. If you squash them between your fingernails, they're quite tough, which is why some people call them 'shellbacks'. Get one on yourself, and you'll end up pretty crook."

After the second spraying, we had 24 hours in which to cross the invisible tick line on top of the Great Dividing Range near Teviot Falls. We'd been told that four different Aboriginal tribes used to walk to a place on the eastern side of the range for meetings and ceremonial rituals. The tracks they made are now used by the locals for mustering cattle. One of the gorges to the north was full of 'moon' caves that had once contained Aboriginal artefacts. But a track was dozed up the gorge, changing the course of the creek the next time it flooded and washing the artefacts away.

By the time we reached the crest, any view of the waterfall was obscured by heavy black thunderclouds and a torrential downpour that soaked us to the skin. Ken had lost his oilskin in the lantana a week before, and mine leaked like a sieve. The horses slipped and skated in the red volcanic soil and nothing, including ourselves, escaped being splattered in red mud. Wet, cold and miserable, we followed the headwaters of the Condamine River into Killarney, thankful for a dry place to camp at the showground and somewhere to hang out the wet gear for a day.

From Killarney, we pressed on towards the Cullendore border gate as we had to arrive within 7 days of our last spraying. *Brown Mare* was lame in the near foreleg, possibly having sprained a fetlock in the slippery conditions when we'd descended the range. It looked like we wouldn't be using her this side of winter.

Crossing the border was hassle free as our paperwork and health certificate from the Queensland DPI were up to date. After a final spraying by the NSW border attendant, our horses were declared 'tick-free'. The big double gates in the dingo fence swung open, allowing our troupe into New South Wales.

Following a stock route towards Tenterfield, we camped in the drizzling rain beside a fallen down set of yards one night. We were so cold and tired that we nightlined the first two horses we caught. *Anvil* was a good nighthorse, having excellent night vision, but *Poddy* had not been broken in to ride and was virtually useless. Too exhausted to realise our error, I crawled into the tent and made some cheese and kabana sandwiches while Ken collected a pile of saturated wood, coaxed a flame with a firelighting cube and fanned it with his hat. Two hours later, he produced two quart pots of hot coffee.

In the morning, only our nighthorses remained. There were ten sets of tracks on the road heading back the way we came, so Ken saddled *Anvil*, and headed off. When he'd been gone an hour, I started to worry and discovered the mistake we'd made. If I had to go and look for him, I didn't

Saying goodbye to the Cullendore border guard in NSW

have a horse to ride. If Ken was in trouble and miles away, it could be half a day or more before I reached him on foot.

Distressed at being left on her own, *Poddy* had been running up and down her nightline singing out for the past hour. She didn't have hobbles on because a broken chain had left us one pair short. When she quietened down and pricked her ears, I heard the faint sound of horses galloping and watched with relief when Ken appeared with the horses.

"The mongrels had hobbled 6km back up the road," he growled, "and they were still heading!" There was no substance in the wiry old forest grass we'd camped on, so they'd gone to find something better to eat.

I let *Poddy* off to graze and we sat down to have breakfast. A horse whinnying from the roadway interrupted our meal.

"I'd better go have a look," said Ken, putting his porridge aside. He came running back a minute later. "*Anvil's* standing in the road, singing out, and there's one set of tracks heading back across the bridge. I bet it's that bloody *Poddy*, I can't see her anywhere."

Catching *Easton*, Ken saddled him and headed off.

"You'd better hurry," I called out, "she hasn't got any hobbles on!"

Tracking *Poddy* at a canter, he caught up with her at the same spot he'd found the other horses. She'd been so agitated at being left behind earlier, that she hadn't realised all her mates were back at camp and had followed their scent down the road. When he returned, poor Ken had ridden 24km and still had the day's ride ahead of him!

We found a paddock near Deepwater to winter our horses, but after the first couple of frosts, we realised it was going to be too cold for them and there wouldn't be much feed about. It would have been cheaper to stay where we were and handfeed, but the horses needed a decent holiday where they could roam about and graze at will. Taking local advice, we booked a 24 foot tray truck and paid the driver $400 to take the two of us, our 12 horses and gear to Moree.

The winter temperature at Moree is 5 degrees warmer than Deepwater and the whole district was covered in rich green feed. Cattle were being railed in from as far away as the Gulf of Queensland and everywhere we looked there were drovers with mobs of sheep and cattle on the stock routes.

We'd made the right decision, but the only hitch in plans was finding a paddock for the horses. Within a couple of days we had a job fencing, but spent two weeks camped at the showgrounds until we found agistment on Weebollabolla Station, the breeding ground for some of Australia's finest Shorthorn cattle.

Our tired, leg weary horses grew long, shaggy coats and thrived on the rich black soil plains at Moree. They well deserved their rest.

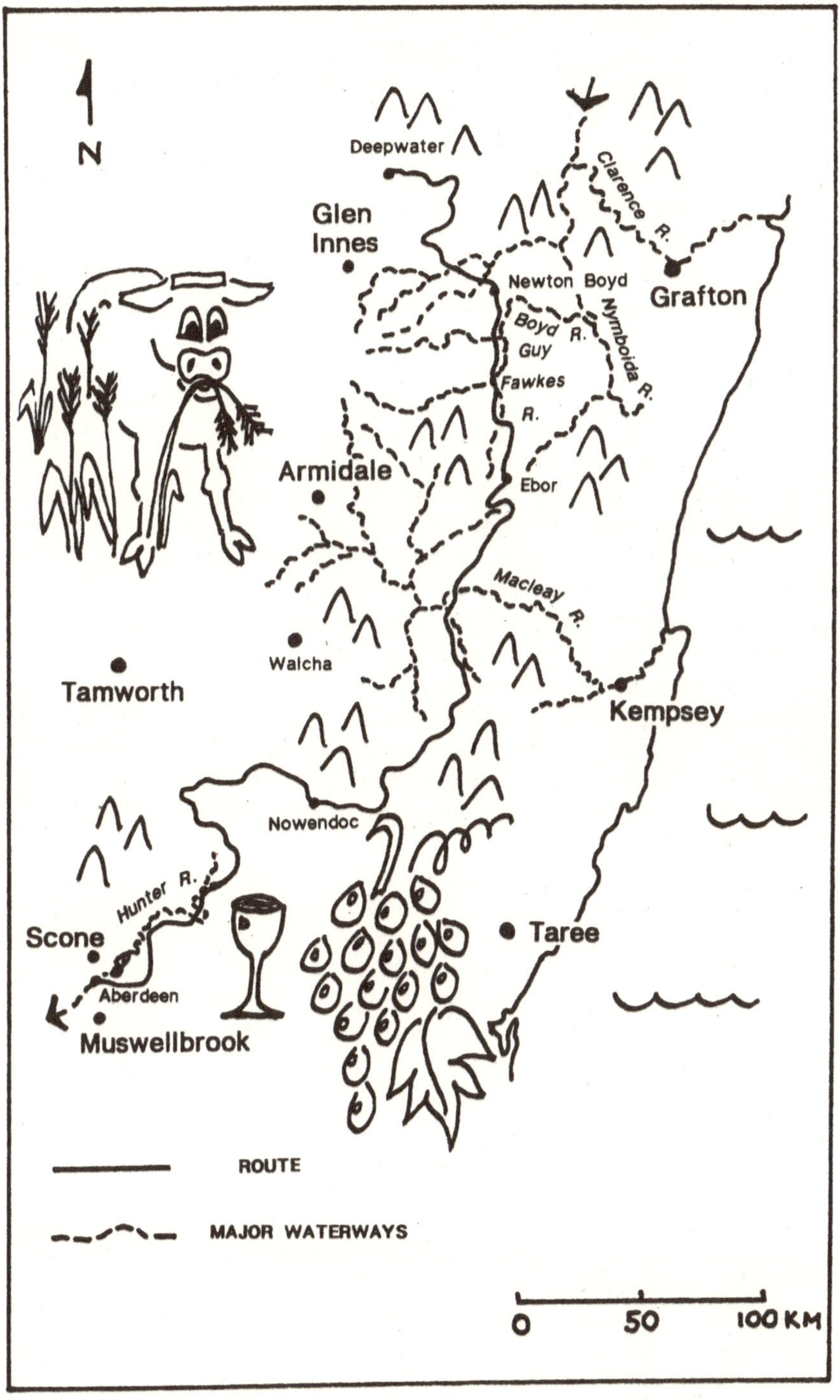
N
Deepwater
Glen Innes
Clarence R.
Grafton
Newton Boyd
Boyd R.
Nymboida R.
Guy Fawkes R.
Armidale
Ebor
Macleay R.
Walcha
Tamworth
Kempsey
Nowendoc
Hunter R.
Scone
Aberdeen
Muswellbrook
Taree
ROUTE
MAJOR WATERWAYS
0
50
100 KM

Chapter 17:
ALONG THE GUY FAWKES

AFTER A FOUR month winter spell at Moree, we'd earned enough money fencing and droving sheep to finance the rest of our trek. The horses had gained so much weight we barely recognised them. Catching sight of us, they galloped off into the distance, but I managed to coax them back by rustling an empty plastic shopping bag. "Aha," thought old *Mal*, "there might be a bit of corn in that bag." I slipped a lead rope around his neck before he discovered otherwise.

Realising it was a trap, the other horses took off so I saddled *Mal*, mounted without being thrown and caught *Brown Mare* for Ken. She bucked when the girth was laced up and snorted while Ken hopped on.

"I hope we don't have to gallop around these horses," said Ken, keeping a tight rein on his horse. "I reckon this mare will pelt me to hell as soon as she gets out of a walk!"

Expecting trouble, I headed off toward the gate at a walk. To our amazement, the horses fell into single file behind me like a group of well behaved school children on an outing. It was as though they hadn't had a day's break from this routine. *Brown Mare* pranced and snorted along at the tail, with Ken looking most relieved that we didn't have to increase our pace.

On arrival at the Weebollabolla yards, each horse was drafted into the round yard and nguru burrs pulled out of manes and tails to prevent the spread of this weed. The outside top and inside bottom of the horses' molar teeth had ground to a sharp edge, so we filed these edges off with a tooth rasp. This helps the horse chew fodder more finely so that the maximum goodness can be extracted in the digestive tract.

With the extra bulk the horses had gained over winter, it was a squeeze to load them into Max Thompson's truck again. Saddles were tied to the top rail of the truck, pack bags jammed into dog boxes, passengers and paraphenalia whisked into the cab and off we headed to Deepwater.

We'd arranged to offload at Peter and Deeny Morton's property, and were just in time to help mark 1600 lambs. Unaware that their back boundary was not a fence, but the

Deepwater River, we released the horses for another week's holiday without hobbling them. After a couple of days lamb marking, we thought it strange that we hadn't sighted the horses since turning them out. Investigation revealed 12 sets of hoofprints heading across the Deepwater River and off into 20,000 acres of mountainous, unfenced forestry!

Peter made some phone calls that evening and discovered that a neighbour working on a boundary fence had spotted strange horses in the forestry. When lamb marking was finished, we borrowed horses and spent several days tracking through the mountains until we found our escapees and drove them back to Morton's.

Our horses' hooves were broken and quartered from running in the rocky hills all week and several were limping. We were on a tight schedule to complete our journey by the end of February to avoid exposing our horses to the freezing alpine conditions of a possible early snowfall in March. Since our start had been delayed, we opted to shoe half the horses in Morton's yards and do the rest along the way.

We'd worked out a good system of shoeing that minimised the strain on our backs. I shod the quiet horses while Ken had shoes, nails and tools ready to pass as soon as I required them. I helped Ken collar rope the difficult horses, passing him the shoeing gear and sometimes rasping or hammering in nails while he held the hoof in position.

I'd been having nightmares about fresh packhorses bucking into fences, tearing pack bags apart and bolting off dragging wrecked saddles behind them. If nothing else, a week in the Deepwater hills had taken the sting out of our horses and we left Morton's on the 20th October, 1990 with no major drama apart from a few pigroots. My fears were replaced with the thrill of riding into country we'd never seen before and wondering what adventure awaited us.

EARLY SPRING RAINS followed by warm, sunny days had brought an abundance of rich new growth to the New England Tableland. Our recent purchase of a portable electric fence allowed us to fence off enough feed to graze 12 horses overnight. We couldn't have done this in Queensland, as feed was scarce along the Great Divide and the horses had to forage some distance from camp. As a necessary precaution we still nightlined a horse inside the fence and kept them all hobbled.

The beautiful sunny days faded quickly to chilly evenings, where forays away from the campfire were as brief as possible. Snuggled into a snow sleeping bag inside my tent, the icy tendrils of frost still managed to sneak in and wake me at 3a.m., the coldest time of the morning. With the exception of *Trotter*, our horses were from inland Queensland, where the summers are unbearably hot, yet winter nights are subject to extreme frost. The NSW spring climate was comparable to a Queensland winter.

On the gravel road into Newton Boyd, a huge black cloud rolled into the valley and sent us diving into pack bags for oilskins. The rainstorm was on us so quickly, we were half soaked by the time we got into our cumbersome raincoats. The horses turned their rumps into the driving rain, refusing to budge. Hunched up in the saddle trying to keep warm, I noticed what looked like flakes of dandruff in *Jordie's* mane. It was snowing!

The storm disappeared as quickly as it came, leaving us with chilled fingers and faces. We were only 7 riding days south of the Queensland border. I hadn't realised that the alpine climate extended this far north.

"Crikey, yes!" exclaimed Ken. "I was surveying once near the Bunya Mountains out the back of Toowoomba. I was only wearin' a Jackie Howe singlet and it snowed on me."

An abandoned school house, a couple of sheds and a grassy rodeo arena were the only man-made features in Newton Boyd. Nestled deep in a mountain valley alongside the Boyd River, it was a picturesque spot to camp and we took a day off to worm and shoe horses. The difficult horses were much quieter to shoe after three days of running barefoot, but *Anvil*, *B2* and *Jack* put up such a struggle when their front shoes were nailed on that we left their back feet for another day. Not only was their behaviour caused by the 4 month winter break, the Monto Greys were mature horses, set in their ways and they'd only had two sets of shoes nailed on in their entire lives. But the improvement in their manners since we had first bought them was remarkable, highlighting the intelligence in their breeding.

Following the Boyd River upstream, we left the last of the cattle properties behind and rode into the Guy Fawkes River National Park on a cattle pad. The river floodbanks merged into steep sided mountains, leaving no space for vehicle

One of the many Guy Fawkes River crossings

access. It was a true wilderness experience, weaving our way upstream as best we could, criss-crossing the stony river where cattle and horses before us had found the easiest access over the years.

"Hey! Look out on your left!" Ken cried in warning, snapping me out of a daydream.

Glancing over my left shoulder, I spotted a chestnut stallion lurking behind a thicket of lantana.

"Get away!" I shouted, wheeling *B2* and cracking the stockwhip Ken had bought me at Moree. Shaking his head, the stallion pranced off, circling in behind Ken where he stamped his foot and snorted a challenge. Ken drove him away with the whip, but he didn't go far and followed along for a short distance.

From then on we were constantly on the watch for brumbies. Some stallions quietly edged their way through the lantana in the hope of stealing our mares. Others were more defiant, sending their mares off to safety while they came forward to defend their territory. Yelling and cracking stockwhips managed to drive them off, but most didn't go far, circling around to sneak up behind us. Surprisingly, our own horses took no interest in the brumby mobs. They obviously considered themselves a family group, sticking together while we hunted the wild horses away.

Each stallion had two or three mares in his harem, some with foals at foot. We'd often encounter stallions within 200m of one another. Their territorial boundaries had a short river frontage but ran a long way back into the hills.

Occasionally we'd see a small group of renegade colts, kicked out of the mob by the stallion when they started to take an interest in the mares, but too young to fight for leadership. The colts had banded together for protection from predators. Many of these brumbies were inbred, but they were good on their feet and a clean limbed strain of buckskins caught the eye.

While we were crossing one of the numerous green river flats, a brown stallion shepherded seven mares and a few foals away up a ridge. It was the largest number of horses we'd seen in any one mob. The stallion snorted from the ridge top and to our horror, *Brown Mare* and *Jordie*, neither of whom were loaded, peeled off and trotted away up the ridge towards him!

Why these mares liked this particular stallion when they'd ignored all the others we'll never know, but we had to act fast.

"Git up boy!" bellowed Ken, urging *Easton* up the ridge in pursuit. Only 14hh, the little skewbald brumby displayed the agility of a mountain goat as he leapt and bounded up the stony hillside. He managed to get ahead of *Jordie* who was finding the grade too steep and didn't need much coercion to rejoin her own mob.

Brown Mare was determined to go with the brumbies and Ken had the ride of his life galloping close behind on her tail. The stallion swung downhill onto the river flat, where our mare picked up enough speed to join the weaner foals at the back of the mob.

"Bring those horses over here!" shouted Ken above the drumbeat of pounding hooves. To cut *Brown Mare* out of the brumby herd, we needed to force her in amongst our own horses to hold her. We risked losing them all, but by the time I pushed them back through the lantana, Ken and the brumbies were nowhere to be seen.

Our own horses were getting stirred up when our lead

mares picked up the scent of the stallion and cantered off towards the hills. I pushed them hard from behind, trying to keep them in a bunch so I didn't lose the mares in front.

The stallion had taken his mares way off up the mountain, but we emerged from the lantana just as the weaner foals and *Brown Mare* with Ken in pursuit came charging across on our left. Horses and foals collided as the two mobs merged and the confused foals decided to stay with us until Ken cracked the whip and drove them away, leaving us with *Brown Mare* again.

"Keep them running uphill until they're buggered!" yelled Ken. When our horses finally tired and came to a standstill, they'd lost the urge to gallop off with the wild horses.

"That was a close one," gasped Ken, wiping the sweat from his brow while the horses puffed and blew. "If I'd had to go one more lap, I would have had to let her go. *Easton* was knocking up and we were close to losing the lot."

Past the junction of the Sara and Boyd Rivers, the terrain grew more rugged and the valley narrowed as we travelled upstream along the Guy Fawkes. Cliff faces on either side often forced us to ride up the middle of the river bed.

'Little Plain' was our first camp on the Guy Fawkes, a delightful clearing set back from the river oaks against the start of the timber. A wire yard of half an acre provided us with a night paddock. Tying our rogue mares *B2* and *Anvil* to nightlines inside the yard, we headed down to the river for a bath.

During the day, we'd been too busy warding off brumbies to enjoy the tranquility of the mountain valley. Relaxing by a glowing bed of coals, we watched the sun sink behind lofty timbered ridges and listened to the musical flow of water tumbling over river stones. Mixing flour and water in a billy, Ken poured the damper mix into a Bedouri camp oven, placing it on a bed of coals and hot ash beside the fire. A stew of split peas and bully beef simmered in a billy while we discussed the day's events, looked at the next day's map and decided which horses to use in the morning.

The horses snorted, pranced and misbehaved when we saddled them after breakfast. The worm mixture had done its job, giving them a fresh spurt of energy. Rid of last winter's parasites, *Joe* was so full of beans that he pulled away as Ken girthed up the packsaddle, plunging in hobbles and pigrooting down the fenceline where the other horses were tied and saddled. They pulled back in alarm, but with a flick of his tail, *Joe* changed direction and cavorted off across the flat before any halters or bridles were broken.

B2 gets out of Joe's way at Little Plain

After three glorious days along the Guy Fawkes, the horses zig-zagged their way out of the valley on McDonald's Spur. There was no track to follow and the turnoff could have been easily missed if we hadn't been taking notice of the landmarks around us. McDonald's Spur is a designated stock route, but how they manage to persuade cattle to make this climb is beyond me.

Brown Mare and *Jordie* must have veered off the ridge and gone around the side, because they suddenly popped up beside me, followed by Ken on *Anvil*.

"Jeez, that was steep!" he muttered with a shake of the head. "I followed those two mares, but when I got below and roused on them, they swung straight up the face of the ridge and bloody *Anvil* followed. It was so steep that when I leaned forward, I had to grab a handful of mane behind her

Commencing the 4 hour climb up McDonald's Spur

ears and I was lookin' down into her eyes. All I could think of was Jack Anger tellin' us his horses were good on their feet. Thank goodness he was right!"

The spur levelled out in places, making travelling easier. Halfway up, we were rewarded with magnificent views of Marengo Falls, plummetting off the face of a distant mountain. Further along, a koala shinnied up a Blue Gum and gazed down at us from the safety of its high perch.

After an arduous 4 hour climb, we reached the top of McDonald's Spur and wound our way through thick timber and boggy creeks to the Marengo Station boundary fence. The fenceline led to a gravel road which we travelled in drizzling rain to reach a stock reserve on the Blicks River. Electric fencing the horses in a corner of the reserve away from the road, we made camp using a fallen tree as a shelter from the biting wind. How lucky we were to have seen the Guy Fawkes River valley in fine weather.

The morning dawned fine and sunny, and after a 10 minute ride down the road, we met Dave and Lyn Williams. They'd taken many people on packhorse trips down the Guy Fawkes over the years, and were keen to hear about our journey.

"Stick your horses in that paddock and come in for a coffee," invited Dave. "You're not in any hurry are you?" he asked.

"We've got plenty of time," grinned Ken, always willing to make new friends.

"Well, offload your horses and stay the night; I'll invite a few friends over for a barbeque."

Travelling with packhorses, we seemed to meet the most fantastic people. We put two horses in the paddock offered and hobbled the rest out on the stock route. The Williamses lived in a cosy stone cottage with the most homely atmosphere and we enjoyed their hospitality and tales of the Guy Fawkes.

Far removed from the hustle and bustle of civilization, this serene river valley tucked away in the wilderness gave us a sense of timelessness. Centuries could have passed without leaving their mark. We agreed that it was definitely the most awe-inspiring section of the National Trail so far. Our earlier hardships and misadventures paled into insignificance as we recalled the sheer pleasure it had given us to ride along the Guy Fawkes.

Chapter 18:
THE VALLEY OF DEATH

LAUNCHING HIS RUMP skyward, our appaloosa erupted through the gates of the Ebor showground, amusing a couple of council workers who paused to watch. Horses collided with gate posts and ran into each other as they hustled out of the way. Swishing his tail, *Joe* changed course and picked up speed as he cavorted down the stock route. With the packsaddle well anchored by a tight flank girth, the dinner packs clung to his heaving sides like the brand on his hide.

"Come on girl!" Urging *Brown Mare* into a fast canter, we went wide then angled across to cut off the surly, spotted demon. As I swung the stockwhip vertically and brought it down with a mighty crack beside the mare, she lost all thought about pulling the rogue packhorse into line. The thrill of pursuit and ring of the stockwhip sent her plunging and pigrooting, while I struggled to hold the reins and coil the plaited red hide.

Joe skidded to a halt on the spongy grass, spun around and trotted meekly back through the snow gums.

"Easy girl," I soothed, trying to untangle reins, whip and mane as *Brown Mare* snorted and danced in circles.

Laughing so much it was a wonder he stayed in the saddle, Ken brought the rest of the horses over. *Brown Mare* settled immediately, quite content to walk off in the lead. *Joe* had happily assumed his travelling position behind one eyed *Jack* as though nothing had happened.

The horses had their own social hierarchy and usually travelled in the same order. *Trotter* was the boss, but he didn't travel in the lead of the loose horses. *Anvil* was first in line, followed by *B2*, if Ken wasn't riding her, then *Poddy*. These mares were *Trotter's* favourites and he always herded them before him. After *Trotter* came *Jack*, who travelled as close to his sisters as *Trotter* would allow him.

Morgan and *Joe* alternated positions behind *Jack*, depending on who was feeling the most energetic on the day. Being a young horse, *Morgan* occasionally got cheeky and tackled old *Jack* for his position. The young chestnut had two broken ribs from an unsuccessful attempt. Next in line travelled three more geldings, *Riley*, *Easton* and *Mal*, followed by *Jordie* then Ken on *B2*.

Power plays were constantly on the go and rarely was there a dull moment. *Morgan* and *Jack* squealed and lashed out with hooves and teeth at one another's rib cages. Half asleep, *Easton* ambled past *Riley*, stumbling in fright as a sharp set of teeth nipped him on the rump. Ken cursed as *Jordie's* back hooves whistled dangerously close to his kneecap, striking *B2* in the shoulder instead.

While I juggled maps out of my saddle bag and concentrated on navigation, *Anvil* would sneak up behind and sink her teeth into *Brown Mare's* rump. Flinging maps into the air, I'd dive for a handful of mane as *Brown Mare* lashed out to give *Anvil* a good boot under the jaw.

The crisp Ebor air put a spring into the horses' step as we left the New England Tableland. Stunted alpine trees gave way to tall eucalypts on the bone-jarring descent and we were grateful for the extra shade in the afternoon heat. We'd followed many historic roads on the National Trail, but the path taken by the George's Creek fire trail had to be the oldest route used by humans. Well before the landing of Europeans in Australia, this hot, waterless ridge was the route chosen by Aborigines to get from the New England Tableland to the coast.

The spring in the horses' step gradually degenerated to a toe-dragging shuffle. It was an exhausted, dusty cavalcade that paused to wet parched throats in the crystal cold waters of George's Creek. We'd travelled 42km and dropped from an altitude of 1563m to 290m. Allowing the horses only a passing sip, we forced them out of the water as it was time to camp. Letting them get a bellyful of cold water would give them stomach cramps that might prove fatal.

Once the horses were unloaded, hobbled and had been grazing half an hour, we hunted them down for a drink. Their body temperatures were back to normal and they didn't gorge themselves like they would have done earlier.

The horses weren't likely to wander back up the ridge during the night, but we still tied up two nighthorses and put the others behind electric tape. There was not a fence within miles of these rugged ridges and thickly timbered valleys. If a mob of wild pigs or brumbies spooked our horses, it would be near impossible to track them in such rugged terrain.

A leisurely ride down George's Creek the next day brought us out into a cleared paddock where we stopped to eat our sandwiches. The horses didn't graze for long before they started shaking their heads and stamping about in agitation. I glanced down to see a swarm of grass ticks crawling over my legs.

"Let's get out of here!" I shrieked. Brushing the wretched creatures off my limbs, I dashed for my horse. Ken wasn't far behind me!

Camping at George's Junction Stock Reserve beside the Macleay River, fat Hereford cows dotted the river flat where we hobbled the horses on 5 acres of rich kikuyu. Lighting the campfire and boiling the billy, we propped ourselves up against a pack bag and sipped coffee as the twilight faded over this serene river valley.

To our surprise, a set of headlights followed by a six wheel drive truck emerged from the river bed. Noticing the strange horses and pile of saddles, the driver stopped at our camp. The manager of Kunderang Station introduced himself and explained they'd been out chasing scrubber cattle for three days. Much of the station's land had been resumed for the Oxley Wild Rivers National Park and they only had a certain amount of time to clear the country of livestock. Any animals remaining after that period would be shot from a helicopter under National Park instruction in an effort to clear the park of introduced species.

Seven wild bulls sulked and shuffled in the back of the truck, so it had been a successful trip.

"I've got a stallion that usually comes down here at night to feed," the manager warned us, before driving home.

The last thing we needed was a stallion fighting our geldings and chasing our mares around. Catching and saddling the nearest horse, Ken rode around the boundary of a small holding paddock, making a few repairs to the fence. The feed wasn't as good as that on the river flat, but we hoped our horses would be out of harm's way.

The stallion left our horses alone during the night, but we kept a close eye out for him when we let the horses down onto the river flat in the morning. When two strange horses approached, Ken drove them down into a gully away from ours. As we were getting packed, the Kunderang manager drove up in a ute.

"Seen any horses about?" he enquired.

Ken described the two in the gully.

"That sounds like them, but there should be another somewhere. I don't suppose you've seen seven bulls?" he laughed, shaking his head.

When he'd driven into his yards to offload the bulls last night, his kids had left the paddock gate open and the horses all took off down to the reserve. As soon as the bulls came off the truck, they smashed through the yards, flattened the fence and kept going.

"Oh well," he sighed, "I suppose they'll be back where we found them by now!"

Sharon & Jordie plunging across the Macleay River

IT WAS AN easy day's travel up the Macleay River, criss-crossing and following the tracks of the truck. Fish darted between the horses' legs as they waded across on water-worn river stones. The weather was warm and the water inviting, tempting us to stop for dinner and let the horses graze while we had a swim.

Further upstream, the beautiful old solid cedar Kunderang Homestead was falling into disrepair. Leaving the abandoned building, we crossed the Macleay for the last

Our horses gallop across George's Creek in hobbles

time and branched off up Kunderang Brook. We felt like dawdling along the bottom of this majestic, sheer sided gorge, but the height of flood debris indicated an unpredictable danger. There was not a cloud in the sky, but who knew how much rain was swelling the headwaters? Over the years, several locals had fallen victim to the violent gully rushers of the Kunderang and we didn't wish to add to the statistics.

Finding a small clearing where the brook swung in a horse shoe shape, we pitched our tent near a hut and put the horses in a small holding paddock. A few wispy clouds had begun to gather.

"I hope it doesn't rain," I said to Ken, feeling claustrophobic with the big cliffs towering over us.

"Don't worry," he reassured, "we're well above the normal flood level."

By nightfall, storm clouds rolled in, lightning flashed and deafening thunder rumbled up and down the gorge. Stirred by the storm, the horses whinnied and galloped around in hobbles, making me uneasy and raising the hair on the back of my neck.

"Let's pack up and go!" I urged.

"There's nowhere to go," he replied. "It's too dangerous to be riding in the creek bed now; the safest place is right here. They wouldn't have built a hut here otherwise."

His words made sense, but when the wind started to roar, it sounded like a wall of water rushing down the gorge towards us and I felt trapped inside the tent. Lightning flashed nearby, and the heavy rain turned to hail. It was a terrible night to be outside, but the thought of being washed away and drowning inside a tent scared hell out of me.

In a river bend next day, we passed a deep, shaded swimming hole under a cliff where a massacre had taken place in the mid 19th century. As punishment for sheep steeling, graziers rode up on a group of Aboriginal men, women and children swimming in the waterhole, shooting and bashing all of them to death except one fellow who escaped to tell the tale.

Riding through a bottle-necked gorge, there was no access to the cliff tops. It looked like a death trap. The thought of all those Aborigines that had been murdered made it feel even more like the Valley of Death. I failed to enjoy the stunning beauty of the Kunderang until the gorge opened up and offered escape routes and we were a long way from that swimming hole.

Youdale's Hut twitched up with wire to stop it sliding down the hill

Chapter 19:
BEYOND THE BARRINGTONS

GRATEFUL FOR THE cool mountain air, we walked beside our mounts while the packhorses puffed and sweated under their burdens. The gravel road zig-zagged its way out of the Kunderang Valley, with the closest to level ground being on the outermost edge of each bend. After every steep pinch we pulled up on the next bend to give our 12 horses a few minutes spell. Staging our way upward, it took two and a half hours to cover the 6km to the top. The horses were relieved to be on level ground again when we reached the lush grazing pastures of the Yarrowitch district.

Meeting local pastoralist Jim Williamson, he introduced us to a couple of adventurous New Zealanders who were staying with him. John and Kevin had set out on the National Trail from Killarney with no horse riding experience whatsoever!

Three horses, two riding saddles and a packsaddle had been purchased from a Brisbane horse dealer who'd trucked the whole outfit to Killarney. The lads had loaded up their packhorse and saddled up their mounts. John managed to scramble on O.K. but Kev put one foot in the stirrup and ended up flat on his back with a saddle on top of him.

"You know that thing that was hanging down?" John had directed, "Well, I think you're supposed to do it up."

Kev had tried to mount without buckling up the girth!

Concerned locals along the trail had given them invaluable lessons in horse husbandry. Noticing their horses were footsore, one chap was horrified to find them unshod. He explained that horses need shoes to stop their hoof wearing away and gave a 15 minute shoeing lesson. John and Kev bought some farriers' gear and did a reasonable shoeing job on their horses without pricking them. Not a bad effort when you consider that some people with years of horse experience are not capable of tacking on a shoe.

Farewelling our friends at Yarrowitch, we travelled through forestry then more grazing country to reach the town of Nowendoc. A store comprising post office, liquor sales and general merchandise was the business centre. Half a dozen houses, a hall and a police station made up the rest of the town. Offloading and hobbling our horses, we turned them out into a huge stock reserve that hadn't been grazed since last summer.

"Horse travel would be a piece of cake if you had a paddock like this every night," grinned Ken as the horses disappeared into a waving sea of rye grass, phelaris and clover.

Arriving in a small town with a team of packhorses never goes unnoticed, and before long a few people came by to investigate. Several families were from the Northern Territory, but wives were expecting babies and they'd moved down to Nowendoc to be close to medical facilities. Ken had spent some time in the Territory and shared mutual acquaintances with these people, which led to all-night talking sessions.

When we left, Shane Webber came over to see us off, and helped Ken bring the horses in from the reserve. Riding *B2*, Shane was amazed when she ploughed straight across a deep, boggy creek without any encouragement.

"She's as fearless as a Territory horse!" he exclaimed. "The horses around here are so gutless they shy at their own shadow."

Shane was delighted when we packed *Joe*, who windmilled his tail and pigrooted off around the flat.

"Good to see some horses with a bit of life about them," grinned Shane.

A landholder had refused us access through to the Barrington Tops National Park, so we left Nowendoc on a 100km detour via Hanging Rock. We could have legally ridden through on a stock route, but the owner had had problems with people who strayed off the trail and camped where they shouldn't. We left her alone in peace; her property was her livelihood whilst our ride was only recreational. By doing so, we avoided problems with brumbies and thick lantana; instead, we followed gravel roads and camped in well grassed stock reserves.

Trotter had become such a tough little packhorse that we rarely travelled without using him. His only setback was that he kept belting up *Jack*. We decided to break *Trotter* in so he could be ridden occasionally, leaving *Jack* to run behind his sisters in peace.

Awaking to a mid-November frost one morning in the Nundle forestry, I bridled and saddled *Trotter*, leaving him for a few minutes to get used to the feel of the bit. Running the reins through the stirrups, I stood in front and pulled steadily on each rein until he turned his head. Good, I should have steering. Leaning over the saddle, I pulled both reins and made him back up a step. Good, the brakes worked. Hobbling him, I mounted and dismounted a few times and he stood placidly as I'd hoped he would. I undid the hobbles, mounted and reined him a step backwards.

Trotter took about fifteen steps backwards and I couldn't get him to go forwards! After much flapping of legs and reins, he finally got the idea and went forward a few paces.

"I'll try riding him in the lead today," I told Ken, so we packed and readied the horses. Impatient to start travelling, *Joe* pigrooted out onto the road and the loose horses followed. Mounting *Trotter*, it felt like riding a camel as we trotted off after the mob, but when he broke into a canter, he was so comfortable that I barely moved in the saddle.

Keen to be in his usual spot, *Trotter* plunged in behind the mares and I had a hell of a job trying to get him out into the lead. Pulling gently on the rein, I turned *Trotter's* head, but he just walked in a straight line with his head bent, like any 'green' horse that hasn't been properly mouthed. With insistent kicking and slapping, I coaxed him to the lead.

A couple of hours later, my legs and arms ached and I was exhausted from trying to keep *Trotter* moving forward in a straight line. It had been a successful first ride for him, so we called it quits and I swapped my saddle onto *Brown Mare*. In comparison, riding *Brown Mare* was like floating along on a cloud.

SEVERAL LARGE GOAT properties were the only hazard on the Hanging Rock detour. Our horses hated the sight and smell of goats. Riding through Barry Station, they caught sight of a mob of shaggy highland cattle. Saddle and packhorses alike shied off the road, disturbing a herd of resting goats. The goats jumped to their feet and the horses came close to all out panic, hemmed in by walking floor rugs on one side and bearded gremlins on the other.

Approaching a huge motel style complex behind an expensive span of chain wire fence, the remote bush trails faded into the distance while civilization loomed near at hand. Letting the horses graze, we watched as a neatly dressed young man on a smart grey horse appeared inside the compound. Seeing our motley band of horses, he rode over to the fence and said hello.

"This isn't the sort of place you'd expect to find a motel," remarked Ken.

After a startled look, the young man nearly fell off his horse laughing.

"I guess it is a motel, but it's one for horses," he chuckled, finding it hard to believe that we didn't know where we were. "You're looking at Kerry Packer's Quarter Horse barn! This is his personal riding horse that I'm exercising."

Rounding a bend in the road, the vastness of the Ellerston complex below took our breath away. Row upon row of 'motel-like' stables with arched doorways formed a central hub while modern brick buildings clustered nearby. Outlying stands of eucalypts housed stylish private residences while sunlight sparkled on the lazy waters of the Hunter River, rolling sluggishly through the valley. But the most dominating feature by far was the opulent green polo fields dotting the valley as far as the eye could see.

Riding down the ridge, our dusty appearance, well-worn saddlery and rugged bush horses looked embarrassingly out of place. When we rode past the secutity-guarded entrance, a bloke in a ute pulled up from a construction site opposite and asked us where we were headed.

"Melbourne," I replied.

"And where have you come from?" he grinned, certain I was having him on.

"Cooktown."

He shook his head, not sure whether to believe me. "Go down the road a kilometre and you'll find a reserve for your horses," he directed. "Someone will come down for you about 6 o'clock and we'll see about getting you a feed and a bed for the night."

Instead of being ridiculed, we'd been invited to spend the night at Ellerston! At the reserve, we watered and hobbled the horses and were packing some clean clothes into an overnight bag when the chap we'd met earlier arrived. Jim was the manager/captain of the polo team. He took us on a tour of the complex, before leaving us with Lance Shephard, another team member who'd be our host. Five of the polo players lived on the grounds.

Ken talks to a man exercising Kerry Packer's horse

"Is this all part of the one house?" asked Ken, when Lance led us down a lengthy passage to the guest suite.

"Yeh," replied Lance casually, "It's not a bad sort of a shack."

It was more like a palace. The guest bathroom was so big you could have fitted a band and a dance floor in there. Scrubbing up, we put on our cleanest and best clothes, but they didn't quite match the standard of our surroundings.

Lance took us down to 'The Club' for tea and we spent the evening with Kerry Packer's polo players and grooms. Theirs was a different world altogether, often spending more time overseas than in Australia. Conversation swung from polo matches in England to Florida and then back to the Argentine, touching on the elite lifestyles of the rich and famous equestrians.

We spent a night of luxury in the visitors' suite at Lance's place, had breakfast with him in the morning and returned to our horses. Having enjoyed the opportunity to see how 'the other half' lives, we were grateful to be back in the Australian bush with our station nags.

In my former life as a computer operator in the city I would have felt quite at ease with the people and glamour of Ellerston. But somehow, my whole perception of life had changed. Battling the jungles of Far North Queensland, suffering thirst, hunger and deprivation, overcoming those first dark days when I thought I'd end up dead, had all helped to change my sense of values and way of thinking. The simple things in life had become the most important: Water, food, shelter, good health. The lace and frills were discarded: unecessary trash which cluttered up one's life and were an extra burden to the horses.

Our horses had become the most important thing of all. We depended on them for our existence. The world revolved around their stomachs. Every injury or illness which befell them was like a knife wound to our hearts. When the horses were hungry, we were miserable. When they were fit and well, we were on top of the world. They played up and could be a handful at times, but when things got really tough they gave their best and we all worked as a team. I never dreamed that two people and twelve horses could have such a special relationship. It was priceless.

Leaving Ellerston, we headed south on the National Trail once more. There was no other place in the world we would rather have been.

Sharon propped up against pack bags writing diary

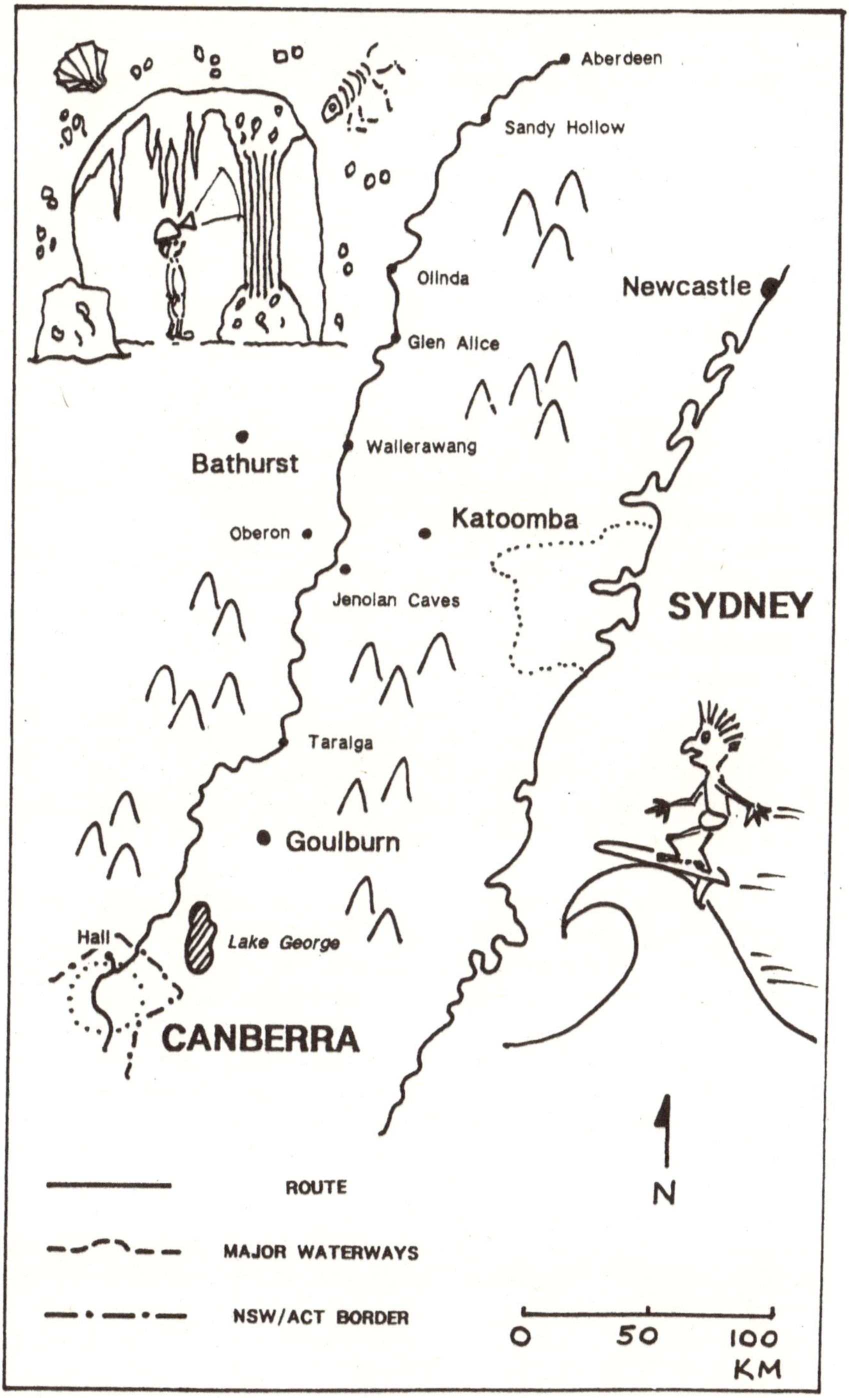

Aberdeen
Sandy Hollow
Olinda
Newcastle
Glen Alice
Bathurst
Wallerawang
Katoomba
Oberon
Jenolan Caves
SYDNEY
Taralga
Goulburn
Hall
Lake George
CANBERRA
ROUTE
MAJOR WATERWAYS
NSW/ACT BORDER
N
0
50
100
KM

Chapter 20:
BUSHRANGERS AND LANDSLIDES

THE WARM NOVEMBER sun made us drowsy as we rode along the banks of the Hunter River. Heavy spring rains had ensured a good season and the horses could fill their bellies with grass after a couple of hours feeding. It was easy travelling compared to the drought and scorching heat we had encountered through most of Queensland.

The only problem was that so much country had been freeholded and cleared for farming that we were restricted to riding down roads. Many of the old stock routes had been fenced in by farmers, leaving a narrow verge and forcing us out onto the roadway to risk being skittled by fast traffic.

Riding in the lead and studying the trail map, I looked with suspicion at our designated approach to Aberdeen township. We had to cross a railway line, turn left on the New England Highway, ride over the Hunter and camp in a paddock behind the caravan park. Cresting the railway line, my suspicions were confirmed by the ceaseless stream of trucks and cars whizzing along the highway and the diminutive ribbon of nature strip alongside.

Wheeling around, I blocked the horses and pushed them back to Ken, who turned and led them into the safety of a laneway. While the horses grazed, we had a closer look at the highway approach and found a maintenance track beside the railway that headed towards town.

Unnoticed by speeding motorists barely 50m away, we nervously trotted the horses across the line and swung hard left onto the maintenance track. The railway track brought us out on the high flood bank of the Hunter, within view of the paddock behind the caravan park. It was full of horses and not a blade of grass, so we camped where we were.

The first coal train whistled past within 10m of our camp. The ground trembled under our feet and the noise frightened hell out of us, but the horses were busy munching behind the electric fence and never lifted their heads. They'd grown accustomed to being passed by log trucks on one-lane timber tracks, so the train didn't bother them.

Supplies were purchased in Aberdeen, properties phoned

to request access, shoeing attended to and we were on our way in a couple of days.

Climbing over Bell's Gap, we left the Hunter Valley behind and followed the path of the mighty Goulburn River. Veering off into the Widden Valley, rugged sandstone peaks towered on either side and thoroughbred studs lay nestled in sheltered hollows. The National Trail literally took us through the backyard of the Widden Stud, where even though on a public road, we felt quite out of place with our station bred horses.

A magnificent black stallion pranced up to the fence beside us. We found out later that he had a $45,000 service fee. Any temptation to back our mares up to the rails disappeared when the owners came out to see who we were. We chatted for a few minutes, then decided to make a quick exit when a male peacock strutted up and the horses became edgy. Trains, trucks and air brakes were no threat, but our horses were still jumpy around goats, pushbikes and peacocks. A display of plumage would leave a trail of torn turf and flattened shrubbery as the horses bolted.

Bill Tindale was waiting for us at the gates of Myrtle Grove.

"I figured you'd be along shortly," he smiled. "Follow me and I'll show you to a hut where you can camp."

Built on a concrete slab, to us the hut had every conceivable luxury, extending to provision for a hot shower.

"Some shooters who come here regularly built this place," commented Bill as he showed us around. "Once you get the wood stove going, warm up this pot of water and take it around here," he instructed, walking outside. At the rear of the hut, three logs made into stepping stones gave access to a black plastic container fixed to the roof. "Pour the water in, then you can go inside, turn on the tap and have a shower until the water runs out."

Myrtle Grove is private property, so we thanked Bill for the use of the hut and allowing us to ride through.

"Our house is only a mile up the road," he directed. "Come over aftea tea and meet my father."

The horses were in a large paddock, so we put three behind our electric fence and left the others loose when we rode over to meet Mr Noel Tindale. His family have lived at

Myrtle Grove for generations and he entertained us with tales of the bushranging that went on in the early days.

"Last century, our family owned a prized thoroughbred stallion named *The Duke of Athol*," recalled Mr Tindale. "He was stolen by the notorious bushranger, Harry Redford, also known as 'Captain Starlight'. Well, they whisked him away over Nullo Mountain, pausing to camp in a small sandstone cave, where one of Redford's men drew a charcoal picture of the stallion over some Aboriginal cave paintings. That's why the cave is now called 'The Livery Stable'. There was no trace of where they took the horse after that, but a few years later, some foals started appearing in Queensland that looked a lot like him."

Returning to our camp later that evening, the electric fence had been flattened and the nighthorses were gone. With thoughts of bushrangers still lingering in our minds, we walked the fenceline to investigate. Surely nobody would steal our horses when they had the pick of the Widden thoroughbreds next door?

"I tied the fence down to a big chunk of wood in this gully, and I can't find the wood," muttered Ken. "Something must have spooked the horses and they've got tangled in the fence and dragged the log away."

Fixing the fence, we put our two riding horses inside for the night. The other horses were grazing nearby in the morning and we returned to our electric fence to look for clues as to what might have happened.

"There's a big wombat hole near this gully," discovered Ken. "Maybe the wombat popped out of his hole and frightened the horses, but I'm buggered if I can find that hunk of wood the fence was tied to. The wombat must have dragged it down his hole or ate it or something," he muttered illogically.

Wombats don't eat logs, but strange things sometimes happen in the bush and the fate of the missing log remained a mystery.

Following the path of the bushrangers, a steep fire trail carved into the craggy sandstone of Nullo Mountain wound upwards through Wollemi National Park. Nearing the summit, the horses were glad to stand and rest while we wandered into 'The Livery Stable' and looked at the historic cave art.

The front girth on *Riley's* packsaddle had broken during

the climb, but we left it hanging and hurried along to reach a gateway that had been left unlocked for us until midday. Access to this rugged section of National Park was a privilege granted to trail riders by the private property owners at either end. To prevent vehicle erosion, the National Parks had destroyed all previous access routes.

Making it through the gate in time, we stopped to thank the owner, who informed us that the water was poisoned at our next campsite. We would have to push two days' travel into one as there was no water until we descended Nullo Mountain.

It was our longest day on the trail and we had ridden 60km when our tired, dusty outfit pulled up in the Cudgegong River stock reserve. *Riley's* load with the broken girth had sat perfectly all day. It proved beyond doubt that the flank girth and surcingle hold the packsaddle in place; the front girth only keeps everything in position until the surcingle is buckled. From then on, we left the front girth loose, lessening the incidence of girth galls.

B2, Sharon & Jordie in the Livery Stable

We stayed on the Cudgegong for a couple of days to let the horses recover from the ride over Nullo Mountain. We were busy shoeing one morning when a wiry, bowlegged little bloke swaggered into our camp.

"Howdy!" he drawled in a musical bush twang, "I'm Cowboy Webster."

He knew the history of every National Trail traveller who had passed across the Cudgegong.

"They's all carryin' too much on their packhorses," he told us. "One bloke was carryin' everything except the kitchen sink on this poor little mool. I had ta help 'im out, 'cos the mool had fallen down luggin' so much weight. His knees were gashed and all the fluid run out."

Mules were much hardier pack animals than horses, but there was still a limit to what they could carry.

"I better go check me kangaroo snares," said Cowboy. "I'll put me ferrets to work and bring you over a couple of rabbits before you leave."

WITH TWO FROZEN bunnies in our pack bags the next morning, we had a lovely shaded ride following the Glen Alice Trail along narrow sandstone rock ledges. Ferns and moss exploded from damp crevices where the sunlight rarely touched. Reaching the summit of Grassy Mountain, we dropped steadily down to the wide open expanses of the Capertee Valley where black thunderclouds rumbled and threatened.

Spring showers made the ground greasy underfoot as we struggled up towards Baal Bone Gap on a steep fire trail. Near the top our progress was blocked by a recent landslide. The right hand embankment above had collapsed and a mass of rubble and uprooted trees lay in our path. To the left, I could see clear to the bottom of the gorge where the landslide had mown a path through the timber. If any of the horses fell over the edge, they'd roll all the way to the bottom.

It was too steep and overgrown to leave the track and too late in the day to turn back, so Ken went ahead on foot to find a way through. Our only option was to lead each horse up the face of the landslide, turn around the base of an uprooted tree, squeeze through a narrow gap then jump down onto the track. Feeling insecure when their hooves slipped on the loose, shaley surface, they needed much encouragement from behind to follow Ken. *Mal* made it halfway up the slope, lost his footing and skated back down, nearly shunting a few horses over the edge of the track.

"Come on *Mal*," I urged on his second attempt, flicking the stockwhip at his heels. He clambered shakily up to Ken and disappeared behind the root system of the fallen tree. It was almost dark when the last horse scrambled to safety, and we quickly rode the one kilometre to the top of the range, camping on the edge of a swamp in the drizzling rain.

It was a miserable place to camp, and whilst the rain cleared overnight, most of the horses had coughs and runny noses in the morning. The day heated quickly, steaming our horses and wet gear dry in the first hour of travel. We reached the coal mining town of Wallerawang, accompanied by hordes of biting Aussie bush flies. Summer had arrived with a vengeance!

Chapter 21: MUTMUTBILLI

NESTLED IN A deep cleft between two mountains, the little village was partly obscured by dense green foliage and towering pines. The tiled chalet rooves were pitched high to shed snow in winter. One could imagine we were gazing down on an Austrian ski resort.

On the contrary, we were viewing this scene from horseback in the Blue Mountains within a stone's throw of Sydney. On foot, we wandered down amongst the European style buildings of the Jenolan Caves Resort. Originally called the 'Fish River Caves', these limestone tunnels were used as hiding places by bushrangers in the 1820's and 30's. Officially discovered by farmers in 1838, they soon became a popular tourist attraction even though the final descent to the Jenolan Valley was so steep it could only be reached on horseback or foot.

After a guided tour of Lucas Cave, we returned to where we'd left *B2* and *Brown Mare* tied up in the scrub, riding back to our base camp, where the National Trail had brought us within 8km of the caves. To our relief there were still 10 horses hobbled and feeding behind the portable electric fence. We'd only had this device for 7 weeks and found it ideal when we had to leave the horses for some reason. It wasn't infallible however, so the horses were always hobbled and two were nightlined. Our saddles and pack gear were still safely stashed in an old shed, so apart from a dozen horses, there was no visible sign of our camp.

Rummaging around in the dinner packs, I looked for something to concoct an evening meal out of. A loaf of heavy rye bread we'd carted from Wallerawang, some rancid butter, an oily lump of cheese and some plum jam were whipped up into a jaw crunching hunger stopper. The mild December weather had not reached heatwave conditions, but the build-up of dead plant litter over the forest floor only needed a hot wind and a spark to transform it into a raging inferno. Ken could heat up enough water for a shave by filling a piece of plastic tube and leaving it in the sun for an hour, but our meals during fire risk periods had little culinary value and were washed down with cordial instead of black tea.

In the morning, I noticed *Mal* standing around listlessly

and looking closer, found he had a badly swollen chest and a sack of fluid hanging between his front legs.

"Look at these marks on his neck," pointed Ken. "I'd say that mongrel *Trotter* shepherded him into the corner of the electric fence and booted hell out of him."

Some people from a nearby guesthouse gave me a lift into the vet at Oberon where I bought some anti-inflammatory medication for *Mal*. *Poddy* and *Riley* still had bad coughs from the miserable night on Baal Bone Gap and the glands under their jaw were swollen.

"Could they have strangles?" I asked the vet. He didn't think so, because they were 7 and 8 years old and strangles tends to infect only young horses.

"It sounds like a bad cold," he diagnosed, prescribing penicillin.

The next morning, *Mal* was stiff in the front legs and his chest had gone rock hard. He loosened up when I led him down to the creek for a drink, so we decided the best thing to do was pack up and keep riding, leaving *Mal* to run empty.

The National Trail zig-zagged through the bushland and pine forests of the Blue Mountains on a broad network of major gravel roads and minor fire trails. Trail markers were scarce in a few critical places, our route description was vague and the labyrinth of forestry roads was not shown on any of our maps. Logging operations can make a minor road appear to be a major road in a matter of days. Even if I'd had a compass, it wouldn't tell me which was the right track.

The only way I could navigate was to work out our destination in regard to a landmark (such as a distinct hill or microwave tower), treat every turnoff with suspicion and only continue down a road if it seemed to head in the right direction. If it didn't, we'd backtrack and try another road.

Turning around created havoc because the horses that normally travelled in front ended up at the back and vice versa. There'd be a mad scramble as *Trotter* headed for his position near the lead, biting and kicking any horse within range. Most took a wide berth of him, squabbling amongst themselves like a mob of hens in a chicken coop until they were back in the right order.

Several days' travel left the bush and rough stony ridges behind. Rolling hills and open grazing country accompanied us into the historic wool growing town of Taralga where an avenue of tall poplars lined the main street. On the nearby Richlands property, John McArthur helped establish Australia's wool industry early last century and the sandstone and basalt buildings of that era remain standing throughout the town.

We'd been invited to stay with Clive and Narelle Thomas when we reached Taralga.

"You can't miss our place when you get to town," informed Clive, a burly truck driver who'd been carting gravel past our campsite at Wiarborough Creek. "Just keep headin' down the street and you'll come to a split slab house. You know; one made of old trees!" he added with a roar of laughter and a sparkle of devilment in his eye.

Packed and ready to travel early the next morning, we'd planned on reaching Taralga by midday until a vehicle pulled up beside our camp.

"Have you got time for me to look at your pack gear?" questioned the driver as he walked over. "I've got an old packsaddle I want to fix up and I'm after ideas."

If it weren't for the people who'd given us their time and knowledge, we wouldn't have been there, so we had all the time in the world for someone who wanted to learn.

Hobbling the horses, we caught and offsaddled *Riley*, pulled his gear apart and spent the morning demonstrating stitching and rivetting techniques whilst explaining how we'd restored our old packsaddles.

"We thought you must have got lost!" greeted Narelle Thomas when we reached Taralga late that afternoon. "You can put your horses in our paddock, here," she invited.

Hobbling *B2* and *Brown Mare* in the Thomas's small paddock, we hunted the rest down a laneway where there was an abundance of feed. *B2* promptly jumped the fence and bounded down the road after her mates. After much haring about on foot, we cornered the little pony and led her back to the paddock. To prevent her jumping the fence again, we put an additional side line from her front hobble strap to one back fetlock.

"Hey mum, dad; can we go for a ride with Sharon and Ken?" quizzed the Thomas children as we told a few tales from our journey that evening.

School holidays were about to begin and they were eager for adventure. After hearing Ken's tall stories on bush tucker and eating witchetty grubs, Rhana decided it might be safer to stay home, but 10 year old Colin remained keen, even if he had to put up with Ken's cooking.

We stayed in Taralga for a couple of days until school finished and Colin was ready to go. The last school bus brought more penicillin for our sick horses from the vet in Crookwell. They needed the rest and *Mal* didn't stiffen up too badly, wandering unhobbled around the laneways.

Everyone agreed that Colin's horse *Candy* was too fat to accompany us and wouldn't last half a day in the December heat. Our skewbald brumby, *Easton*, was the only reliable horse small enough for Colin to mount.

"I'll give *Easton* a quick ride before Colin gets on," Ken said to Clive on the day of our departure. "He's had a few days off, so I'll make sure he's going to behave." Kicking the pony into a canter, *Easton* humped his back and jumped around a bit.

"He's never done that before!" exclaimed Ken in surprise.

"Ah, he'll be right," said Clive casually, "That horse looks quiet enough to me; throw the young fella on board."

Much to Colin's disgust, Ken put a lead rope on *Easton* and led him alongside for the first hour. It must have been the longest stretch Colin had ever walked a horse, and when Ken let him loose, he kicked the pony into a canter and joined me in the lead. *Easton* probably did twice the distance we covered that day, continually cantering between the lead and the tail and haring off into the distance when a gate came into view.

The mercury soared to 39°C and after riding 35km it was a hot, tired and dusty boy who willingly climbed off his pony at a stock reserve on the Wollondilly River. Unsaddling *Easton*, he was amazed to find only two small patches of sweat on the horse's back where the saddle pads had rested.

"If this was *Candy*, she would have been dripping with sweat and just about melted away," he exclaimed. Not many 10 year olds would be so observant after a long, hard day. Ken cooked up some mutton chops and potatoes for tea and Colin stayed awake long enough to eat them before falling exhausted into his swag.

Buzzing, biting flies woke us early next morning, but Colin was still out to it like a light, so we let him sleep while we made the dinners and packed. It wasn't worthwhile to unload the horses and stop for dinner, as we lost too much time catching, hobbling and unloading. At midday, we'd dismount, hold onto our riding horses and eat the sandwiches we carried in our saddlebags. All the horses grazed while we ate, and if they wandered too far, we swung onto our mounts and got around them.

"Hop into that creek and have a bath," Ken told Colin when the heat finally woke him.

"You don't have a bath when you go camping!" Colin protested.

"Well hop in have a swim then," ordered Ken, "and wash your clothes while you're in there." Changing the word 'bath' to 'swim' had the desired effect, especially when the young boy found out there was no soap involved.

I handed him a corned meat and salad sandwich for breakfast when he'd finished.

"What's this green stuff?" he shrieked, examining the contents.

"Green capsicum," I replied.

"Yuck! I'm not eating that stuff," he announced.

"If you don't eat your greens," lectured Ken, "you'll get crook in the guts and we'll have to leave you behind."

"Oh no!" cried Colin, purposefully dropping the sandwich on the ground, "I can't eat it now!"

"Oh yes you can!" declared Ken, picking up the filling, dusting off the grass and slapping the sandwich back together, "and you've got a few extra greens in there now!"

We were invited to stay with people for the next two nights. Spared from the evils of capsicum sandwiches on the Cormack's property, Colin gorged himself on icecream instead.

The McLeans on 'Mutmutbilli' shared some wonderful photos and stories with us of previous horse treks through the NSW high country. One of the things that intrigued us most, was how they acquired such a unique name for their property. Apparently a bullock driver had a regular route across their creek which got boggy at certain times of the year. The lead bullock's name was 'Billy', and whenever he got to the boggy crossing, the bullocky would sing out 'mud mud Billy', so that the beast knew to take up the strain in order to pull through. However, the bullock driver had a speech impediment so what actually came out was more like 'mut mut Billy' hence the name of the creek and the property it runs through.

Our next day's travel was one of the most dangerous on the entire ride from Cooktown. We had to cross the Hume. This highway is the main artery between Sydney and Melbourne and echoes to the ceaseless roar of semi-trailers, cars, trucks, buses and motor bikes, twenty four hours a day, seven days a week. The black spot of the Hume is the Cullarin Range as more people have died in accidents on this short stretch than on any other. To our dismay, our crossing was on a short straight on the Cullarin Range. We had to cross the main railway, then only 5 metres of gravel before we reached the highway. To our left, there was 50 metres of visible bitumen until it disappeared over a hill. To our right there was 100 metres in sight before the highway swung around a bend. A treacherous place to make a crossing with horses, but there was no alternative.

We were fortunate to have a good set of young ears with us. Colin could name the make of a truck by the sound it made and a far off glimpse of the rig, as he'd done many trips on the road with his father. Ken crossed the highway on foot and opened up a set of double gates we had to go through. Colin came up front with me and we waited for a lull in the traffic.

"Can you hear any trucks?" Ken called out to Colin.

"Nope", he yelled in reply.

After a quick look up and down the line for trains, we took off at a canter across the railway, and as we hit the Hume the crack of the stockwhip resonated down the bitumen, encouraging the horses to hurry across. Colin and I made it safely through the gateway, just as a semi-trailer roared over the crest of the hill on our left. The mob of horses were still on the far side of the highway, so Ken flicked the whip at the heels of the last two horses spurring them to gallop through the gateway only seconds before the semi howled past. One-eyed *Jack* didn't quite judge the opening properly and sideswiped the gate post with a pack bag on his blind side. It nearly swung him off his feet, but he regained his balance and trotted after the other horses.

I wiped a bit of nervous sweat from my brow while Ken closed the gates and we continued on our way, only to be nearly run over by a vehicle speeding through the paddock. The driver ignored my frantic hand signals to slow down, roared up the crest of a hill and locked his brakes up when he saw the mob of horses on top. He spun onto the edge of the gravel, coming to a halt in a cloud of dust.

"Hey!" he yelled out to Colin, "You better slow those horses down; other people use this road you know." We'd been travelling at 5km/h and he was travelling at about 105, which was way too fast in a paddock full of livestock!

After two nights of luxury, Colin was delighted when we camped in a laneway next to a stock reserve.

"Have you got any of that green stuff left?" he asked, wanting a piece of capsicum to eat.

"I thought you didn't like it?" I queried, getting a sheepish grin and shrug of the shoulders in reply. Perhaps he thought we'd decline all further offers of accommodation if he ate capsicum. He much preferred camping out.

It started to rain, so Ken lit a small fire down in a sandy-bottomed creek and cooked some corned meat and potatoes for tea. I pitched my emergency two-man tent and the three of us managed to cram inside and get a good night's sleep out of the rain.

The morning dawned hot and steamy, and the air buzzed with the whirring wings of millions of Christmas beetles. Flying from tree to tree, they munched the eucalyptus leaves to ragged skeletons, while the ground beneath was littered with pieces of gum leaf and beetle droppings. Donning hats to keep the droppings out of our hair, we packed up, had breakfast and left.

By midday we reached the Marked Tree Road along the top of the Lake George Range. Magnificent views over Lake George could be seen, but the wind was so strong we clamped our hats down and kept away from the edge of the drop-off.

On the descent into Gundaroo, we came across Clive and Narelle who'd driven out to meet us. It wasn't much further to the Gundaroo sports ground, where we offloaded the horses and electric fenced them in a corner full of phelaris grass.

Colin gave his parents a whip cracking demonstration off *Easton*, who didn't seem to mind when the whip flicked up under his belly and was dragged across his rump. He'd behaved better for Colin than he did when Ken or myself rode him.

"Sit down and have a drink and something to eat," said Clive, as Narelle produced a hamper full of food. "I hope you behaved yourself," he grinned at Colin.

"I even ate green capsicum!" Colin proclaimed, pulling a face at his parents.

The young lad had ridden 140km in 5 days (plus the extra distance from cantering back and forth along the road). He'd been a terrific travelling companion, nearly always cheerful or full of cheek and been no trouble whatsoever.

We waved goodbye when they drove out of the sports ground, imagining how much quieter it would be without Colin. One extremely tired skewbald pony seemed to nod his head in relief as the car disappeared down the road.

Sharon & Easton make a phone call home to Perth

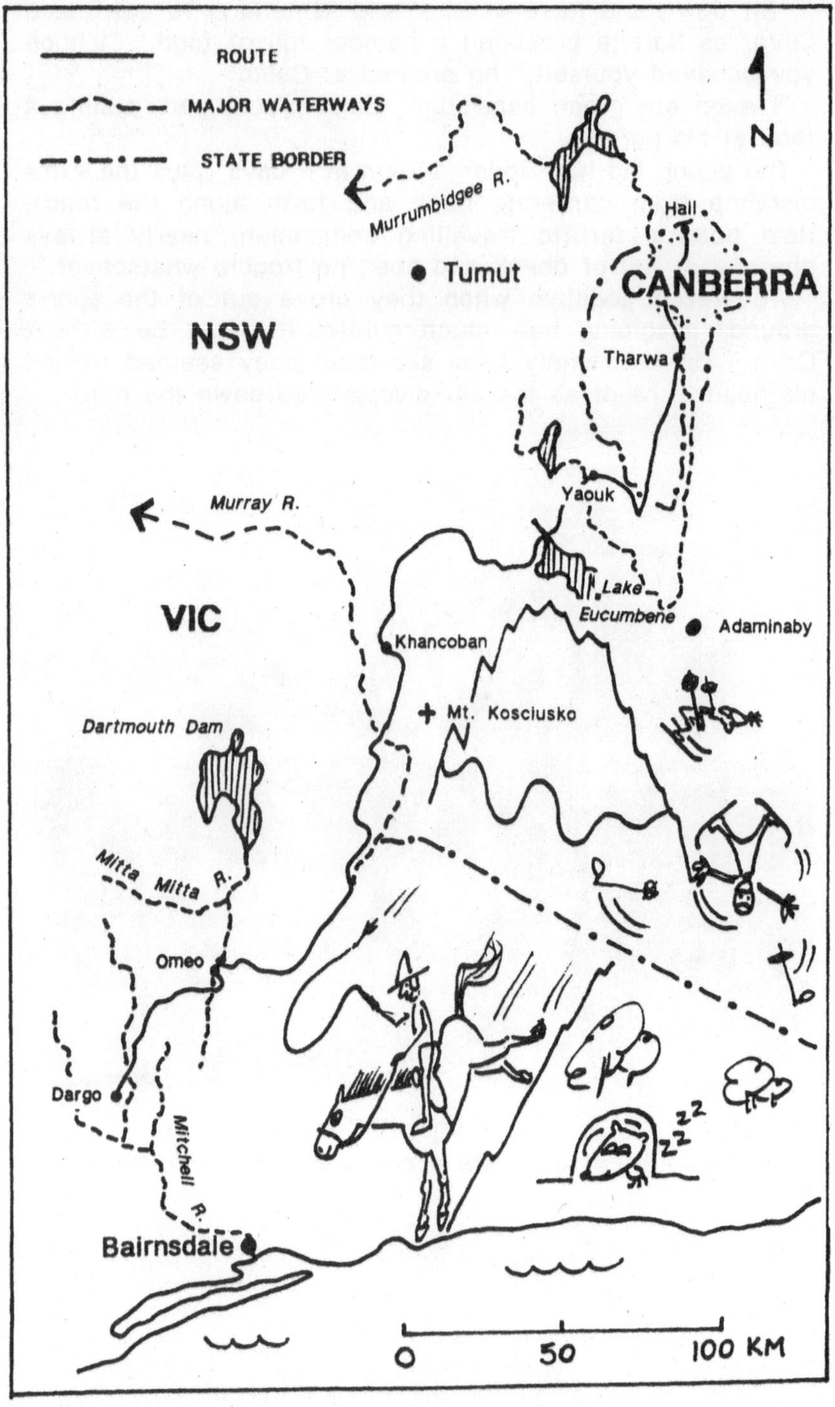
ROUTE
MAJOR WATERWAYS
STATE BORDER
N
Murrumbidgee R.
Hall
Tumut
CANBERRA
NSW
Tharwa
Yaouk
Murray R.
Lake
Eucumbene
Adaminaby
VIC
Khancoban
Mt. Kosciusko
Dartmouth Dam
Mitta Mitta R.
Omeo
Dargo
Mitchell R.
Bairnsdale
0
50
100 KM

Chapter 22: KOSCIUSKO COUNTRY

"YOU HAVE TWO choices; put him down now or give him massive doses of penicillin for a week and if there's no improvement, then put him down." The Gundaroo vet delivered his verdict as he felt the grotesque hardness of *Mal's* swollen chest. The stricken grey piebald from Cloncurry barely responded to the poking and prodding.

"This hard lump is a massive 'cellulitis'. The kick to his chest caused this enormous tissue reaction and there's probably some fluid in there that will form an abcess and burst to relieve the pressure."

Neither Ken nor myself wished to give *Mal* the death sentence. He was still eating and drinking O.K. and didn't seem to be in any great pain. He was just very stiff in the front legs. We might not be able to use him for the rest of the trip, but felt we owed him a chance. Whilst he never over-exerted himself *Mal* had been a faithful, quiet-natured work horse. He was such a tough battler, he probably had the tenacity to survive and recover.

"How much penicillin do we give him?" I queried.

"Twenty mls, twice a day" smiled the vet.

Spending Christmas in Gundaroo, our vet's bill for worm mixture, vaccinations, drugs and lotions came to over $500, but at the end of the week, *Mal* had transformed from the easiest horse to catch, to the most difficult. Little wonder, as after two needles a day he must have felt like a pin-cushion. As the vet predicted, an abcess formed on his chest, burst and drained the excess fluid, much to *Mal's* relief. The main danger was that if he stood around for too long, the abnormal tissue might fuse with the muscle causing a permanent injury, so it was time to get moving again.

Mal was quite happy running loose without a load and his front legs worked much more freely after he'd warmed up. After an hour on the bitumen, we swung right onto the gravel Gininderra Road and crossed the border into the Australian Capital Territory about mid-afternoon. Shortly after, we rode under the Barton Highway bridges to find ourselves in the Canberra suburb of Belconnen. Down in a gully alongside the Gininderra Creek there was not a sign of a house anywhere. It felt peculiar. We knew from the roar of traffic near at hand that we were in the nation's capital city, but there was nothing visible. There was just us and our 12 horses wandering peacefully through the dense, green creekside vegetation.

We came to the creek crossing, but the bridge had been washed out and the vertical scour marks on our side of the bank indicated a dangerous depth of water. Looking for another spot to cross, we continued along the bank and found ourselves under a bridge at the intersection of two major roads. A group of teenagers riding skateboards across the concrete paving on the far side of the bridge paused and gazed dumbfounded. We'd come to a 'dead end' and would have to cross the creek.

Brown Mare unwillingly took me across the boggy depth of silt, but the rest of the horses baulked and a couple ran in behind a bridge pylon. I came back to help Ken and with the ring of our stockwhips echoing around the concrete jungle we managed to push the horses through the slimy water. The skateboarders were still staring speechless, not believing this could be happening in civilized Canberra, as I shot to the lead to block the jittery horses before they were up on the bitumen.

We reached our night camp at the village of Hall on the outskirts of Canberra unscathed, after fairly close contact with fast traffic and a hair-raising ride down a concrete storm water drain.

Our next day's ride to the Yarralumla Equestrian Centre was far more relaxed. The National Trail linked up with a network of equestrian trails that criss-cross the city. We travelled through the 'green' belts that separate suburbs, crossed the major roads via underground subways and met with only a few cyclists, joggers and walkers. Our entry into the nature reserves and forests was over a row of poles placed close together. These 'cavaletti' are designed to keep out motorbikes and vehicles.

Pausing on the crest of a hill, we gazed down on Lake Burley Griffin with Parliament House in the distance. Canberra has been designed so that the houses are almost invisible. From our vantage point we couldn't see a single roof-top. It seemed like we'd stumbled across Parliament House in the middle of a wilderness.

We rode through a Corkwood Plantation then into the Stromlo Pine Forest before crossing the Molonglo River. A

Riley crosses 'cavaletti' into a nature reserve

large woolshed drew our attention and since we had no directions on where to go once we'd crossed the river, we naturally headed for it. We were in a vast open expanse of grassland dotted with thickets of timber and a distinct lack of people.

When Tom and Carol strolled past the empty woolshed walking their dog, we pounced on them for directions. "Can you tell us the way to Yarralumla?" I enquired.

"You're sitting right in the middle of it," chuckled Tom.

For some reason I'd envisaged lots of buildings, paddocks, horses and signs everywhere proclaiming 'Yarralumla' and 'Trail Riders Camp Here'. The couple directed us to some buildings used by the Pony Club of which their daughter was a member and we camped under the verandah and set up the electric fence for the horses.

"Come over to our place for a shower," they invited. "We're only 10 minutes walk away." It was hard to believe we were so close to suburbia.

There was a noisy party at the woolshed overnight, and when I checked the horses in the morning I found a set of hobbles lying on the ground. Not far away, I spotted another set and it dawned on me that someone had unhobbled our horses.

"Quick! Come over here!" I cried to Ken in panic.

If our horses had got out of the electric fence there was nothing to stop them galloping off to create havoc in the Canberra traffic. Luckily we found all 12 horses safely behind the fence. Only the quiet ones had been unhobbled. The irresponsible offenders hadn't been able to catch *Jordie*, *Joe* and the Monto Greys, who were most likely to jump the fence without hobbles.

Leaving Yarralumla, we rode past several housing areas and a local horse paddock. Horses belonging to Canberrans are kept in a horse paddock designated for their suburb. The agistment of $5/week per head is very reasonable and rangers keep an eye on the feed conditions and shift horses into adjoining paddocks when necessary.

Once past the Arawang horse paddocks we rode through cleared grazing country, glad to be out of Canberra and back in the bush, or so we thought. Pulling up on the brow of a hill we were greeted by the sprawling outer suburb of Tuggeranong. The equestrian trail took us alongside a busy thoroughfare. The roadside was fenced off around a constuction site and we had to ride on the bitumen in amongst fast traffic. Several vehicles pulled over and their passengers jumped out to take photos of our team of horses as they trotted along in single file down the left hand lane.

Crossing the Murrumbidgee River on the Point Hut causeway, Canberra lay behind us at last. In the evening we arrived at the village of Tharwa and camped by the river. Mrs West heard horses clatter down the main street, and going out on the verandah, caught a glimpse of us through the houses and yards that blocked her view. At 90 years of age she had enough sight with one good eye to notice the packhorses. She sent her son down to invite us up for a shower and tea.

"It's been a long time since I saw a packhorse," she reminisced. "My family were pioneers in the high country of the Kosciuskos and all supplies used to come in by pack team."

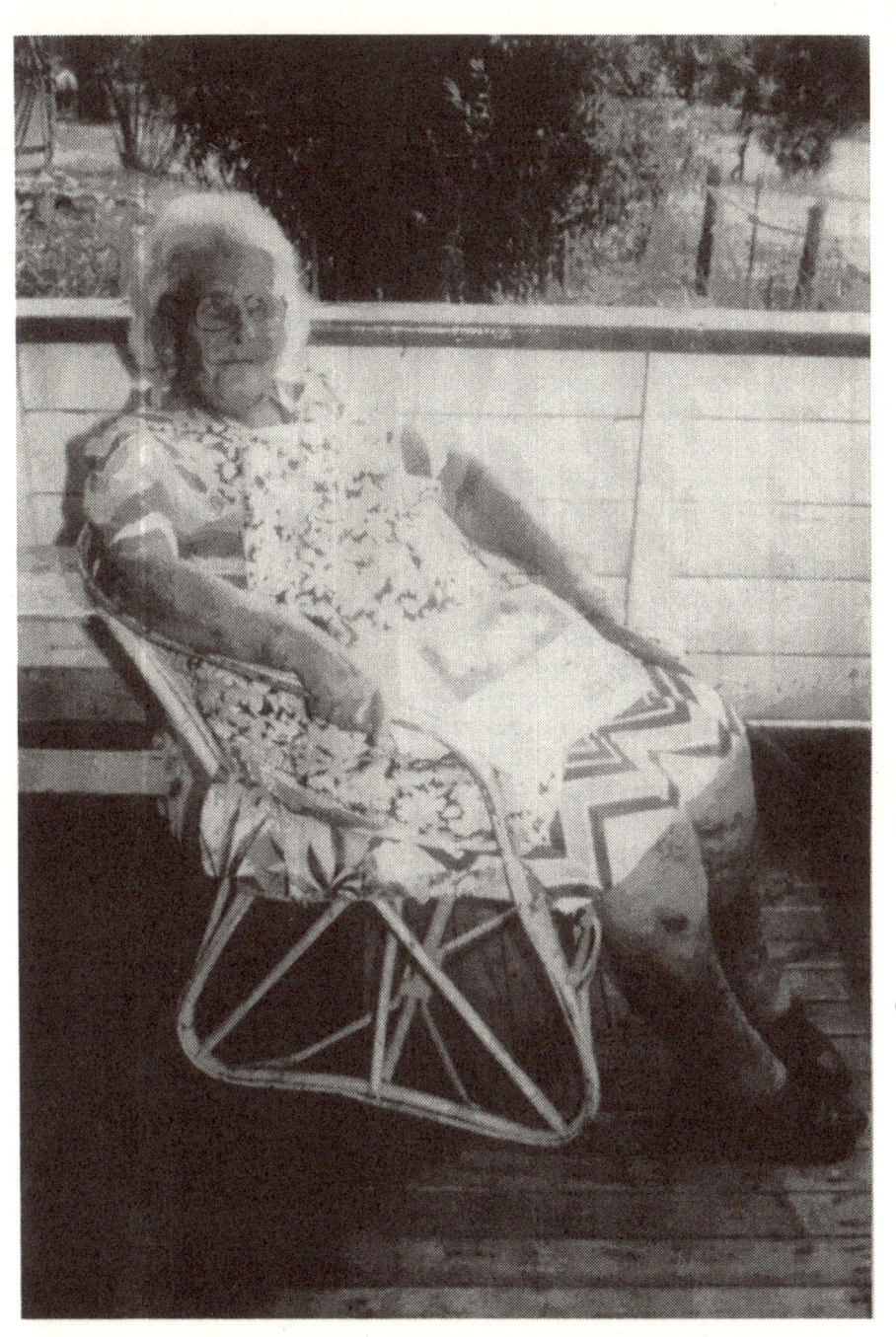

Mrs West on her verandah in Tharwa

We stayed in Tharwa for New Year's Eve which we spent with Cathy and Paddy across the road from the Wests'. A National Park ranger paid us a visit the next morning as we were leaving.

"Years ago," he told us, "When we used to take cattle up to the high country in summer, we'd break in horses by packing them and loadin' them up with Murrumbidgee river stones. They'd buck and carry on at first, but by the time we hunted them to the top of a mountain, they were buggered from cartin' these heavy rocks. We'd tip all the stones out, and the horses'd be that quiet we could put a riding saddle on and ride them home."

"There must be a lot of river stones on top of the mountains," I grinned.

"Yeh," laughed the ranger, "Because they're so far from the river, the tourists think they're Aboriginal artefacts and lump all these bloody heavy rocks home in their backpacks!"

Mal's injury had been steadily improving. His front legs showed only a trace of stiffness as we took a gravel road down onto the Gudgenby River and let the horses graze at midday. While we were cooling off in the water a vehicle pulled up beside the horses and out hopped Cathy laden with a couple of bottles of Coke and a pecan pie for us!

That evening, we offsaddled the horses at 'Caloola Farm'. All land in the A.C.T. is owned by the government and Caloola is managed and run as a children's camp. The farm was currently host to Dr Gary Jones' "Mountain Trails", a Christian camp for children with a range of outdoor activities. In the morning Gary harnessed a slab-shouldered roan Clydesdale called 'Alby' up to a slide and towed groups of delighted children around the paddock.

Leaving Caloola on a 4-wheel-drive track, we followed the Naas River upstream into Namadgi National Park. As the altitude increased, so did the biting March flies. We'd been forewarned and bought bottles of pump action insect repellent for the horses. But each horse jumped away from the 'pfft pfft' and the mist of spray drifted uselessly away in thin air. Only by spraying it onto our palms could we smear repellent over the horses' legs.

At Horse Gully Hut, we paused to admire our first 'high country' clearing amidst wiry snow grass and gnarled, twisted snow gums. There was nothing here for the horses to eat; kangaroos had chewed the clover down to ground level and the snow grass was old and rank. We pushed on to Mt Clear where the rabbits and kangaroos were in plague proportions. A fenced paddock of about 15 acres offered us night-time security and the horses could forage in amongst the snow grass for new shoots that rabbits had missed. Introduced by early European settlers, the voracious appetite and breeding ability of these cotton-tailed burrowers has decimated more native vegetation than the kangaroo and created more soil erosion than the wombat ever will. We'd had beautiful feed conditions through most of N.S.W. but now that we'd hit the Australian Alps it looked like the horses wouldn't fare quite so well.

Sharon, Jordie & Morgan about to cross back into NSW

Crossing the A.C.T. border back into N.S.W. our spirits lifted when we reached a huge, grassy stock reserve on the Murrumbidgee at Yaouk (pronounced 'Yi-ack'). We hobbled our horses out to graze on the treeless plain, left our gear in a heap and sat in underneath the bridge. It was the only shade in the scorching afternoon heat.

Men in rubber waders walked the river bank looking for

the telltale signs of feeding trout. The peculiar casting action of the fly fishermen was fascinating. Flicking the hollow nylon line back and forth through the air like a lasso, they paid out enough line to land the fly in the water above the trout. I'd tried it once, but the hook had nearly pierced my ear on its way past and had ended up lodged in my hat. Making my way back to the riverbank, I'd stepped in a deep hole and my waders filled up with water. Quite irate by this stage, I'd grabbed a fishing knife and cut the line, leaving the fly in my hat, emptied the water out of my waders, then driven to town and bought fish and chips instead.

"How do you cook your fish?" I asked one of the fishermen who stopped to say gidday.

"I don't eat fish," he replied with a laugh. "I release them back into the river or give them away if their mouth has been damaged by the hook and they're unlikely to survive. Would you like a couple if we catch any?" he added, noticing our loose fitting clothes and gaunt faces.

"That'd be great," I responded. Under my shirt, I could feel every rib bone sticking out and I knew Ken was in the same condition. Fresh fish would be a nourishing change to our basic diet of rice, porridge and pasta.

The fishermen continued their sport late into the night and we were asleep when the cry rang out, "Hey Ken! Do you want these coupla fish!"

Ken lept out of the swag and struggled into his strides.

"Bugger!" he cursed at the sound of tearing fabric. "I've put me foot through the knee of me jeans."

He ran down towards the river with the leg of his strides flapping about his knees.

"Holy bloody hell!" I heard him call, "Get out of the way you mongrel big coot!"

"Hey! Do you want these fish or not!" called the fisherman.

"Yeh," replied Ken, "I'll be there as soon as I get untangled from this bloody wombat!"

The lumbering, furry creature had been heading for its burrow when Ken walked in between. Making a frenzied dash for safety, the wombat butted Ken in the kneecaps trying to get past, while Ken jumped around in bare feet, trying to avoid teeth and claws!

"The things I do to get you a feed!" he grinned, returning after a few minutes bearing two delicious trout!

THE PACKHORSES STRAINED against their breastplates as they struggled up the steep Gurrangorambla Range in the Kosciusko National Park. When the Blue Gums gave way to stunted Snow Gums, the grade levelled out and we came across delightful little pockets where clover and snow grass grew along icy brooks. The soft turf had been ripped up in several of these natural clearings along the Lone Pine Trail where vehicles had been bogged. The high country with its spongy, fragile soil was easily damaged by the passage of wheels.

As storm clouds gathered in the late afternoon, the timber slab walls and iron roof of Oldfield's Hut were a welcome sight. Built in the 1920's by the Oldfield family, it sheltered them from the elements when they came to 'salt' their cattle or muster the high plains before the snow season. These 'snow leases' were used to graze cattle in the summer months as the graziers' selections below the snow line were not large enough to stock sufficient cattle year round to support their sizeable families. Decades have passed since the government put an end to summer grazing in this district. A dilapidated set of stock yards to the east of the hut was the only reminder of this past activity.

Easton rolled with the packs before I could catch him,

breaking one of the welds on the camera case frame. The case had withstood a great deal of rough treatment during the trip, but on checking the contents I found my camera lens jammed on the wide angle setting. Ken bound the broken weld with a strip of redhide, but the camera repairs were a specialist's job.

Hobbling our 12 horses out to graze we stacked the gear under the verandah. The naturally cleared plain outside the hut was thick with snow grass and we figured the horses would happily stay put while we set up the electric fence. Ten minutes later, there was not a horse in sight.

"Quick!" cried Ken, "Back the way we came!" He was already tracking the horses at a run. We found them hobbling frantically along the track, swishing their tails at the hordes of biting March flies. They didn't like this place; the grass was old and sour and the insect repellent wasn't having much effect on the flies. They were heading back to the Murrumbidgee River flats at Yaouk where we'd camped the night before and bounded off like a mob of jack rabbits when they heard us coming.

Joe swishing March flies outside Oldfield's Hut

Hobbled horses can travel much faster than people on foot, so we veered off into the bush, going wide to cut them off. The snow gums didn't offer much cover and the horses in the lead spotted us when we drew level. They bounded off along the track and we scrambled off through the scrub again, finally intercepting the leaders and turning them back to Oldfield's hut. We'd made it a rule to keep a night horse secured at all times, but every so often, we'd get overconfident and break it. The horses racked off every time.

The January days were warm and pleasant as we followed the National Trail across the high plains. Ken had to cut the toe out of a sock and pull it over the leg of his jeans to stop his knee getting sunburnt. We were fortunate to have horses in such good condition, because the natural grasses were low in feed value and they had to draw on their reserves to keep warm at night, as the temperature dropped sharply on sunset.

How much easier it would have been if we were regularly passing through towns and buying handfeed. But for us, there was more challenge in being self-sufficient. Travelling with our 12 horses, keeping them all shod and making their welfare our number one consideration, we'd formed a unique bond with each and every animal. Not only did they depend on us; we depended entirely on them. Should anything go wrong, we were all in it together.

Between each sunrise and sunset and into the fading glow of evening, we learnt something new. Sometimes, a little thing; *4 nails held on a horse shoe on the flat, but the same shoe slipped backwards in the hills unless it had a toe clip. A toe clip was as good as two nails.* Sometimes, a major revelation; *If there was more than a pound difference between the two when we weighed each set of pack bags in the morning, the load would slip and the horse would have an injured wither at the end of the day.*

By mistake, experience and observation, we were slowly but surely gaining a true impression of what horse travel would have been like in the early days. Even the local cattlemen had little idea of the difficulties our horses faced. They were used to doing packhorse trips for no longer than a couple of weeks, after which their horses were turned out in a paddock to spell. In the north we'd met many retired drovers who understood the logistics of long distance packhorse travel and the associated problems with injuries, leg-weary horses and lack of feed. In this district, it was only a few people in their nineties who remembered stories of the overland journeys.

"IS THAT AN old football injury, or has the knee gone out of your jeans?" asked George as he sauntered across. The sharp-witted Scotsman was camped alongside us in the caravan park on Lake Eucumbene.
"Yeh," laughed Ken, "If we can get a lift into Adaminaby today, I'll buy a new pair."
"We'll give you a ride," offered George, "But it'll be a slow one."
It was. With four people on board and a heavy caravan in tow, George nursed the Mercedes over the range on the Snowy Mountains Highway to Adaminaby. It was a small town, with most shops serving a dual purpose. The Post Office was incorporated into the newsagency and the grocery store sold hardware and clothing. Ken couldn't buy a pair of jeans his size, but the real estate agent had a few pairs of horse shoes for sale. A chance meeting with our friendly fishermen from Yaouk provided a lift back to the caravan park.

With the hazy purple hills of the Monaro Range behind us the next day, our horses waded chest deep across the rocky bed of the Eucumbene River. A steep climb on the Grey Mare Trail brought us out onto the Happy Jacks High Plains. Picking our way carefully across the treeless plain I watched out for narrow mountain brooks camouflaged by gorse that could swallow a horse's leg right up to the knee. Shaded by vegetation, the water was so cold that the horses wouldn't drink it.

The vivid green banks of a wider creek were lined with soft, spongy sphagnum moss. In places along its length, the ground had been transformed into a brown, muddy mess as though it had been turned over with a rotary hoe. *Brown Mare* threw her head up and snorted at the culprit: a sleek, glossy black pig nosing his way along the creekbank, ripping and shovelling the beautiful moss aside with his snuffling snout. The destructive feral pig had adapted even to the alpine environment, leaving only the true desert of Australia untouched.

When we made camp, there were no trees from which to

string the electric fence. Ken stacked a packsaddle on a packbag and propped it up with dead gorse sticks. Patching up an ancient, rotting fenceline that ran for 20 metres, I reeled out the electric tape from the fence to the precarious pile of saddlery, then back to the fence to make a triangular paddock. There was nowhere to tie up a night-horse, so we front hobbled and sidelined *B2*. If the horses escaped, we would hear them go and have time to catch *B2*, saddle her and bring them back. During the night our wonky anchorage toppled over, shorting the fence out on the ground, but miraculously the horses didn't discover this. For once, our luck was in!

Bridge over the Tooma River

FOR OVER 12 months, Ken had been trying to convince his brother, Pete, to join us on the trail. Although he'd had little riding experience, Pete finally agreed, bussed his way down from Queensland and was waiting at Khancoban to greet us. *Mal* had recovered from the bad kick in the chest by now and we decided to recommission him. He was our quietest horse and would barely notice Pete's light weight and small riding saddle.

Our departure from Khancoban was delayed when a load of hay on the Alpine Way caught fire and the truck driver heaved the burning bales over the road embankment, setting the bush alight. The fire was fuelled by the debris and fallen timber that had accumulated over the years and posed a serious danger to anyone caught in its path. Station hands were sent out to look for campers and bushwalkers, instructing them to evacuate the district. Helicopters brought in loads of water and firefighters battled the blaze for days while we watched its progress from Khancoban. It was burning very close to our proposed route and the National Park rangers were relieved to hear that we intended to stay put until it was safe to move.

Once the fire had been beaten, we waited another couple of days before the 'all-clear' was given and the Alpine Way reopened. It had been a good opportunity to re-shoe a few horses, repair some broken equipment and make new friends. We left Khancoban in the company of Lennie Ceccheto, a linesman with the Snowy Mountains Authority. With Lennie on *Easton* and Pete riding *Mal*, we wound our way down the Geehi Walls track and across the Swampy Plains River.

It was terrific having people join us on our trek. A surprise visit from friends, Rob and Jenny Braddy, swelled our ranks that evening. Surrounded by pals, we spent a memorable night within the smooth river stone walls of Keeble's Hut, where the rocky peaks of Mt Kosciusko towered over us to the south-east.

Saying goodbye to the Braddys next morning, we joined up with the Alpine Way, where the Sunday traffic was fast and dangerous. Travelling along this busy gravel road for most of the day, we were relieved to finally turn off at the Tom Groggin gate post.

Taking a last look at N.S.W. we plunged into the swirling waters of the Murray River, just as a group of rubber rafts appeared upstream. There were too many horses in the water to try turning them back, so I reined my mare to a standstill while the bulk of the rafts whizzed past under her nose.

"Get going!" yelled Ken.

I looked upstream to see a solo rafter bearing down on us. The horses were overtaking me from behind, so I booted the mare forward and made for the opposite bank.

Lennie, Ken & the horses at the Tom Groggin gate post

The raft was zipping along on an imminent collision course for the last few horses who were struggling slowly across the current in chest deep water. Its occupant began frantically backpaddling, but the raft responded with loop-de-loops and kept coming, whizzing straight between two horses and off down river.

We emerged onto the Victorian side of Tom Groggin Station, a small freeholding of 1800 acres on the Murray River flats with an adjoining snow lease in the mountains. Jack Riley, who the locals claim was 'The Man From Snowy River' in Banjo Patterson's poem, managed Tom Groggin Station for many years. Riding up onto the high flood bank, we sat astride our dripping horses and gazed awe-struck at the magnificent circle of timbered mountains around us. It was easy to imagine 'The Man From Snowy River' galloping down these rocky slopes, jumping logs and ducking branches as he chased a mob of wild horses. The National Trail had succeeded once again in giving us ringside seats to view Australia's mountain grandeur.

Chapter 23:
STALLION ON THE HIGH PLAINS

DRIVING RAIN LASHED the sides of our tin shelter on Tom Groggin Station, howling in under the verandah and soaking our pile of saddlery within seconds. Ear splitting thunder rumbled around the hills and the ferocious sky was so black it could have been nightfall instead of 10a.m.

"I'd better cover the campfire with a sheet of iron," yelled Ken, as Pete and I dragged the sodden gear into the shed. Lennie had gone home to Khancoban the day before.

Donning a raincoat, Ken ran out into the storm, splashing barefoot through sheets of water as a bolt of lightning hit the ground nearby.

"Yie, yie, yie!" shrieked Ken, and we looked up to see him jumping from one foot to the other. "I just got zapped by lightning!" he grinned, dashing back under the shelter. "It hit me in the ankles and kept jumpin' back and forth between them. Felt like hangin' on to an electric fence and me ankles are still ticking."

He put his rubber soled boots on before going outside again to stoke the fire. It was the heaviest rain I'd ever seen and the storms continued to roll around the mountains for the next few days. The horses were hobbled out in a large paddock and had plenty of trees to shelter under. If we'd been camped in the bush, we wouldn't have been able to use our electric fence, as the energiser was likely to conduct lightning and be blown apart. I was glad we weren't camped out in the tent and that the horses were safely behind a fence.

Fine weather eventually replaced the storms, leaving everything hot and steamy. We said goodbye to Pete who was heading back to Queensland, packed up and rode off on our own again.

SLEEPING IN A swag beside a cattleman's hut on Davies Plains, I woke to what sounded like a rusty gate hinge squeaking. Squinting in the early morning sunlight, I located the noisy culprits directly overhead. Several pairs of Gang Gang cockatoos perched in the branches of a tree next to the hut. The male birds had a bright red head in contrast with their soft grey body, while the breast feathers of the females were etched with a pale, translucent pinky-green sheen, resembling fish scales. Instead of taking fright at our movements, the feathered comedians put on a show. They bobbed up and down, sidled back and forth, kissed one another, clowned about on one leg and squawked for attention if we turned away.

The long climb to Davies Plains was the original path of the National Trail and had been well worth the detour. A local cattleman had taken us over the current trail up Tom Groggin track in a 4 wheel drive. It had little to offer in the way of views and there was no grass or water for the horses. Being the long weekend in January, Davies Plains track hummed with the engines of 4 wheel drive vehicles. Our progress was slow, continually stopping to chat with fellow travellers and to admire magnificent views of the mountains and valleys. One elderly lady beat a group of small children out of a vehicle in her eagerness to see our horses.

"I was one of the Nankervis family when they owned Tom Groggin Station," she explained. "It's wonderful to see horses here. I haven't been on Davies Plains for nearly 50 years. My last trip here was in 1942 and we came by packhorse!"

As we wound our way south through the Alps, the piles of stallion dung where they'd marked their territory became more frequent and fresh. Our horses needed to forage for feed as much as possible, during which time they were most vulnerable to a brumby attack. All the horses were hobbled, the mares had an additional short rope running to one back fetlock and we kept them close together. A saddled horse was left on a nightline in case the horses strayed or a stallion appeared and had to be chased away. At nightfall, the horses were electric fenced and two were tied on nightlines. Ken would wait up till 11p.m., then tie all the horses up short to trees except *Mal*, the lowest gelding in the pecking order and a prime target for a vicious stallion. I'd arise before daybreak and let the horses loose inside the electric fence to feed again.

"I don't like the feel of this place," remarked Ken one afternoon when we pulled up at a campsite on Brumby Hill. Nestled in a hollow amongst the snow gums, it contained a small spring fed dam that was the only water supply for

Davies Plains Hut

miles according to my map. The grass in the clearing was cropped short like a bowling green, there were piles of stallion dung with steam rising off them and a dust bath dug by hooves and smoothed out by rolling horses. We were about to camp in the favourite spot of a brumby stallion!

Our own horses were so hungry they forgot about the electric fence, frequently pushing against it and getting zapped. After tea of damper and roast potatoes, I crawled into the swag which we'd placed at the base of a tree which could be climbed to safety. Ken waited up to watch the horses, fitting a new cracker to his stock whip as it was the only protection we had.

Not long after he'd tied the horses up and gone to bed, I heard a horse's footstep.

"There's a stallion out there!" I hissed to Ken.

"Nah, it's probably old *Mal* shuffling around," he replied, half asleep.

But there'd been no clink of hobble chains so I lay awake, ears straining for another soft footfall. I'd nearly dozed off when a spine-chilling snort shattered the still night air.

"That's him!" I cried, but Ken was already up with

stockwhip in hand. He let fly a mighty crack and we heard the stallion snort and crash off through the timber. I shone the torch around our horses who were standing quietly, undisturbed by the incident.

"Thank God we don't have a mare in season," I declared.

"He'll be back," stated Ken. "We're challenging his authority by camping here, plus he'll be interested in pinching our mares."

Half an hour later the wild horse returned. Ken frightened him away with the whip which sounded like a cannon going off in the bowels of the clear, starry heaven.

We were both so tired that we didn't hear the stallion return a third time until he was just outside the electric fence. Ken cracked the whip, but the horse snorted in defiance and moved closer. A glint of moonlight off his eye drew my attention and I focussed on the black shape lurking around in the shadows. He was only 15 metres away on the opposite side of the spring. The sharp report of the whip no longer kept him at bay.

"Get up that tree!" yelled Ken, "He's coming in! Get out of here you black mongrel!" he hollered, cracking the whip and dancing around the flat in his jocks in the sub-zero temperature. The sound of Ken's voice must have done the trick, because the stallion wheeled around and galloped off up the track, leaving us in peace for the few hours of night that remained.

We sighted the wild horses next day, having followed their tracks down the road. Three mares and a foal vanished into the bushes while the heavy-boned black stallion stood his ground until they were safely gone.

The gradient into Hell's Gates on the Tambo River was so sharp that our packhorses skated down on their haunches, turning broadside to slow their pace then trying to sneak off around the contour of the hill. Our riding mounts worked double time, slithering back and forth as we tried to keep the mob together. The steep grade was a deterrent to wild horses and once across the Tambo we would have no further encounters.

There was no suitable campsite near the river, so we urged our weary horses on and camped outside the back boundary of Bindi Station. Dating back to 1837, Bindi is one of Victoria's oldest properties. In the morning we met the owner, John Armit.

"You look like an Afghan camel train, carting your bundles of possessions along with you," he laughed at the sight of our horse team stringing along single file.

We'd just started our day's travel, but John invited us to stop overnight. He took us on a tour of the station buildings which are classified by the National Trust and have been painstakingly restored by his family.

"To my knowledge, this is the oldest brand registered in Victoria," said John, showing us a heavy branding iron. "The initials that make up the symbol are PCB, and it was probably registered in 1837 when P.C. Buckley took up the Bindi run."

While the summer hills of Bindi are yellow-brown and dry, the river flats are lush and green from a gravity fed irrigation system. John's fencing and tree planting efforts have also helped to make Bindi a role model in land conservation, especially for a property that was overcleared in the early days and has run sheep for over 100 years.

Reaching the town of Omeo, we camped at the caravan park and electric fenced the horses in knee-deep grass. The grazing had been poor since leaving Canberra, so we bought a bag of horse feed and stayed a couple of days until it was eaten. It was the first time we needed to handfeed and had the opportunity to do so since Monto in Queensland.

Leaving Omeo, we were back to climbing up and down mountains again. It was much colder than we'd imagined the February climate to be, but there were plenty of snakes basking out on the track to avoid. We camped a night at a place called 'Dog's Grave' on the headwaters of the Wentworth River. A cattleman once lost his dog to a dingo bait here, and a monument was erected on the grave site by a stonemason as a touching remembrance to the bond between stockmen and their dogs.

From the summit of Mt Birregun we gazed down from a clearing used as a firefighting helipad and were amazed to see clouds below. Distant mountain peaks rose up through the blanket of cloud like islands in the sea. We'd reached an altitude of 1320m but it was an unexpected sight as we'd been gradually climbing for days and roadside timber had hidden the view until now.

On the long descent to the Dargo River we met Froggy

McMahon spraying blackberries.

"You should make the river by tonight, but it's another 14km before you get to town," he informed us. "I'll have a place lined up for youse to stay when you get there tomorrow."

When we crossed the Dargo River that evening, Froggy and his wife Rita were sitting on a bale of hay waiting for us.

"Thought youse might like a beer and a steak before you get to town," grinned Froggy.

Unloading the horses, we scattered the hay amongst them and sat around the campfire half the night, exchanging horse tales with the McMahons. Their horse, *Blue Rag*, had won the Mountain Cattleman's Cup the previous weekend, a race where cattlemen and horses pit their skills against the mountains and each other to gallop around a course that most would not be game to tackle at a walk.

Reaching Dargo the next day, we stashed our gear in McMahon's paddock and hobbled the horses out on beautiful rich feed growing along the road. That evening, Rita put on a video of the Cattleman's Cup. To my surprise I found I was watching myself trying to load *Bob* (the horse I had started with in Cooktown) in the packhorse race. It was an old video from 1989 and the first big packhorse trip I'd ever done had been a 9 day ride to this particular Cattleman's Cup. I was absolutely hopeless, barely able to lift the pack bags, and coming in last with my surcingle flopping around all over the place and the packsaddle about to fall off. Froggy, Rita and Ken were having a good chuckle at the pathetic sight on the TV screen while I cringed in embarrassment.

"We thought it was you," laughed Rita. "We reckoned we knew your face from somewhere!"

Two years ago I needed a horse that would hold his feet up for me to shoe and my pack bags were lucky to stay level for 5 minutes. Now, I could shoe a horse that was trying to kick my head off, I could load 3 packhorses in the time it once took to load one, and the bags would sit perfectly and comfortably on a horse all day.

"I really have come a long way and not only in distance," I thought to myself.

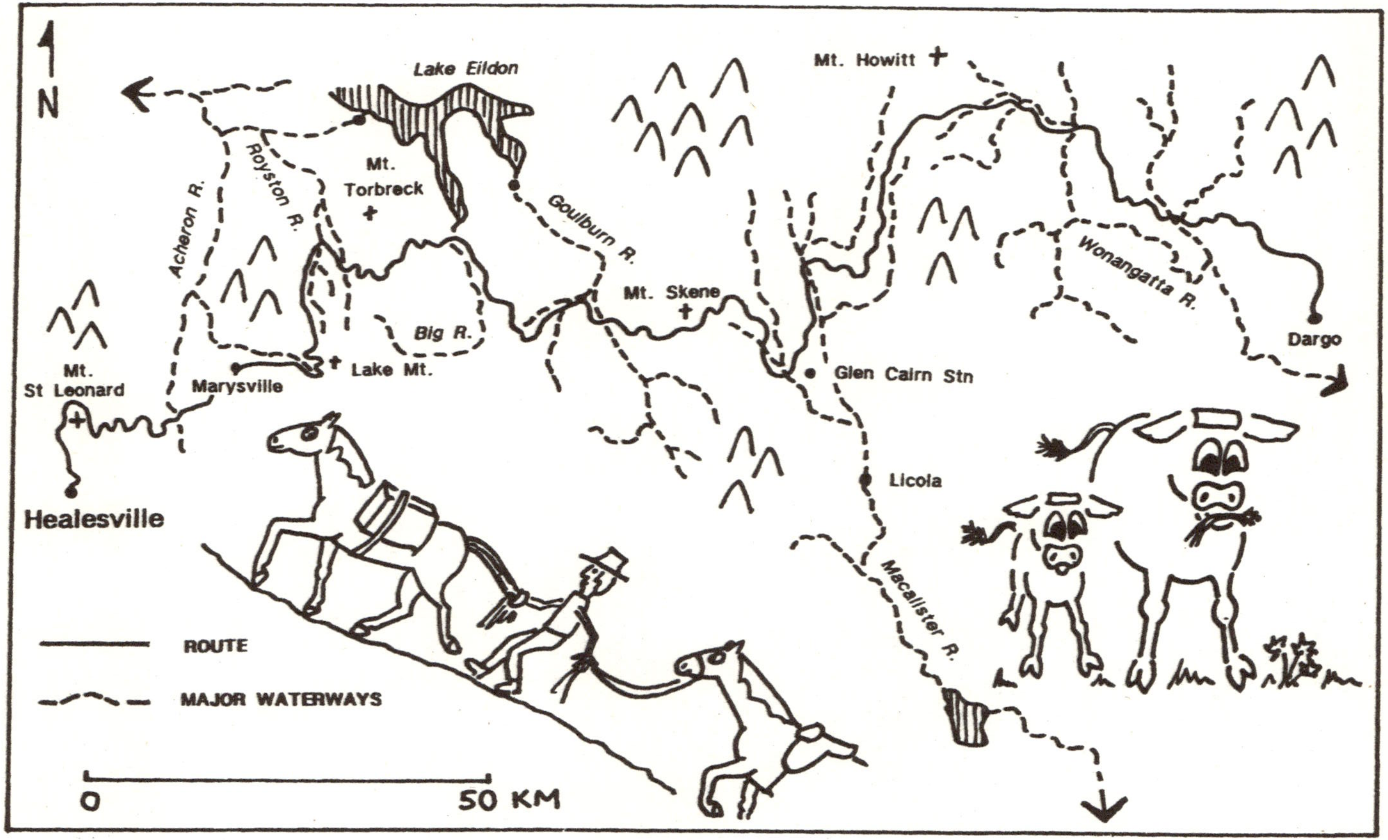
N
Lake Eildon
Mt. Howitt
Mt. Torbreck
Royston R.
Acheron R.
Goulburn R.
Mt. Skene
Wonangatta R.
Big R.
Dargo
Lake Mt.
Glen Cairn Stn
Mt. St Leonard
Marysville
Healesville
Licola
Macallister R.
ROUTE
MAJOR WATERWAYS
0
50 KM

Chapter 24:
BUTCHER COUNTRY SPUR

DRIVING THE HORSES before us, we ducked and shielded our faces from whipping thorny tendrils as we pushed through a dense thicket of blackberries. The old packhorse track we'd been following around the hillside had been engulfed by the wicked vegetation when it dropped down to the Wongungarra River. The lead horses were bulldozing a path for those behind.

After a couple of minutes of shoving and trampling, the leaders halted and the others bunched up behind. Peering over the crush of horses I saw that they were jammed up against a log 3 feet high.

"We'll have to push them over it," figured Ken. "If we try and detour we might do a lot of extra distance then come up against another log 4 feet high; at least they can hop over this one." The blackberry bushes towered over our heads and it was impossible to see through them. We had no idea how far we were from the river and could easily lose horses if we didn't keep them close together and moving in the same direction.

"Git up there!" boomed Ken, unable to crack a whip in the confined space. *Anvil* leapt over the log, knocking down a swag of blackberry fronds before disappearing completely. A definite 'splash' followed her exit, so we knew we'd reached the river. *B2* and *Jack* jumped the log, but the rest of the horses baulked and pushed away to the left.

"Push 'em in or we'll lose them!" shouted Ken and we shunted them through the last of the bushes and down into the water. I leant so far back in the saddle that my head must have nearly touched my horse's rump as she slid down the river bank with her back hooves tucked up under her stomach.

The mountains were wild, rugged and beautiful but were proving such an obstacle course for our horses that we felt only concern for their welfare instead of wonderment at the scenery around us. We were only a day's ride from Dargo, but the comforts and security of civilization seemed a million miles away. Dismounting, we zig-zagged our way up the timbered Wombat Spur, stopping frequently for the horses to have a breather. Walking at the rear, Ken had the easiest climb by hanging onto the tail of the horse in front. After two hours we reached a rocky track at the top of the spur, then began the bone-rattling descent to the Wonangatta River.

Tired and cranky, the horses kicked and fought as they travelled. *Trotter* swung his head when *Joe* walked past, tearing a huge gash in the fleshy part of *Joe's* front leg with his teeth. We were drawing close to the end of our ride, but the horses were growing leg-weary, their reserves were diminished and they were more prone to injuries and illnesses. The toughest part of the trip was still ahead.

The horses had a day's respite near the site of the old Wonangatta homestead beside Conglomerate Creek. The buildings were long gone, except for a hut, a few old split rail fences and a cemetery which stood as reminders of the days when cattle grazed the open plains of the Wonangatta valley.

Joe's leg became stiff and swollen as his wound turned septic and fly blown. Tipping a capful of hydrogen peroxide into the open gash to kill the infection, it bubbled and disappeared down into the flesh. Ken ran his thumb up from the horse's knee and to my horror, pushed a seething mass of wriggling maggots and peroxide out of the wound.

The horses take a last few mouthfuls of good feed as we leave Dargo

"Don't worry," he reassured, grinning at the shocked look on my face. "If we weren't here to treat this gash, these maggots could possibly be doing a lot of good. They've saved many a leg from turning gangrene by eating away all the rotten and infected flesh."

Ken rinsed the wound with warm water until there were no more maggots, then smeared it with antiseptic grease to keep the flies off. *Trotter* was a terrific packhorse, but he'd injured so many of the other horses that we might have been better off without him. We wouldn't be able to use *Joe* for the next few days as his body would need all its resources to fight the infection and begin the healing process.

After our day off, the horses had to battle through more blackberries as we left the Wonangatta valley on the Dry River Track spur. This same route was once used to walk the Wonangatta cattle up to the Howitt High Plains for summer grazing. No doubt the cattle would have gone willingly up the steep ridge because they knew they were heading for sweet grass. Our horses had no such knowledge and gave us endless trouble trying to sneak off and follow the contours. They were absolutely fed up with mountains and when we pulled up at a level clearing near the top, we were one horse short.

"Bloody old *Mal!*" cursed Ken, as we gazed back down the mountain and saw a grey piebald rump poking out behind a tree. *Mal* ignored our calls and Ken had to go fetch him.

I nearly fell off my horse when a girl stepped out of the snow gums and started taking photos. Ken had just begun to hurl a colourful stream of insults at one of the horses that wouldn't stay with the mob, but he was too far back to see the girl and his voice carried plainly.

"Hi! I'm Sandy from *'The Age'* newspaper," she said, as I drew closer, politely ignoring Ken's bad language. "I hope you don't mind me taking photos. I drove out from Melbourne and I've been camped here since last night waiting for you."

"How on earth did you know we were out here and where to find us?" I asked in amazement.

"I had a tip from a friend in Omeo," she explained. "I couldn't get a guidebook on the National Trail to find where it went, so I rang the forestry people in Heyfield. They rang all their field workers on the radio telephone and a couple of guys spraying blackberries in Wonangatta had seen you and knew you were heading for Howitt Hut. There's only two possible tracks you could have taken, so I've been checking them for signs of horses all day."

There was no way we could have got past this dedicated photographer unnoticed! The rolling open expanses of the Howitt High Plains with their little timbered copses and crystal clear brooks were a welcome sight and after a photography session we set up camp beside Howitt Hut. A thick fog rolled in on nightfall, making it too dangerous for Sandy to drive back to Melbourne, so she camped out with us. The horses were hobbled in a fenced paddock where they grazed on patches of clover and sweet pick in amongst the wiry tufts of last season's snow grass. They would have loved a week's spell here, but even in mid-February the chilly evening temperature was too severe for Queensland horses with summer coats and the energy required to keep warm would negate the benefit.

Just on daylight we were hit with a shower of hail. So suddenly does the weather change in the high country that by the time we scurried into the hut there were masses of hail stones lying on the ground. With snow falls possible at this time of year, we were not prepared to chance our luck. Packing the horses in drizzling rain seemed the lesser of two evils as we donned oilskins, said goodbye to Sandy and headed down the Butcher Country Spur.

Hard, rocky and narrow, the track was perched on top of a ridge like a dinosaur's backbone and the wind howled up from the valley on either side, trying to pluck us off and hurl us down into the chasm below. A forlorn pile of bones just off the track told the sad story of a horse that had died from dehydration. It was hard to imagine on such a wet, miserable day, but the owner had lost a second horse not far away and had only just managed to walk to a forestry camp in time to summon a vet and save the third horse.

Another northbound traveller suffering from dehydration had lost his way at the top of the Dry River track. Both his horses had tumbled over a cliff to their deaths and he'd been lucky to find his way out alive.

The National Trail campsite in a small clearing on Pine Creek was 1200m above sea level. There was no water in the shallow depression which served as a creek, even though it was raining. It would have been a depressing dry weather campsite for northbound travellers, their horses thirsty after the steep climb from the Macalister River.

There were enough puddles for easy water collection, but there was little feed and the ground was saturated and spongy. Horses dislike standing on unstable ground and the added discomfort of the cold wind that whistled around the mountainside made it quite likely that they would try and escape. It was a dangerous place to lose horses from, because they would travel a fair distance before they found somewhere comfortable to stop. Looking at our maps, we anticipated finding a better campsite 19km downhill on the Macalister. Hopefully there would be good feed and shelter along the river, as there were on most rivers. If only we'd known what lay ahead, we would have stopped right there and averted disaster.

We pushed on instead, while the track fell sharply away into a wet, greasy mud slide. I gave *Brown Mare* her head when she slithered sideways into a 4-wheel-drift but she lunged forward for traction and smacked her hoof against a protruding slab of rock. There was no blood and she seemed OK but I hopped off and led her, trying to stay out of the way of her sliding hooves.

The track seemed to go down forever, torturing muscles and jarring every bone in our bodies. Dispirited, exhausted, plastered in mud and soaked to the skin, we finally reached the river and the most soul-destroying campsite we'd ever seen. Not one blade of grass grew in amongst the dank, musty timber and the river bank was a greasy white clay that dropped vertically before reaching the water. We would have been better off at Pine Creek which at least had a little grass. The valley was too narrow downstream to camp, so we set up our electric fence and watched our poor horses eating dogwood bushes and lily leaves. We didn't feel like eating while our horses went hungry, so set up the tent, crawled out of the rain and went to sleep.

During the night we heard steel shod hooves crashing amongst the river rocks and something splashing in the river. Ken got up to investigate and found *Anvil* and *Jack* down in the riverbed grazing on a coarse, broad leaved grass. Nothing seemed amiss, so he returned to bed.

"How on earth did they get down there?" I puzzled, looking at the steep, slippery bank the next morning.

"Here's *Anvil's* hoofprints where she's hobbled up to the

edge," said Ken. "You can see the slide marks where she's skated down on the clay."

It was going to be interesting getting them back up the bank again.

"Holy hell!" exclaimed Ken. "Come and have a look where *Jack* went down!"

A fresh pile of earth and a cherry tree sapling were strewn over a big flat river stone about 8 feet below. *Jack's* rounded, size 4 hoofprints led to the spot where the river embankment had given way.

"He was probably looking for a way to get down to *Anvil* and went too close to the edge on his blind side," mused Ken. "He must have fallen onto that slippery rock; probably lost his footing and landed on his stomach. He's lucky not to have broken his neck."

We carefully climbed down into the river and examined *Jack* for broken ribs and exterior wounds, but he didn't have so much as a scratch on him.

"Jeez, I bet he's horribly bruised inside," muttered Ken, as he unhobbled him.

We left the hobbles on *Anvil* as I couldn't catch her and hunted the two horses back up the bank. Even in hobbles, *Anvil* bounded up the slippery embankment with easy agility and grace, followed more cautiously by her brother. *Jack* seemed O.K. and travelled along quietly when we got going, but he bailed up on the long climb out of the Macalister in the afternoon and we had to camp where he stopped.

Brown Mare had gone lame from the whack to her hoof, *Joe's* wound was turning septic and *Riley* had cut his fetlock. We'd lost the large cooking billy, the tent pole broke and my watch stopped. In just under 2 years we'd travelled over 5000km, but now, with only 200km to go, our horses and equipment were starting to pack it in and it felt like we weren't going to make it.

But we HAD to make it. We were stuck. We couldn't just let our horses go and walk out on foot. They'd given us their best, so we had to give them ours and make sure we all got out of there alive. There was no going back. Not with the dreadful Butcher Country Spur behind us. It was easier to go forward, so on we plodded.

Using sheer determination, Ken put his shoulder in behind *Jack's* stifle and physically pushed and prodded the horse up the side of the mountain. A procession of 4-wheel-drives roared along the track and pulled up. Whilst we were talking to the occupants, *Jack* leaned against the bonnet, visibly distressed.

"That horse is gunna die!" said one driver sadistically.

"Garbage!" replied Ken. "He's too bloody tough to die; he's just crook in the guts."

Having kept a close eye on *Jack* since his fall into the river two nights ago, we were aware that the horse hadn't relieved himself. He must have had massive bruising to the stomach from landing on the rock, and it hurt too much to pee. Stimulated by Ken massaging his stomach every time he stopped, *Jack* eventually relieved himself and the torrent just about flooded the roadway.

Jack's condition steadily improved, allowing us to reach a reasonable campsite on Mt. Skene Creek at Rumpff's flat. We stayed here for several days, hoping that *Brown Mare's* injury was only a stone bruise. But we couldn't find any bruising and the mare deteriorated to such a state that she couldn't put any weight on her injured foot.

There was very little feed value in the grass along the flat and we rationed ourselves to a couple of spoonfuls of porridge for breakfast and a slice of damper and cheese for tea. We had to move on, but there was no way *Brown Mare* could keep travelling. I'd seen a fence on top of the last ridge, so we decided to put *Jack* and the mare behind it and return for them in a few weeks. It turned out to be nothing but a block fence, as the wires only stretched a kilometre back into the bush. It was still our only chance to trick the horses into not following us. We left them near water, then strung up some old wires where we'd come in, hoping it would confuse them into staying put.

Thankfully, it worked. The two injured horses didn't turn up at Rumpff's flat by the next morning, so we stashed a bit of gear in a rock cave to lighten our loads, packed up and began the long climb up Mt. Skene. The horses were hungry and exhausted when we reached the Jamieson–Licola Road. We stopped to let them graze on a small patch of grass, before taking the Lazarini Spur track to our campsite near an old dog trapper's hut. A spring across the road was a welcome water supply, but the only feed was a scant spattering of clover along the edge of the road. It hadn't been used by a vehicle for some time, so we electric fenced the horses on the narrow track.

During the night, we were woken by something trying to roll us out of the swag.

"Don't move!" whispered Ken, waiting for his eyes to adjust to the starlight that filtered down through the timber. "It's alright," he said, after a few moments, "It's only *Easton* trying to eat the grass growing under the swag." The poor horses had quickly eaten all the available grass and were still hungry. *Mal* had escaped from the electric fence at some stage and we found him in the morning feeding on woody dogwood bushes and lilies. While the other horses picked fussily at these barely palatable plants, *Mal* tucked into them with great gusto.

Another tiring day was in store, pushing our way through thick wattle down the Lazarini Spur. Hoping to find a patch of feed when we reached the Goulburn River, we were disappointed to find nothing but blackberries and a few tough old bits of bladey grass. There was no point camping there, so we pressed on.

Riding through an open gateway near the Mansfield-Woods Point Road, a white envelope tied to the gate with a piece of string caught my eye. Turning it over, I found it addressed *"Sharon & Ken"*. Inside was a note from Jamieson policeman, Bernie McWhinney, telling us we'd reached Knockwood, to put our horses in a partially fenced paddock nearby, get a lift into Kevington or Gaffney's Creek and make an urgent phone call home to Mum.

It gave us a real buzz to receive a letter in this fashion but the unknown reason for the urgent phone call worried me. To our relief the paddock had the best feed the horses had seen since Dargo. We risked not tying up a nighthorse, certain they wouldn't want to leave, had a quick bath in the Goulburn River and hitched a ride to Kevington.

We arrived at 10 minutes to 5 on a Friday afternoon without a brass razoo in our pockets to find a pub and a phone box, but no bank, post office or any other means of drawing cash. Nobody at the pub believed we'd ridden down from Cooktown and had a dozen horses 20km up the road. Except for one knight in shining black leather, Ernie Smith, who rescued us from our cash crisis by arranging credit with the publican and gave us his bed for the night while he slept beside his motorbike out in the paddock.

Chapter 25: HEALESVILLE

IT WAS SLIGHTLY unnerving, sitting on a bag of corn in the middle of the scrub with a TV camera trained on my face and a woolly microphone hovering nearby. The urgent phone call I'd made from Kevington had been nothing drastic; it only concerned the media who'd been trying to contact us.

I struggled to answer Bronwyn Kiely's questions, a bit over-awed that Channel 7's Hinch program rated our journey interesting enough to send a film crew bumping and jolting over rough roads a couple of hundred miles out from Melbourne. Unknown to me, my mother had organised them to bring horse feed, and they were two hours late because of this. The filming further delayed our departure from Knockwood until late afternoon. We would normally have stayed on camp, but our arrival in Healesville was scheduled for Sunday 3rd March, 1991, so we had to keep going in order to meet our deadline.

Joe had been tossing his head all morning and climbing Mt. Terrible on the Moonlight Spur track, he became so agitated that he all but threw himself over backwards. We'd noticed earlier that he was a touch sunburnt on the nose, but closer investigation revealed the pink skin on the leopard spotted appaloosa to be red and swollen. The touch of the saddle having further added to his discomfort, we pulled it off and went to transfer the load onto *Easton*. Catching the skewbald I was alarmed to discover that all his white patches were raised above the chestnut ones and the pink skin beneath the white hair was also inflamed. Examining the other horses, we found that even the blue-skinned greys were burnt on the end of their noses, where they lacked pigment.

There was something drastically wrong. It looked like our horses had been poisoned but we didn't know the cause. Ken was feeling a lot worse than the combined effects of hunger, fatigue and the nightmarish foot-slog up the mountainside should have made him. Perhaps the river water was contaminated? Maybe the blackberries they'd all been eating had been sprayed with poison? I was the only one not to touch them, but I wasn't sure whether the dizziness I was feeling was from sickness or heat exhaustion.

Joe showed instant relief when unsaddled and we took the halters off the horses with a blaze, as the nose band had been aggravating the sensitized skin. Without *Brown Mare* and *Jack*, we were down to 10 weary horses. *Easton* was one of the few that *Joe's* packsaddle fitted so we transferred the pack since he didn't have pink skin under the saddle line. Since he was no doubt feeling off-colour, we spared him the burden of the swag and strapped it onto *Poddy's* load.

"What on earth are we going to do?" I asked my stricken partner.

"There's no point going back," he replied, wiping the feverish sweat from his brow with the back of his wrist. "We'd only end up stuck at Knockwood, and the horses might cop another dose of whatever made them crook. *Joe* seems O.K. without the saddle on, so the sooner we get going, the sooner we get out of this mongrel hill country. Just keep a close eye on the horses to see if they're getting better or worse."

The National Trail took a dreadfully steep and rocky track over the top of Mt. Terrible, but our horses were in no condition to follow that route when we reached the top of the spur at about 6pm. It had been a hot afternoon and there was no water for our thirsty horses at the overnight camp beside the fire tower on the summit. We took the only humane alternative, descending the Matlock track to the Big River. *Joe's* tender skin seemed less inflamed as the heat faded into evening and the horses had a much needed drink before we turned them back to the road and set off in search of a campsite. The undergrowth was so thick between the river and the road that we didn't find a clear patch to camp until 11.30p.m. judging from the position of the Southern Cross (my watch had stopped working a week ago). Shivering and hunched in the saddle, my fingers were so cold that I had to prise them off the reins with the hand that I'd kept warm under my armpit. My coat was in the bottom of a pack bag and we didn't have the heart to hold up the horses for 5 minutes to attend to our own comforts.

Our horses desperately needed a day's spell: they were sick, exhausted and their sleeping and feeding patterns had been thrown into confusion. But we'd arranged to meet a fellow at the Royston River about 40km away the next evening. He wanted to ride through to Marysville with us and we'd asked him to bring out some lucerne hay and a bag of corn.

To our relief, *Joe's* sunburn-like symptoms had eased the next morning, but we had a long uphill haul ahead of us and it was nearly dark when we reached the base of Mt Bullfight with 10km left to go. A clearing of knee-high grass offered an ideal camp site and we were tempted to stop for the night and let the horses fill their bellies. But the thought of the fellow camped at the Royston with his horse and the lucerne and corn that awaited our hard working team kept us going.

The track to Mt Bullfight had a locked vehicle barrier and was no longer maintained. Trees had fallen across the road and we spent much time detouring through the scrub around them. Dismounting, we walked to give our riding horses a spell; something we'd been doing a great deal in the last fortnight.

It was pitch black when we reached the summit of Mt Bullfight and began the descent. The moonshadow made it impossible to see any obstacles until we were right on top of them. After barking my shins a couple of times walking into fallen branches I mounted *Anvil* and rode down, as she could see in the dark. Riding in total darkness seems to affect a person's balance and every time the mare hopped over an unseen obstacle I had no idea whether I was falling off or not.

Within a stone's throw of the Royston River, we struck a huge log about 3 foot 6 inches high blocking our path. A steep dropoff loomed on the downhill side of the track, but the rising moon illuminated a narrow squeeze around the base of the log to our left. I rode *Anvil* in and felt her bog, but she kept going and made it around the log. The horses behind baulked at the sound of squelching mud and no persuasion from Ken could convince them to follow.

Tying my mare to a bush, I returned and attempted to lead each horse around on foot, scrambling to keep out of their way when they panicked and lunged forward through the quagmire.

"Hop out the way," ordered Ken, "I'll try and drive the rest through." He pushed them into a bunch and cracked the whip, but only two horses wallowed around the log. The rest wheeled about, ducked past Ken and took off up the hill. Ken disappeared to return with the horses 10 minutes later. He tried pushing them through, but they got past him and galloped back up the hill again.

Ken's patience exhausted, I went after the horses on foot and brought them back. With both of us on the ground behind them, we managed to drive most of the horses around the log. *Jordie* and *Joe* hesitated, but when Ken lost his temper and launched himself bodily towards them, they both jumped the log from a standstill.

Fifty metres ahead lay the dark shadow of the riverbed but there was a huge, gaping emptiness where the bridge should have been. Hunting the horses away from the riverbank, I tied my mare up again, cautiously walked across and shone a torch over the edge. There was a 6 foot drop to the water and the soft riverbank was honeycombed with rotten bridge timbers, hidden by layers of silt. The water level was low, but the bank was unstable and the horses would need much persuasion to make the crossing.

Finding a strip of firm ground to the left of the old bridgeworks, Ken led *Riley* down into the river. The horse's rump wedged in the furrow made by his hooves, but a tug on the reins compelled him to slide the rest of the way into the river bed, making a neatly smoothed track for the other horses. Ken mounted, letting *Riley* pick his way across the slippery river stones in fetlock-deep water.

"Git up there! Git up!" yelled Ken as they climbed out through blackberry bushes on the far side. I could see the vague outline of horse and rider plunging up to the road.

"It's too boggy over there to lead horses through," explained Ken when he returned.

We led a few horses down into the river instead, then drove the rest in after them. Cracking the whip and yelling encouragement, we kept the horses at the tail moving and when the leaders baulked, they were pushed through the bog by the tail enders. Not wanting to be left behind, the last few horses lunged willingly through the soupy mud.

It was another hour before we reached the Royston campsite. Well before our arrival, the absence of woodsmoke and non-existent glow of a fire told us we'd pushed on needlessly. A fresh set of vehicle tracks showed that someone had been there earlier and we searched about with the torch, failing to find any sign that horse feed had been dropped off. The globe in my torch blew and we were plunged into darkness and total disappointment.

Tea-trees and broad leaved lilies were all that grew along the river while the dogwood and towering alpine ash covering the hill behind us offered little for the horses to eat. We didn't have the heart to tie any up. They were so hungry we let them hobble off into the darkness to scavenge whatever they could, hoping we'd find them again in the morning.

During the early hours we woke to the sound of *Trotter* whinnying as he hobbled back and forth along the road. I had the horrible feeling that the horses had 'headed out', but there was nothing we could do until morning. At first light, we tracked the horses and found them feeding along the roadside. My heart sank when I realised the three Monto greys were missing. *Trotter* had 'adopted' these mares and had woken us earlier when he couldn't find them. They could be miles away by now.

I hunted the other horses back to camp while Ken scoured the road for hoofprints. How relieved I was when three grey mares galloped over the hill in hobbles a short time later. They'd turned up an old track and Ken had found them grazing some distance along it.

Taking the horses down for a drink we discovered that the vehicle tracks we'd seen last night went across the river. Wading over to investigate, I found an old set of yards and a derelict hut with 3 bales of hay in the doorway and a couple of loaves of bread dangling from the rafters! It was dry, grassy hay and there was no bag of corn, but if we'd found it last night, the horses would have been able to fill their bellies and get some rest.

When the horses finished the hay we were packed up and gone by dinnertime. Logging operations were under way, and I stirred up clouds of bulldust created by timber trucks, which settled over the horses behind me and formed a thick mantle on Ken at the tail. He was more relieved than anyone when I picked up a faint track on top of the Blue Range and turned off the logging road. Following the ridge top, it was a short day's ride of 20km to our camp at Keppel's Hut on the side of Lake Mountain. There was good pick in places along the track, so we travelled slowly, allowing the horses to graze.

We'd dispensed with the electric fence batteries when

Giving the horses the last of our food at Keppel's Hut

they'd gone flat over a week ago, so it was only a flimsy strip of white tape across the track either side of Keppel's Hut that contained our horses.

"I wouldn't have believed it possible that you'd get sub-zero temperatures in Australia at this time of the year," said Ken, huddling around a roaring campfire that evening.

He'd lived most of his life in Far North Queensland, where the late February conditions are sweltering. The horses normally kept as far away from us as possible, but there was standing room only around the fire on Lake Mountain that night. We woke at one stage to find *Anvil*, our worst kicking horse, straddling one corner of the swag!

The horses looked terrible in the morning, their ribs visible and their short summer hair standing on end. Placing a canvas pack cover on the ground, I emptied the remnants of our food into it. Split peas, pearl barley, rice, sugar, muesli and dehydrated peas were snuffled up hungrily. Ken cooked a sugary raisin damper with the rest of the flour and we saddled the horses while it cooled. Very few of our horses would eat bread, but they all devoured a chunk of damper before beginning the descent from Keppel's Hut.

Keen to reach Marysville to buy horse feed and something to eat ourselves, we barely noticed the surrounding splendour. Towering beeches and giant tree ferns dwarfed our tired procession as we followed the tinkling clear waters of the Taggerty River. We paused to say hello to a carload of people and a lady visiting from England hopped out to pat the horses.

"I'm so glad you stopped to talk to us," she smiled in wonderment, "I've never seen anything like this at home."

"We'd normally stop and talk all day if you wanted, but we're keen to reach Marysville and buy some feed for our horses," I replied.

"Oh dear!" remarked the driver, Val Stafford. "I'm afraid Marysville doesn't have a produce store."

Seeing our disappointment, she promised to try and organise some feed for our hungry horses.

We were still waving goodbye to Val and her friends when Ann Thomas, a local historian and writer for the Alexandra newspaper, pulled up to take photos. A bus driver we'd met earlier in the day had phoned Ann of our whereabouts and her brother, Dan Gould, had driven her out to meet us. A horseman who'd contributed to the planning of the National

Trail, Dan was just as keen as his sister to hear all about it, so we promised to tell them the story when we reached town and our horses were tended to.

As Dan and Ann turned and headed back to Marysville, I realised for the first time that the end of our journey was near at hand. The rugged, inaccessible wilderness lay behind at last and civilization had extended out to meet us. I shed a silent tear for the lonely places that Ken, myself and our team of horses had travelled.

Half an hour later, another car pulled over and a lanky, wild-haired looking fellow jumped out to greet us.

"Now, you're only a day from Narbethong; we've got a barbeque tea organised for you there on Friday night; do you want any of your horses trucked into Healesville?" he rattled off, while his wife plied us with fruit, lollies and lemonade. We didn't have a clue who these friendly people were and I interrupted to ask.

"Oh, I forgot you don't know us; we're Joe and Jan Kay from Healesville," he laughed. "We heard you were on your way so we've been comin' out here for the last few days to see if you needed any help."

What a relief it was to see Val waiting at the town oval with a bale of lucerne hay and a bag of corn. At last we could relax, knowing that our horses had something decent on which to fill their bellies. When we'd finished talking to Ann Thomas, Val invited us home to 'The Hermitage,' an historic guesthouse on the Black Spur. We had the first hot shower since Dargo, 3 weeks ago, and the Staffords spoilt us with a beautiful meal in the comforts of their home, before driving us back to camp.

I saddled up *B2* the next day and we set off for Narbethong in high spirits. I could hardly conceive that after coming so far, here we were on the third-last day of our trek.

Only a stone's throw from our destination, disaster struck! Cutting through the bush to avoid the busy Maroondah Highway, a pile of rotting vegetation gave way as *B2* stepped onto it! She crashed onto her side, pinning my leg underneath! Thank goodness for elastic sided boots! My boot was jammed in the stirrup but I managed to pull my foot out and dive to one side before she rolled onto her back and wedged upside down between two branches.

"Get over here!" I yelled to Ken. "*B2's* stuck and she

can't get up."

She just lay there, not even trying to get up! With a terrible sinking feeling that drove to the depths of my stomach I considered the possibility that she'd broken a leg. Poor little *B2*! She was the tiniest, yet the most courageous of our horses! If courage were a colour it would have to be the same hue as this little pony: Not black or white, but shades of grey.

But for the first time in her life, our brave little *B2* had lost her fire. I'd never seen her look as helpless as she did now. I felt absolutely devastated!

A group of people from Healesville awaited us at the Black Spur Inn. They were scrambling across a creek and through the undergrowth to see what all the yelling was about.

"Crikey, how did she get down there?" grinned Joe Kay when he caught sight of the little grey pony lying on her back. "Come on boys, we'll give her a lift."

I hopped out of the way while the men manhandled *B2*, hoping with all my heart that when they set her on her feet she wouldn't collapse with broken bones.

"She'll be right," said Ken who'd just managed to reach me through the scrub. "Look, they've got her up now. She was probably so buggered from all those hills that alls she needed was a helping hand."

The high spirits of our helpers and the fact that *B2* was now standing quietly on all fours lifted my mood.

"Here, is this your boot?" Somebody tossed over my squashed boot.

"We'll get up on the highway and stop the traffic," said one lady. "You'll never get across this creek – it's too boggy."

B2 seemed quite O.K. back on her feet, so I climbed aboard and led our string of horses along the highway and into the hotel grounds. A float load of hay and a bag of oats was a most welcome sight and many hands assisted us pulling the gear off. Jan Kay was busy piling our plates with food while we discussed our arrival in Healesville with Lynne King, the marvellous lady who'd arranged every last detail without even having met us. The whole evening was a blur of talking, laughing, eating and good company and all too soon everybody departed and left us to our own devices.

We had a short distance to travel along the Maroondah Highway in the morning, but there was a small track along one verge and the horses kept away from the bitumen until the track petered out. We trotted them towards the oncoming traffic for a couple of hundred metres then turned onto a side track to be greeted by Joe Kay astride an appaloosa.

"Howdy!" he greeted. "I was starting to think you must have got lost!"

Joe accompanied us over the Black Spur and into our last night's camp on top of the Great Dividing Range. Another barbeque had been organised. Again our visitors departed all too soon and we were left to our own thoughts.

Not far away lay the untamed waters of the Southern Ocean. The day we'd left the tropical mangrove-lined shores of the Endeavour River at Cooktown, I never dreamed that this journey of a lifetime would come to an end. Yet here we were amongst the tree ferns and tall timbers, 22 months and over 5000km later, about to reach our final destination.

The National Trail had become a way of life. I was relieved it would soon be over for the horses' sake, but my thoughts were tinged with sadness. How could I live without our beloved horses? What was going to happen to them? Where would I go from here?

Descending the slopes of Mount St Leonard on the last day we were joined by riders from Healesville. At Donnelly's Weir, we stopped to read the plaque marking the southern end of the National Trail. It was over. At this point, the entire trail lay behind us.

A police escort met us on the edge of town. The white squad car, with its blue light flashing, slowly led a tired, dusty string of travellers and horses into the town of Healesville. The local riders dropped back to the tail and Ken rode up beside me in the lead. He gave me a wink, but didn't expect an answer. He could see my eyes were brimming with tears.

People clapped and cheered as our cavalcade drew up to the busy Sunday market place. The noise dimmed in my ears and the whole scene faded into a blur of activity. Our horses were ushered into the Pony Club grounds and I dismounted for the last time. People were waiting for us. We were whisked across the road, bunked up onto the

Poddy, Sharon, Ken & Riley beside a plaque marking the southern end of the National Trail at Donnelly's Weir

back of a ute, congratulated and presented with plaques by the Healesville Tourist Association for being the first people to ride the entire length of the National Trail.

Feeling self-conscious in front of the crowd, I thanked the people of Healesville for their warm welcome. Ken praised the courage and tenacity of our sturdy team of Queensland horses to whom we owed the success of our trek. As we stepped down from the platform, visions of people's faces and far-distant places flashed through my mind. Our journey had finally come to an end, but those memories of the National Trail will forever linger on in our hearts.

* * * * *

EPILOGUE

With our horses resting in a Healesville paddock, we made two trips by vehicle into the back of Glencairn Station to look for *Jack* and *Brown Mare*. We found them on the second visit and trucked them out to Healesville. *Jack* had fully recovered and *Brown Mare* showed only a trace of lameness.

The bad sunburn on our pink skinned horses at Knockwood was discovered to be 'photosensitisation', a condition caused by the ingestion of certain toxins and plant hormones. It could possibly have been caused by all the 'rubbish' (lilies, blackberries etc) the horses had been eating in the absence of grass. In Healesville, *Joe's* sunburnt skin peeled off in big patches as it was replaced by new skin and hair growing underneath.

Many of the problems we encountered were due to our own inexperience and from riding the trail in its infancy, often using incomplete draft notes that were untested. Feedback from past users of the trail has now provided an improved set of guide books, so that future travellers have more information available and can look forward to a much easier trip than ours.

No longer having a use or a place for twelve horses, we were faced with the heartrending task of parting with our beloved companions.

Riley, the chestnut from Mareeba who'd been with us the longest, was sold in Healesville. *Mal*, the grey piebald from Cloncurry, was donated to the Riding for Disabled at Stanthorpe, Queensland and delivered free of charge by Chapman's Horse Transport.

We kept *Morgan* and *Jordie*, the young horses we'd broken in on the trail, and trucked the remainder to a rural horse sale in Benalla, Victoria. *B2* and *Easton* have turned into wonderful children's ponies while the rest, no doubt, are growing fat and lazy in a paddock somewhere.

Neither Ken nor myself has ever really felt that our ride has come to an end. It had become a way of life. On our arrival in Healesville we changed our pace slightly but didn't come to a conclusive stop. By writing this book, the National Trail has continued to dominant our lives. Once the book goes to the printer, perhaps then we can finally close the door on the trek and start the next chapter.

BIOGRAPHY
KEN ROBERTS

Ken Roberts was born in Hopetoun, Victoria. At the age of 14 he left Warracknabeal High School and went to work on wheat farms in the Mallee.

At 16, he travelled to the Northern Territory and worked with horses on cattle stations. Ken eventually moved to North Queensland to work on the sugar cane, where he cut cane by hand for replanting, hauled cane from the paddocks to the sidings, offsided on the locos and assisted the sugar boiler in the mill. He has lived most of his life in Queensland, working in the sugar and dairy industries, on cattle stations and as a chainman for surveyors.

He had never taken a photograph before setting out on the National Trail and hardly ever puts pen to paper except for the rare poem.

Ken and B2 beside the Guy Fawkes River, NSW

BIOGRAPHY
SHARON MUIR WATSON

Sharon Muir Watson was born in Perth, Western Australia.

Educated at Rossmoyne Primary School, North Kalgoorlie Primary School, Eastern Goldfields High School and Kobeelya College at Katanning. She also attended WAIT (now Curtin University of Technology) where she obtained an Associate Diploma in Valuation.

Sharon's lifelong love affair with horses started with a riding lesson on her eighth birthday at Wyandra Riding School.

She began a career in computer systems support with a building society in Perth, then branched out into the computer operations field, eventually moving to Melbourne to continue this career.

While Sharon enjoys art and photography, writing is an activity only resorted to under extreme pressure and persuasion. With Ken's persistence, she kept a diary whilst on the National Trail and wrote a series of articles for Western Australia's 'Hoofbeats' magazine.

Sharon on Easton beside the old telegraph line over the Connor's Range inland from St. Lawrance Qld.

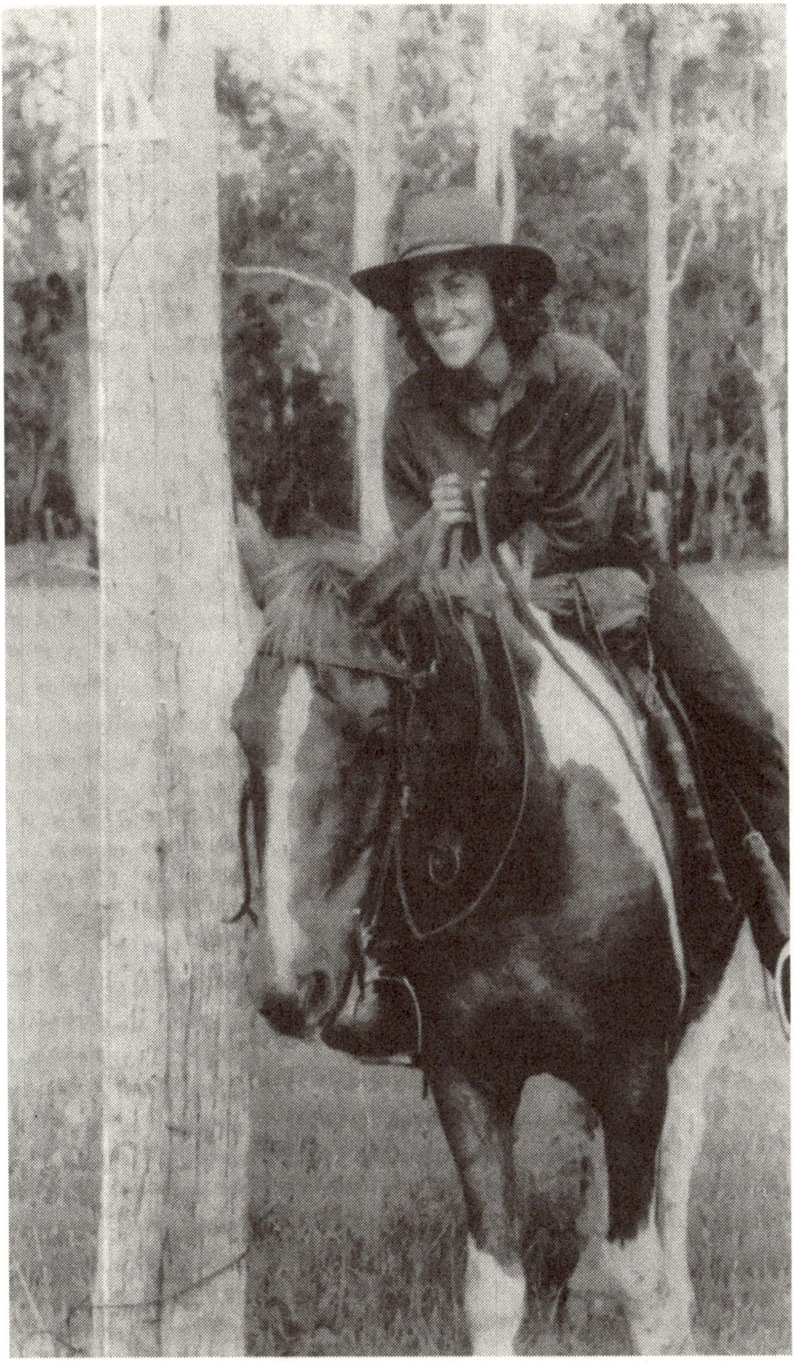

Some of the other titles in the Equestrian Travel Classic series published by The Long Riders' Guild Press. We are constantly adding to our collection, so for an up-to-date list please visit our website:
www.thelongridersguild.com

Title	Author
A Lady's Life in the Rocky Mountains	Isabella Bird
A Ride to Khiva	Frederick Burnaby
Across the Roof of the World	Wilfred Skrede
Adventures in Mexico	George F. Ruxton
Bohemia Junction	Aime Tschiffely
Boots and Saddles in Africa	Thomas Lambie
Bridle Paths	Aime Tschiffely
California Coast Trails	J. Smeaton Chase
Caucasian Journey	Negley Farson
Following the Frontier	Roger Pocock
Horse Packing	Charles Johnson Post
Horses, Saddles and Bridles	W. H. Carter
Journey from the Arctic	Donald Brown
Khyber Knights	CuChullaine O'Reilly
Last of the Saddle Tramps	Messanie Wilkins
Manual of Pack Transportation	H. W. Daly
Mongolian Adventure	Henning Haslund
My Kingdom for a Horse	Margaret Leigh
New Zealand: Bit by Bit	Jacqui Knight
Ocean to Ocean on Horseback	Williard Glazier
On Horseback in Virginia	Charles Dudley Warner
On Horseback through Asia Minor	Fred Burnaby
Ride a White Horse	William Holt
Riding Across Patagonia	Lady Florence Dixie
Rural Rides – Volume One	William Cobbett
Rural Rides – Volume Two	William Cobbett
Saddle and Canoe	Theodore Winthrop
Saddlebags for Suitcases	Mary Bosanquet
Saddles East	John W. Beard
Saddletramp	Jeremy James
Shanghai à Moscou	Madame de Bourboulon
The Abode of Snow	Andrew Wilson
The Art of Travel	Francis Galton
The Courage to Ride	Ana Beker
The Journeys of Celia Fiennes	Celia Fiennes
The Prairie Traveler	Randolph Marcy
The Road to the Grey Pamir	Ana Louise Strong
The Tale of Two Horses	Aime Tschiffely
This Way Southward	Aime Tschiffely
Through Five Republics on Horseback	George Ray
Through Mexico on Horseback	Joseph Carl Goodwin
Through Persia on a Sidesaddle	Ella C. Sykes
Through Russia on a Mustang	Thomas Stevens
Through the Highlands of Shropshire	Magdalene M. Weale
To the Foot of the Rainbow	Clyde Kluckhohn
Travels in Afghanistan	Ernest F. Fox
Travels with A Donkey in the Cevennes	Robert Louis Stevenson
Tschiffely's Ride	Aime Tschiffely
Turkestan Solo	Ella K. Maillart
Vagabond	Jeremy James
Wartime Ride	J. W. Day
Winter Sketches from the Saddle	John Codman

The Long Riders' Guild
The world's leading source of information regarding equestrian exploration!
www.thelongridersguild.com

Printed in June 2019
by Rotomail Italia S.p.A., Vignate (MI) - Italy